Brokering in Education Research-Practice Part

Educational leaders, researchers, and community members have found collaborating on research supports improvement in their schools, districts, and the wider community – but how do we go about developing these partnerships? With essential tools, frameworks, and tips for brokering in research-practice partnerships (RPPs), this practical book provides guidance on cultivating and sustaining impactful relationships and supportive infrastructure with partners. Through the careful brokering of these partnerships, RPP brokers can bridge the gap between education research and practice, bringing people together to build a more equitable educational system.

Written by RPP leaders, researchers, and professionals, this handbook explores how brokering can:

- Support the production and use of partnership research
- Develop and nurture meaningful relationships, even in the face of challenging circumstances
- Build individual competencies to manage an RPP and strengthen the partnership
- Develop partnership governance
- Implement effective administrative structures
- Design processes and communications routines
- Assess and continuously improve the partnership

This is an essential read for any educational leader, higher education faculty, researcher, or other community member who wants to understand the types of activities and responsibilities required of an RPP broker and the strategies to become an effective broker of RPPs aimed at educational improvement and equitable transformation.

Laura Wentworth is Director of the Research-Practice Partnership Program for California Education Partners, USA.

Paula Arce-Trigatti is Director of the National Network of Education Research-Practice Partnerships at Rice University, USA.

Carrie Conaway is Senior Lecturer at the Harvard Graduate School of Education, USA, and Co-Chair of the Education Policy Analysis Master's Degree Program.

Samantha Shewchuk is Research Associate at the Center for Research in Education and Social Policy at the University of Delaware, USA.

Brokering in Education Research-Practice Partnerships

A Guide for Education Professionals and Researchers

Laura Wentworth,
Paula Arce-Trigatti,
Carrie Conaway, and
Samantha Shewchuk

Routledge
Taylor & Francis Group
NEW YORK AND LONDON

Designed cover image: © Getty Images

First published 2023
by Routledge
605 Third Avenue, New York, NY 10158

and by Routledge
4 Park Square, Milton Park, Abingdon, Oxon, OX14 4RN

Routledge is an imprint of the Taylor & Francis Group, an informa business

© 2023 Laura Wentworth, Paula Arce-Trigatti, Carrie Conaway, and Samantha Shewchuk

The right of Laura Wentworth, Paula Arce-Trigatti, Carrie Conaway, and Samantha Shewchuk to be identified as authors of this work has been asserted in accordance with sections 77 and 78 of the Copyright, Designs and Patents Act 1988.

The Open Access version of this book, available at www.taylorfrancis.com, has been made available under a Creative Commons Attribution-Non Commercial-No Derivatives (CC-BY-NC-ND) 4.0 license.

The Open Access version of this book is based on research funded by (or in part by) the Bill & Melinda Gates Foundation. The findings and conclusions contained within are those of the authors and do not necessarily reflect positions or policies of the Bill & Melinda Gates Foundation. The Open Access version of this book was also made possible by the National Network of Education Research-Practice Partnerships (NNERPP), a program of the Kinder Institute for Urban Research at Rice University.

Trademark notice: Product or corporate names may be trademarks or registered trademarks, and are used only for identification and explanation without intent to infringe.

Library of Congress Cataloging-in-Publication Data
Names: Wentworth, Laura, author. | Arce-Trigatti, Paula, author. | Conaway, Carrie, author. | Shewchuk, Samantha, author.
Title: Brokering in education research-practice partnerships : a guide for education professionals and researchers / Laura Wentworth, Paula Arce-Trigatti, Carrie Conaway, Samantha Shewchuk.
Description: New York, NY : Routledge, [2023] | Includes bibliographical references and index.
Identifiers: LCCN 2022058372 (print) | LCCN 2022058373 (ebook) | ISBN 9781032368993 (hardback) | ISBN 9781032358758 (paperback) | ISBN 9781003334385 (ebook)
Subjects: LCSH: Education—Research. | Action research in education. | Educators—Professional relationships. | Educational equalization.
Classification: LCC LB1028 .W37 2023 (print) | LCC LB1028 (ebook) | DDC 370.72—dc23/eng/20230216
LC record available at https://lccn.loc.gov/2022058372
LC ebook record available at https://lccn.loc.gov/2022058373

ISBN: 978-1-032-36899-3 (hbk)
ISBN: 978-1-032-35875-8 (pbk)
ISBN: 978-1-003-33438-5 (ebk)

DOI: 10.4324/9781003334385

Typeset in Perpetua
by Apex CoVantage, LLC

Access the Support Material: www.routledge.com/9781032358758

Online Resources

These resources can be downloaded, printed, used to copy/paste text, and/or manipulated to suit your individualized use. You can access the downloads by visiting this book's product page on our website: www.routledge.com/9781032136158 (then follow the links indicating related resources, which you can then download directly to your computer).

- Appendix E – Internal Review Template
- Appendix I – Shortened EFI Sprint Protocol for RPP Members: Hewlett Deeper Learning Network
- Appendix J – Generic School District DUA
- Appendix K – Data SafeGuards
- Appendix L – DUA Correspondence Template

Contents

Acknowledgments ix
Preface xi

1 **What Is Brokering and Why Does It Matter in Education Research-Practice Partnerships?** 1
  Education Research-Practice Partnerships (RPPs) Help Research and Practice Intersect 3
  Brokers Sustain and Support RPPs 4
  RPP Brokers Activities Framework 6
  Orientation to the Handbook 7
  Conclusion 10
  References 10

2 **The Practice and Research Behind the RPP Brokers Framework** 13
  Practice-Based Reflection 15
  Perspectives From Other Brokers 17
  Structured Reviews 19
  Conclusion 34
  References 34

3 **A Framework: What Do Brokers Do?** 38
  What Do Brokers Do? 40
  Brokering to Strengthen Partners 41
  Brokering to Strengthen Partnerships 54
  Examining Brokering Across One RPP with a Critical Lens 72
  Conclusion 73
  References 74

vii

CONTENTS

4 RPP Brokers in Different Contexts   76
Revisiting the Definition of RPPs and What
  It Means for "Types" of RPPs 77
Mapping the RPP Definition Onto the RPP Brokers Framework 78
Conclusion 97
References 98

5 Cases Describing Brokering to Strengthen Partners   99
Developing Partners' Competency With Partnering 99
Developing and Nurturing Relationships to Weather Partnering
  Challenges 109
References 137

6 Cases Describing Brokering to Strengthen Partnerships   139
Cases About Brokers Developing Partnership Governance
  and Administrative Structures 140
Designing Processes and Communications
  Routines 152
Assessing and Continuously Improving
  the Partnership 168
References 171

7 Using Cases to Support RPP Broker Work and Development   172
In a Course . . . 173
Coaching . . . 174
Onboarding Resource . . . 174
Conclusion 177
References 177

8 The Future of Brokering in Research-Practice Partnerships   179
Brokering Aims to Change the Status Quo Behaviors and Systems
  of Individuals and Institutions 180
Brokering Activities Expand and Spread to All Members as an RPP
  Develops 182
Brokers Learn How to Do This Work Both Explicitly
  and Implicitly 183
Next Steps for RPP Brokering 183
References 185

Appendices   187
Index   248

Acknowledgments

This book would not exist without the community of brokers in the National Network of Education Research-Practice Partnerships who have been slowly developing these cases since the network was formed in 2016. The first compilation of these cases about brokering came out in 2021 as a white paper called the *RPP Brokers Handbook* with almost 40 brokering cases (Wentworth et al., 2021). The second compilation of these cases came out in 2022, with almost 60 cases (Wentworth et al., 2022). The growth in the number of cases demonstrates the incredible work that RPP brokers are doing in education settings. We are so appreciative of all the brokers working across the field of collaborative education research, and especially want to honor the RPP brokers who contributed to this book and versions 1.0 and 2.0 of the handbook. (You can see a list of all the contributors on pages 35–37 in the *RPP Brokers Handbook V.2*, which can be found on the NNERPP website at http://nnerpp.rice.edu/rpp-brokers-handbook/.)

We want to thank our reviewers, Moonhawk Kim at UC Berkeley and Erin O'Hara Block, who was formerly with the Tennessee Education Research Association and is currently a school board member in Metro Nashville School District and adjunct professor at Vanderbilt University. Your insights on how to improve the book were very important to strengthening our final product. We want to thank Norma Ming, Supervisor of Research in San Francisco Unified School District, who was an important contributor to some portions and provided incredible guidance overall as we worked to finalize the book. We want to show appreciation to our editors at Routledge, including Heather Jarrow and Mari Zajac, for support in developing this manuscript and giving us the opportunity to make this book a reality. Finally, we want to thank Ruth López Turley, who launched National Network of Education Research-Practice Partnerships (NNERPP) in 2016 and formed the network of RPPs that lead to products such as this handbook.

We'd like to thank the Bill & Melinda Gates Foundation, whose funding allowed for this open access book to exist. We also note that this work was supported by the Bill & Melinda Gates Foundation [Grant INV-026588]. Under the grant conditions of the Foundation, a Creative Commons Attribution 4.0 Generic License has already been assigned to the Author Accepted Manuscript version that might arise from this submission.

Finally, thank you to our families who love and support us as we pursue our professional careers. We could not do this without you!

REFERENCES

Wentworth, L., Conaway, C., Shewchuk, S., Arce-Trigatti, P. (2021). *RPP Brokers Handbook: A Guide to Brokering in Education Research-Practice Partnerships*. Houston, TX: National Network of Education Research-Practice Partnerships (NNERPP).

Wentworth, L., Conaway, C., Shewchuk, S., & Arce-Trigatti, P. (2022). *RPP Brokers Handbook, V. 2: A Guide to Brokering in Education Research-Practice Partnerships*. Houston, TX: National Network of Education Research-Practice Partnerships (NNERPP).

Preface

This book documents the work of brokers: the professionals who serve as the bridge between researchers and practitioners in partnerships working to improve education organizations. Brokers manage the necessary relationships across the worlds of educational research, practice, policy, and community organizations, bringing people together to build a more equitable and just educational system.

As we write this book, the field of education continues to grapple with its reputation for systematically reproducing inequality. Many members of the education sector have been working to break down existing systems that cause this inequality and to design new systems to produce more equitable outcomes. Leaders in education working to change status quo practices, especially practices and systems that reinforce the existing power structure, are confronted with resistance from people who gain power from existing practices. For example, education researchers may have been trained in practices that are decolonial (Patel, 2015) or humanistic (Paris & Winn, 2013) in nature, but then are asked to study and document phenomena without seeking to respond to or repair historical harms. New educators may enter teaching positions inspired by notions of culturally sustaining pedagogy (Paris, 2012), only to be confronted with resistance from their more senior grade level or departmental colleagues with whom they are expected to collaborate.

Similarly, brokers have to work against existing power structures that favor the expertise of researchers. They will be confronted with resistance when they work to center the research questions of practitioners, students, community members, or people other than those with the title "researcher" or with "PhD" behind their name. They will bring ideas into their practice from research that may seem opposite the routine behavior in schools. They will find that researchers are not accustomed nor expected to present their findings to the communities in which they conduct their research.

The work of an RPP broker is inherently against the grain of existing power structures, and many of their actions will be questioned by people in leadership positions or by people who hold the power. RPP brokers will need to confront efforts to marginalize groups of people through racism, sexism, ableism, xenophobia, status hierarchies, and other mindsets and efforts that marginalize.

While their work is confronted with these multiple barriers, brokers in education RPPs are an essential component. They are found everywhere in partnerships: in all sorts of roles – teachers, school and district leaders, students, parents, community members, and researchers – and across a variety of organizations. Despite their critical connector role, brokers are often undervalued or not given the importance they deserve because their work is invisible. Yet it is brokers who create the conditions that result in socially impactful, collaborative, and community-engaged research.

This book aims to elevate the work of RPP brokers in education by codifying their work, thereby identifying the specific and essential role the work of RPP brokers plays in enabling public scholarship and social impact of research. The book describes brokers' activities through a new and hopefully useful framework dividing the work of brokers into two main groups of activities: 1) *brokering to strengthen partners* through supporting participants' research use and production; developing and nurturing relationships to weather challenges; and building individual competencies to manage an RPP; and 2) *brokering to strengthen the partnership* through developing partnership governance and administrative structures; designing processes and communications routines; and assessing and continuously improving the partnership. This book also attends to the sociocultural, historical, and political contexts where RPP brokering happens. The book includes cases that highlight brokers' work in existing RPPs. The majority of the cases explore brokers' work to manage inevitable power differences and other attempts to marginalize individuals and groups.

It is worth emphasizing what the handbook does not attempt to do. The framework was developed based on existing research on brokering in the field of education and the authors' professional experience, and does not share findings from new research about brokering in RPPs in education. Further, it is a compendium of existing brokering cases, with guidance and resources for individuals engaging in these activities. It does not aim at *reduction or isolation* of brokering activities in and of themselves. Rather, it aims to integrate existing research- and practice-based knowledge on brokering, in order to support individuals doing this work into the context of research-practice partnerships. In doing so, we hope that the handbook provides a common language and puts the often "hidden" activities of brokering in partnerships into the spotlight, for the benefit of practitioners and scholars of research-practice partnerships in education.

The book aims to answer some important questions in the field of education about RPP brokering. Questions like, what practices bridge research, practice, and policy in education? What are effective tools and routines that have been used in an RPP to bridge these research and practice communities? How do participants in RPPs work to change systems in education to support research production and research use simultaneously? How do participants in RPPs upend status quo practices? How do participants in RPPs support change in individual practices and institutional practices and policies at the same time? What is brokering in RPPs? Why are brokering activities important for RPP work?

The "who" of this book is the intended audience of people across different roles in the education sector who are curious about, interested in, currently studying, and actively working in, or aspire to help, research, practice, and policy in education work together to support educational outcomes and systems change through brokering. Here are a few of the audiences we imagine reading this book:

- **People who are already engaging in RPP brokering.** This may include individuals who serve in formal brokering positions or partners who are engaging in informal brokering in RPPs or other forms of collaborative education research.
- **People who are curious about RPP brokering.** You have been working in more traditional roles within the field of education, and you are curious about how your role could evolve to help research, practice, policy, and other parts of the educational communities work together to support improvement and transformation.
- **People who are about to engage in RPP brokering.** This may include new staff that might be interested in learning more about brokering and RPPs, especially those who are novices with respect to developing RPP relationships and infrastructure.
- **People who are working towards or teaching a course in educational research, practice, and policy systems.** The handbook may also prove useful to the growing number of university instructors, faculty, and students who are teaching and learning about brokering within education contexts and, in particular, in RPP settings.
- **People who may be researchers who study RPPs or brokering in education.** We think the handbook is also useful to researchers who are studying knowledge brokering as a concept, especially within the education sector or within research-practice partnerships.

This book contains some special features that will help readers understand the concept of RPP brokering in education as well as see the brokering in action. First, we include cases in many of the chapters describing brokers using tools or making moves in the day-to-day realities of their work in an education RPP. In Chapters 1 and 3, we start with cases of RPP brokers that are more holistic in nature, where a set of tools and moves are used over time in an RPP. In Chapters 4, 5, and 6, we present cases that demonstrate different aspects of RPP brokering, organized in relationship to a framework for RPP brokering. Many of the cases have specific templates and reference materials that can be seen either in the appendix of this book, or at the Routledge webpage for this book (www.routledge.com/9781032358758). Second, in Chapter 2, we include more detailed overviews of specific literature reviews we've conducted related to brokering and RPPs that may be of interest to the research community and practicing RPP brokers who like to read research on brokering. Finally, in Chapter 7, we describe how people in different roles in the field of education use the cases to learn about RPP brokering or to adapt the tools and brokering moves in their work as an RPP broker. These examples could be a model for readers who want to use these cases to help others learn about RPP brokering.

These special features are intended to help you fulfill the needs in your current, future, or newfound role related to RPP brokering in education. Our goal for this book is to help legitimize and strengthen the practice of RPP brokering across the field of education. We see RPP brokering in education as a means to an end; we want RPP brokering to ultimately support better partnerships, better schools, better universities, better communities, and ultimately a better, more equitable and just future for our children.

REFERENCES

Paris, D. (2012). Culturally Sustaining Pedagogy: A Needed Change in Stance, Terminology, and Practice. *Educational Researcher, 41*(3), 93–97.

Paris, D. & Winn, M. T. (2013). *Humanizing Research: Decolonizing Qualitative Inquiry with Youth and Communities, First Edition.* SAGE Publications, Inc.

Patel, L. (2015). *Decolonizing Educational Research: From Ownership to Answerability.* Routledge.

Chapter 1

What Is Brokering and Why Does It Matter in Education Research-Practice Partnerships?

It is June 2020, and the head of the Department of Technology in San Francisco Unified School District, Melissa Dodd, is working with a team of other administrators to figure out their approach to designing and providing online instruction at scale across all K–12 students for the 2020–2021 school year. The sources of evidence and information to consider are limited due to the COVID-19 pandemic's unprecedented scope in modern history and the lack of experience worldwide in teaching K–12 students and engaging with families exclusively through online platforms.

Two years earlier, Dodd and her team started a pilot that helped teachers across a subset of schools implement and employ technology, practices, and mindsets to support personalized learning environments for students. Called the PLE pilot, these personalized learning environments are designed to support teachers leveraging digital tools and flexible environments to enhance student learning, equity, independence, and agency. From the onset, Dodd and her colleagues, Lindsey Blass, Zareen Poonen Levien, E'leva Hughes Gibson, and Ben Klaus, wanted research to inform the design of the PLE program. Blass took the lead, tapping the long-standing research-practice partnership with Stanford University. The partnership between Stanford and San Francisco Unified School District (SFUSD) is directed by California Education Partners, a nonprofit that acts as a third-party broker to develop relationships between the researchers and the leaders and support research development and use. The partnership director, Laura Wentworth, acted as a broker by arranging a meeting with Blass, Hughes Gibson, and Stanford University researchers Amber Levinson and Brigid Barron with expertise in the area. Together, the district leaders and researchers developed an approach to

DOI: 10.4324/9781003334385-1
This chapter has been made available under a CC-BY-NC-ND license.

documenting insights generated by the program and generating formative feedback to aid program iteration and improvement. Wentworth organized their first few meetings and facilitated the establishment of agreements for working together, but soon Levinson and the SFUSD leaders like Blass and Poonen Levien negotiated their own routines for working together and supported the operations and use of the research. Having this RPP in place along with a broker available to manage these initial meetings provided important infrastructure and supported relationship development.

Their investment in this relationship provided unexpected additional value during the pandemic. Dodd and her colleague Blass from SFUSD turned to their "researchers on speed dial" Levinson and Barron to provide insights on how to design approaches to distance learning. The Stanford researchers continued to work with the teachers in the PLE pilot within SFUSD during spring 2020, a critical time for schools during the pandemic. Teachers reflected that their professional development related to this PLE pilot leading up to 2020 on shifting mindsets about instruction enabled them to be more successful during the difficult transition to distance learning. This research highlighted how teachers valued learning with each other in the PLE pilot, learning how to better engage with families and caregivers online, and seeing how student engagement and fluency with digital tools from the PLE pilot supported students' learning during the pandemic. On the last point, teachers described how their students in the spring of 2020 had already learned to be leaders in their classroom all year and had been proactively asking questions and solving problems. When they transitioned to distance learning in the 2020–2021 school year, teachers noticed that students continued this level of agency in approaching this new mode of learning.

Levinson and Barron went on to study the teachers in the personalized learning environments program in the 2020–2021 school year, examining instruction during distance learning. During this time, the PLE leaders added an additional part of the program to supply kindergarten and first grade students at some of the participating schools with home kits of physical materials to use in conjunction with digital tools. The researchers observed virtual classrooms of students using these materials to increase student engagement and participation. Teachers also recorded videos of their instruction to share with the researchers and with other teachers in the program. All the while, the researchers were also sharing findings with Dodd, Blass, Poonen Levien, and their team, who could use this evidence to improve the conditions, support, training, and materials for

> teachers working online with students. For example, an online learning tool, Seesaw, that had been previously only used in this PLE pilot, was rolled out as a districtwide tool during 2020–2021 to support deeper learning for all students. SFUSD's Department of Technology developed extensive training on using Seesaw for all teachers in the district, using many examples from the schools in the PLE pilot.

This story demonstrates the potential of a research-practice partnership (RPP) in education to provide research evidence for practitioners to make timely decisions. It also demonstrates how brokering can facilitate this work. Wentworth's role with the third-party non-profit was dedicated to brokering: she connected researchers and practitioners and helped them negotiate the formation of their relationship by setting up agreements and establishing roles for working together. In parallel, the district and research partners also employed brokering skills to get the necessary work done to inform district practice. They built relationships and created routines and structures that allowed the two sides of the partnership to operationalize the research and discuss formative findings. For example, district leaders like Blass and Poonen Levien managed meeting schedules and maintained a running notes document with shared resources and agendas based on pre-existing district norms, which facilitated providing updates and guiding the timely progress of the research. These relationships helped build systematic evidence from SFUSD's own context about teacher and family needs during the pandemic. Further, these routines also transferred across leadership turnover on both the research and district sides of the partnership.

EDUCATION RESEARCH-PRACTICE PARTNERSHIPS (RPPS) HELP RESEARCH AND PRACTICE INTERSECT

Despite the promise of such collaborative relationships, research production and enactment of practices have historically not worked very closely together in education. Nelson and Campbell (2017) describe the field of education's difficulty in achieving what they call "evidence-informed practice" at a systems level, where evidence, including research evidence, informs decisions that positively influence educational improvements. Nelson and Campbell attribute this challenge to a lack of consensus on key questions about what evidence-informed practice means, what is reliable evidence, what constitutes research, or what are the mediating processes that bridge evidence and practice.

To help research and practice work together towards improvements in the field of education, researchers and practitioners engage in research-practice partnerships (RPPs) (Coburn & Penuel, 2016).

Farrell and colleagues (2021) define research-practice partnerships in education as:

> A long-term collaboration aimed at educational improvement or equitable transformation through engagement with research. These partnerships are intentionally organized to connect diverse forms of expertise and shift power relations in the research endeavor to ensure that all partners have a say in the joint work.
>
> (p. 5)

Farrell and colleagues also describe five principles from RPPs that set them apart from other forms of collaborative education research. They are long term, they work on educational improvement or equitable transformation, they feature engagement with research as a leading activity, they intentionally bring together expertise from different sectors and perspectives, and they employ strategies that shift power and status to make sure all RPP participants have a voice. Consequently, members of RPPs use specific strategies for working together: they build trust and develop relationships to strengthen the work of partnerships (Tseng et al., 2017; Kochanek et al., 2020); they establish roles, routines, and structures of partnerships that support researchers' and practitioners' engagement (Penuel et al., 2013; Farrell et al., 2018, 2019b, 2022); they learn and sensemake together as they work on research together (Penuel et al., 2015; Bevan et al., 2017); they attend to issues around authority (Coburn et al., 2008) and race and power differences (Denner et al., 2019; Tanksley & Estrada, 2022).

Farley-Ripple et al. (2018) describes RPPs as having the potential to support research use in educational organizations as they emphasize "co-construction" of research rather than "dissemination and uptake" (p. 7). (See also Henrick et al., 2018; Farrell et al., 2019a.)

BROKERS SUSTAIN AND SUPPORT RPPS

There is some research and practice evidence suggesting the role of the brokers or the act of brokering is an essential role or activity in RPPs. Brokers and brokering moves are involved in starting, supporting, and maintaining research-practice partnerships. We define the role of a broker as a person who serves as a key connector to help members of research and practice organizations integrate into an RPP by cultivating and maintaining the relationships needed to effectively support research production and use (Cooper, 2014; Neal et al., 2015; Farley-Ripple et al., 2018; Wentworth et al., 2021). The broker may perform these functions as their primary job duty, and/or multiple members of the partnership may take on different dimensions of brokering work.

Davidson and Penuel (2020) suggest "brokering acts are crucial for sustaining RPPs" (p. 154). Brokers support "joint work" between researchers and practitioners by crossing the professional and organizational boundaries between their worlds. This stands in contrast to the translational paradigm of research use, where researchers conduct research in one world and translate findings for practitioner use in another world (Penuel et al., 2015).

If brokering is an essential role within RPPs, then it is even more important that the field understands the activities brokers undertake to support RPPs. One way to think about the work of brokers is to think about brokering as facilitating knowledge mobilization processes, which is an umbrella term encompassing a wide range of activities relating to the production and use of research results, including knowledge synthesis, dissemination, transfer, exchange, and co-creation or co-production by researchers and knowledge users (Social Sciences and Humanities Research Council, n.d.). Brokering helps knowledge mobilization through five processes (Ward et al., 2009; Glegg & Hoens, 2016). First, knowledge brokering manages information by seeking and sharing relevant education research. Second, knowledge brokering can function as links between research and practice by fostering relationships among researchers and education professionals. Third, knowledge brokering builds capacity by developing organizational structures and individual attitudes and skills that support research use, as well as context-specific knowledge (e.g., culture, processes, and barriers) with stakeholders to inform decision-making processes. Fourth, knowledge brokering provides facilitation by guiding and supporting individuals in integrating research, contextual, and experiential knowledge into educational decision-making. Fifth, knowledge brokering helps to assess the local context to inform knowledge brokering activities, evaluating the outcomes of RPP activities, and evaluating the knowledge brokers' own knowledge brokering performance. Within RPPs, some brokers function mostly in one of these role domains, while others may cross all five categories to facilitate the use of evidence within their partnerships.

Another way to think about the work of brokers in RPPs is to think about the spectrum of activities and actors involved in an RPP, with brokers being one of those actors. Some actors are purely research oriented and some actors are purely practice oriented. But many participant activities in RPPs occupy the space in between research and practice and are aimed at sustaining research use and the partnership itself. This is illustrated in Figure 1.1, adapted from Booker et al. (2019). The activities of brokering and boundary-crossing may be done by an actor whose role it is to serve as a broker for the partnership, or they may be done by other members of a partnership with a stronger research or practice orientation to the work. As seen in the opening case, the partnership had a formal RPP director whose role it was to broker partner relationships. However,

Purely Policy/Practice	Brokering	Purely Research

• Advising on existing and anticipated policies and local context
• Anticipating likely concerns of stakeholders
• Advising on the right research design and products to meet stakeholder needs, but also adjusting to meet researcher needs
	• Brokering to support partners
	  ○ Research production and use
	  ○ Building skills and knowledge
	  ○ Building relationships to weather challenges
	• Brokering to support partnership
	  ○ Developing partnership infrastructure
	  ○ Designing processes and communication
	  ○ Assessing and improving the partnership
		• Conducting original analysis
		• Advising on data collection and research design, but also adjusting to meet policymaker needs

Figure 1.1 Brokering activities distinguished from policy and practice or research activities

other practitioners and researchers also used brokering moves when working within the RPP, making brokering an important set of activities that many RPP members enact.

RPP BROKERS ACTIVITIES FRAMEWORK

With this handbook, we wanted to move beyond the theoretical frameworks described earlier to a more practical framework for RPP broker activities to advance how aspiring, existing, and veteran brokers execute their work. As seen in Figure 1.2, the framework addresses six key activities, grouped into two overarching skill sets, brokering to strengthen partners and brokering to strengthen partnerships. Brokering to strengthen partners is the work that brokers do when working with individuals and teams working across different organizations. It includes activities related to creating the conditions to support research production and use, developing and nurturing relationships to weather partnership challenges, and building individual partners' competency for engaging in an RPP. Brokering to strengthen the partnership is the work brokers do when working to build and maintain systems and processes across the partnership that span two or more organizations. It includes activities associated with developing

WHAT IS BROKERING AND WHY DOES IT MATTER?

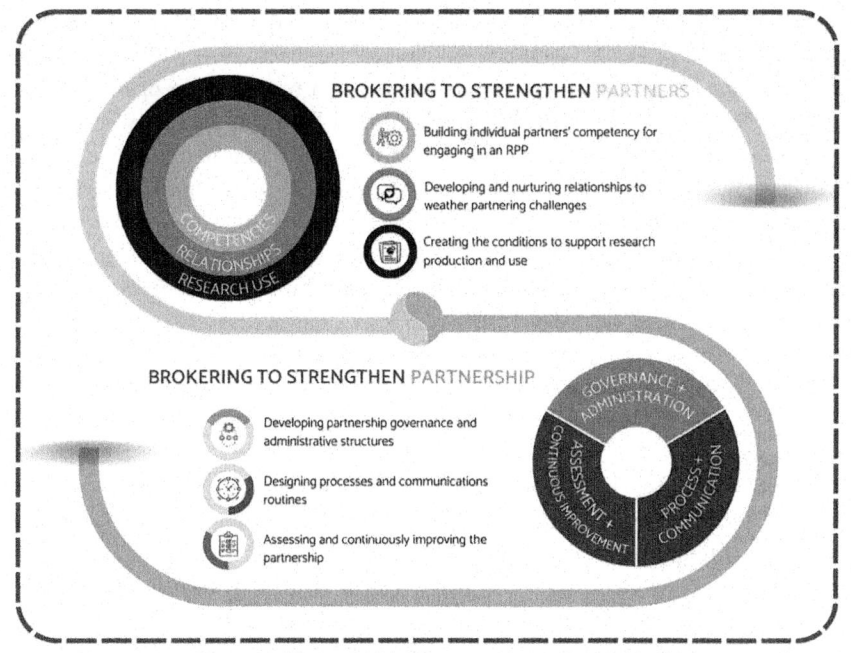

Figure 1.2 A framework to explore the work of brokers in education RPPs

partnership governance and administrative structures, designing processes and communications routines, and assessing and continuously improving the partnership. We also situate the framework in a broader sociocultural context that attends to power differences and tensions between participants because of issues like racism centering white, middle-class norms (e.g., Chavez, 2005; Denner et al., 2019; Henderson & Laman, 2020; Ho et al., 2020; Tanksley & Estrada, 2022) and various efforts to support equity and social justice (e.g., Vetter et al., 2022).

ORIENTATION TO THE HANDBOOK

In Chapter 2, "The Practice and Research Behind the RPP Brokers Framework," we describe in detail the process we used for developing our framework, as seen in Figure 1.2, what we often refer to as the "RPP Brokers Framework." First, we examined RPP broker activities through our own practice-based reflection. Three of the four authors have been active brokers in research-practice partnerships in education, and we based some description of brokering activities on our professional experiences. Second, we examined the activities of RPP brokers through the NNERPP member stakeholder feedback. NNERPP is a network of education research-practice partnerships with a membership of 60 RPPs at the time of publication. NNERPP has an Annual Forum each year where all of its member may gather to learn from each other. Starting in 2019, we hosted a meeting at the Annual Forum about brokers where we gathered information from self-identified brokers attending the event who showed up to the role-alike session for RPP brokers. Third, we triangulated our reflections by conducting a systematic scoping review of the literature. In the chapter, we present the literature collected during our review. Thus, readers will be able to look "under the hood" of the process we used to develop the framework. It's important to note that this chapter includes a description of our methods for developing the framework and may be less relevant for readers who are purely reading this book to get specific practices to use for brokering in their RPPs.

In Chapter 3, "A Framework: What Do Brokers Do?," we explain the RPP Brokers Activities Framework. We describe each part of the framework using a summary of findings from our systematic literature review and examples from practice stemming primarily from RPP broker actions within the partnership between Stanford University Graduate School of Education and SFUSD. The framework adds to the documentation about RPPs by explaining the two levels of activities at play within partnerships – partnering and partnerships. We argue that the individuals and teams engage in activities that involve partnering. "Partnering" is essentially working together with another individual or other team members, who may work for one or multiple organizations. We define the micro behaviors in partnering that brokers can help develop and influence – supporting research production and use, weathering challenges by building relationships, and building individual competencies of partners. We also describe how RPP brokers strengthen partnerships as a whole through actions such as developing partnership governance and administrative structures, designing processes and communication routines, and assessing and continuously improving the partnership.

We end Chapter 3 by describing the sociocultural context in which RPP brokers situate their work. We discuss how racism and efforts to support equity influence the power differences in RPPs. As we further developed this RPP Brokers Framework, and as the literature on RPPs and brokering in education has evolved since we first started working on the framework in 2019, we found that attention to power differences, equity, and racism also sits in RPP brokers' lexicon of responsibilities. Because brokering is about crossing organizational boundaries, RPP brokers must attend to power differences stemming from issues of differential status and authority awarded to different organizations and roles across the RPP (Coburn et al., 2008). Brokers must attend to equity in process – centering voices in communication and structures of groups historically underserved in educational research — as well as outcome — producing and using research that centers on supporting historically marginalized groups that sit outside of the white, middle-class norms usually privileged in our organizations. RPP brokers must inevitably confront and work against racism as they work to decolonize and humanize educational research and move it away from reproducing the status quo of centering whiteness and patriarchy. We will explain in Chapter 3 what the literature and practice say about power differences, equity, and racism in RPPs.

In Chapter 4, "RPP Brokers in Different Contexts," we explain the role of RPP brokers across contexts. We break down the definition of the role of an RPP broker and provide short vignettes demonstrating variations in their roles and organizations. Brokers can sit inside the practitioner institutions, inside the researcher institutions, in third-party organizations, or in many other types of roles and settings. Funding for the broker role could come from different sources like institutional funding or "soft" money grants. Generally, we explore who is a broker, what roles they typically play in their organizations, and how they show up across the field of education. We provide examples of formal job descriptions of various self-identified brokers, as well as illustrating the informal activities they engage in because they identify as brokers. This chapter will help the field understand that brokers come in all types of roles and how their roles and behaviors may differ based on their context.

In Chapter 5, "Cases Describing Brokering to Strengthen Partners," we explain in short summaries the cases, describing the tools and strategies RPP brokers use and how they relate to the concept of brokering to strengthen partners. We identify three important activities a broker must attend to when strengthening the partners, which build on each other. First, brokers must create the conditions to support the partner's research production and use, which are often the central aims of partnership work. Second, brokers must develop and nurture partner relationships to weather challenges that will test the limits of effective collaboration. And third, brokers must build individual partners' knowledge and skills to collaborate effectively. We will have cases that exemplify and explain each of these types of activities.

In Chapter 6, "Cases Describing Brokering to Strengthen Partnerships," we describe the other half of the RPP Brokers Framework. This part of the framework centers around building and maintaining the necessary infrastructure for the partnership to thrive. RPP infrastructure refers to the underlying processes, routines, and protocols that shape how the partnership operates. Infrastructure helps define the system within which the RPP will function. Although it is often invisible once implemented, it is critical to ensuring the RPP runs smoothly. While there are several infrastructural components that together result in the partnership, we focus on three areas here that are especially important for brokering in RPPs. First, brokers develop partnership governance and administrative structures. Second, brokers design processes and communications routines.

Third, brokers assess and continuously improve the partnership. Like Chapter 5, in Chapter 6, we will have cases that exemplify and explain each of these types of activities.

In Chapter 7, "Using Cases to Support RPP Broker Work and Development," we describe how we have seen the cases used to support skills and knowledge building for new, aspiring, or seasoned RPP brokers. We describe approaches to using the cases for 1) brokers to use in their day-to-day work, 2) teachers or leaders to use in university courses or non-profit workshops, 3) supervisors to use as a coaching tool to support aspiring brokers in the field, and 4) researchers to use as part of their study of RPPs and RPP brokering.

In Chapter 8, "The Future of Brokering in Research-Practice Partnerships," we share an essay describing how we envision the future of RPP brokering as the field evolves. We talk about the current and future conceptions of brokering and implications for RPP brokering as the field of education evolves.

CONCLUSION

Brokering activities are to research-practice partnerships as gears are to bicycles. Like gears, brokering is both very practical when it adjust the speed of your bike and very challenging when they break down and stop your ride mid-journey. Consequently, the effectiveness of the brokering in an RPP can make or break the outputs and outcomes of an RPP.

We also want to point out that RPP work is complex, and effective brokering is not the only way to address challenges faced in collaborative education research. We humbly present the cases in this book as a potentially useful resource, and we acknowledge this is not a recipe book for RPP brokering. The work of RPPs is often nuanced, and some RPP participants may find these cases of RPP brokering more helpful than others.

In general, we hope this book describing the brokering activities will support the growing number of professionals in education RPPs identifying as brokers. We aspire for the book to be a resource for future brokers as well as professionals currently acting as brokers who want to strengthen their skills in brokering.

REFERENCES

Bevan, B., Penuel, W. R., Bell, P., & Buffington, P. J. (2017). Chapter 2: Learning, generalizing, and local sense-making in research-practice partners. In B. Bevan & W. R. Penuel (Eds.), *Connecting research and practice for educational improvement: Ethical and equitable approaches*. Routledge.

Booker, L., Conaway, C., & Schwartz, N. (2019). *Five ways RPPs can fail and how to avoid them: Applying conceptual frameworks to improve RPPs*. William T. Grant Foundation.

Chavez, V. (2005). Silence speaks: The language of internalized oppression and privilege in community-based research. Community based research. *Metropolitan Universities Journal*, *16*(1).

Coburn, C. E., Bae, S., & Turner, E. O. (2008). Authority, status, and the dynamics of insider-outsider partnerships at the district level. *Peabody Journal of Education*, *83*(3), 364–399.

Coburn, C. E., & Penuel, W. R. (2016). Research – practice partnerships in education: Outcomes, dynamics, and open questions. *Educational Researcher*, *45*(1), 48–54.

Cooper, A. (2014). Knowledge mobilisation in education across Canada: A cross-case analysis of 44 research brokering organizations. *Evidence and Policy*, *10*(1), 29–59.

Davidson, K. L., & Penuel, W. R. (2020). Chapter 11: The role of brokers in sustaining partnership work in education. In J. Malin & C. Brown (Eds.), *The role of knowledge brokers in education: Connecting the dots between research and practice* (pp. 154–167). Routledge.

Denner, J., Bean, S., Campe, S., Martinez, J., & Torres, D. (2019). *Negotiating trust, power, and culture in a research – practice partnership*. AERA Open.

Farley-Ripple, E., May, H., Karpyn, A., Tilley, K., & McDonough, K. (2018). Rethinking connections between research and practice in education: A conceptual framework. *Educational Researcher*, *47*(4), 235–245.

Farrell, C. C., Coburn, C. E., & Chong, S. (2019a). Under what conditions do school districts learn from external partners? The role of absorptive capacity. *American Educational Research Journal*, *56*(3), 955–994.

Farrell, C. C., Davidson, K. L., Repko-Erwin, M. E., Penuel, W. R., Quantz, M., Wong, H., Riedy, R., & Brink, Z. (2018). *A descriptive study of the IES researcher – practitioner partnerships in education research program: Final report* (Technical Report No. 3). National Center for Research in Policy and Practice. https://files.eric.ed.gov/fulltext/ED599980.pdf

Farrell, C. C., Harrison, C., & Coburn, C. E. (2019b). "What the hell is this, and who the hell are you?": Role and identity negotiation in research-practice partnerships. AERA Open.

Farrell, C. C., Penuel, W. R., Allen, A., Anderson, E. R., Bohannon, B. X., Coburn, C., & Brown, S. L. (2022). Learning at the boundaries of research and practice: A framework for understanding research – practice partnerships. *Educational Researcher*, *51*(3), 197–208.

Farrell, C. C., Penuel, W. R., Coburn, C., Daniel, J., & Steup, L. (2021). *Research-practice partnerships in education: The state of the field*. William T. Grant Foundation.

Glegg, S. M., & Hoens, A. (2016). Role domains of knowledge brokering: A model for the health care setting. *Journal of Neurologic Physical Therapy*, *40*(2), 115–123. https://doi.org/10.1097/NPT.0000000000000122

Henderson, J. W., & Laman, T. T. (2020). "This Ain't Gonna work for me": The role of the afrocentric praxis of eldering in creating more equitable research partnerships. *Urban Education*, *55*(6), 892–910.

Henrick, E. C., Klafehn, A. B., & Cobb, P. (2018). Chapter 14, assessing the impact of partnership recommendations on district instructional improvement strategies. In P. Cobb, K. Jackson, T. M. Smith, & the MIST Team (Eds.), *Systems for instructional improvement: Creating coherence from the classroom to the district office*. Harvard Education Press.

Ho, D., Dawene, D., Roberts, K., & Hing, J. J. (2020). A systematic review of boundary-crossing partnerships in designing equity-oriented special education services for culturally and linguistically diverse students with disabilities. *Remedial and Special Education*, 42(6), 412–425.

Kochanek, J., Scholz, C., Monahan, B., & Pardo, M. (2020). Chapter 12: An exploratory study of how to use RPPs to build trust and support the use of early warning systems. *Teachers College Record*, 122(14), 1–28.

Neal, J. W., Neal, Z. P., Kornbluh, M., Mills, K. J., & Lawlor, J. A. (2015). Brokering the research-practice gap: A typology. *American Journal of Community Psychology*, 56(3–4), 422–435.

Nelson, J., & Campbell, C. (2017) Evidence-informed practice in education: Meanings and applications. *Educational Research*, 59(2), 127–135.

Penuel, W. R., Allen, A. R., Coburn, C. E., & Farrell, C. (2015). Conceptualizing research – practice partnerships as joint work at boundaries. *Journal of Education for Students Placed at Risk*, 20(1), 182–197.

Penuel, W. R., Coburn, C. E., & Gallagher, D. J. (2013). Negotiating problems of practice in research practice design partnerships. Yearbook of the national society for the study of education. *Teachers College Record*, 112(2), 237–255.

Social Sciences and Humanities Research Council. (n.d.). *Guidelines for effective knowledge mobilization*. www.sshrc-crsh.gc.ca/funding-financement/policies-politiques/knowl edge_mobilisation-mobilisation_des_connaissances-eng.aspx#:~:text=and%20 related%20activities.-,What%20is%20knowledge%20mobilization%3F,by%20 researchers%20and%20knowledge%20users

Tanksley, T., & Estrada, C. (2022). Toward a critical race RPP: How race, power and inform research practice partnerships. *International Journal of Research & Method in Education*, 1–13.

Tseng, V., Easton, J. Q., & Supplee, L. H. (2017). Research practice partnerships: Building two way streets of engagement. Social policy report. *Society for Research in Child Development*, 30(4).

Vetter, A., Faircloth, B. S., Hewitt, K. K., Gonzalez, L. M., He, Y., & Rock, M. L. (2022). Equity and social justice in research practice partnerships in the United States. *Review of Educational Research*. https://doi.org/10.3102/00346543211070048

Ward, V., House, A., & Hamer, S. (2009). Knowledge brokering: The missing link in the evidence to action chain? *Evidence & Policy: A Journal of Research, Debate and Practice*, 5(3), 267–279. https://doi.org/10.1332%2F174426409X463811

Wentworth, L., Khanna, R., Nayfack, M., & Schwartz, D. (2021, Spring). Closing the research-practice gap in education. *Stanford Social Innovation Review*, 19(2).

Chapter 2

The Practice and Research Behind the RPP Brokers Framework

Our RPP Brokers Framework aims to describe the professional activities RPP brokers engage in when bringing together education researchers and practitioners to work collaboratively on research. In elaborating on the framework, we drew upon our own experiences working as brokers in RPPs and those of NNERPP members who identify as RPP brokers, in addition to examining research about brokering in RPPs and knowledge brokering in education more broadly. In this chapter, we present our approach to developing the framework. The context within which the framework was developed is key to understanding its contribution to the preparation and support of brokers in education RPPs.

The groundwork for what eventually came to be the activities identified in the RPP Brokers Framework was laid via extensive RPP initiatives in education that took place within the U.S. during the 2000s. These included the relatively rapid expansion of RPPs in education settings (Arce-Trigatti et al., 2018; Penuel et al., 2018), the development and study of brokering roles more recently (e.g., Hopkins et al., 2019), and new offerings from the National Network of Education Research-Practice Partnerships focused on training and development opportunities for those interested in pursuing or extending their capacity to broker (NNERPP, nnerpp.rice.edu). Those involved in developing the framework had themselves worked in brokering roles in RPPs best characterized as research alliances. The authors of this handbook playing those roles were Paula Arce-Trigatti, formerly a postdoctoral student working in an RPP; Carrie Conaway, a director of research within a state education agency; and Laura Wentworth, a director of a research-practice partnership within a third-party, non-profit organization.

At the time we developed the framework (and still today), outside of NNERPP's efforts named earlier, few professional development and training opportunities within the U.S. prepare education professionals for brokering positions. Seeing this gap in capacity-building, we aimed to develop materials that would equip both novice and experienced brokers with knowledge and tools to support everyone's meaningful engagement in the collaborative education

DOI: 10.4324/9781003334385-2
This chapter has been made available under a CC-BY-NC-ND license.

research process. The aim was not to prepare individuals serving in a specific role, such as researchers aspiring to work in RPPs. Rather, it was to support anyone (including education professionals, researchers, community members, and other RPP participants) involved in an RPP who either currently acts as a broker or aspires to become a broker.

Because the framework is meant to influence and guide practice, it was essential for us to include knowledge from actual brokering practice as part of our development process. Experiential and practical knowledge and expertise are important in many professions, notably in education, where practice-based knowledge and expertise are recognized as vital complements to research-based knowledge that, together, can provide viable solutions to local problems (e.g., McMahon et al., 2022). In the context of education RPPs, a broker's knowledge and skills are a key part of the research use process as well as the collaboration happening among RPP participants. The personal scope of practice consists of activities undertaken by an individual broker that are based on one's own education, knowledge, competency, and experience. Individual brokers also have to contend with a larger ecosystem within the field of education where institutions and systems have reproduced power differences among individuals as a result of racism, sexism, xenophobia, and other social harms. Identifying, valuing, and sharing professional knowledge from these experiences are essential for continuous improvement of brokering practice, *as well as* for developing and improving the theory and science of RPP brokering.

To gain a comprehensive understanding about the field of brokering in education RPPs, we also worked to locate the framework within the body of research on brokering in education RPPs. Literature on this topic is international, originating from the United States (e.g., Davidson & Penuel, 2019; Farrell et al., 2018; Miller, 2007; Wilcox et al., 2017), and to a more limited extent Canada (e.g., Campbell et al., 2017; Fenwick, 2004) and Europe, including Germany (e.g., Hartmann & Decristan, 2018) and the Netherlands (e.g., Akkerman & Bruining, 2016). Developments in education RPPs within the USA have occurred in a completely different practice and policy context from that in other countries. As such, research literature stemming from the U.S. is important for building an understanding of the context in which brokering in RPPs has developed here, as well as how the concept of brokering has been interpreted and used in the academic community. However, international literature can assist with broadening knowledge of brokers' skills and activities and can add discoveries from other contexts that are relevant for professional practice in the U.S.

Combining practice and research expertise to develop this framework maximizes the potential contribution of both forms of expertise. In the following paragraphs, we provide more detailed information about how we integrated both research and practice knowledge to develop the framework.

THE PRACTICE AND RESEARCH BEHIND THE RPP BROKERS FRAMEWORK

PRACTICE-BASED REFLECTION

In the first phase of creating the RPP Brokers Handbook, Laura Wentworth and Carrie Conaway engaged in practice-based reflection to explore their experiences as brokers in education RPPs. During these meetings, Wentworth and Conaway reflected on their activities, their main achievements as brokers, and where they had met particular challenges or conflicts they faced in their roles. They cross-referenced these experiences with relevant academic literature to understand how practices identified through reflection were discussed in the academic contexts. This initial literature review was not structured or comprehensive but instead looked for work that illustrated how their experiences (identified through reflection) showed up in the research literature. At the end of the reflection exercise, Wentworth and Conaway generated the first draft of the Brokering Activities Framework, which would eventually be presented at the NNERPP Annual Forum in 2019. As seen in Figure 2.1, Conaway and Wentworth landed on seven themes, or what they called "broker moves." As described in Table 2.1, each theme has a definition and an example of what the broker move looks like in action.

RPP Broker Handbook: Definition and Framework

Broker: Brokers help members of a partnership navigate the cultures, languages, and conditions faced when working together. (See NNERPP definition of knowledge broker.)

RPP Broker Moves

1. Negotiating
2. Designing social interactions
3. Forming partnership infrastructure
4. Building skills for partnering
5. Establishing partnership culture
6. Supporting knowledge mobilization
7. Blending in

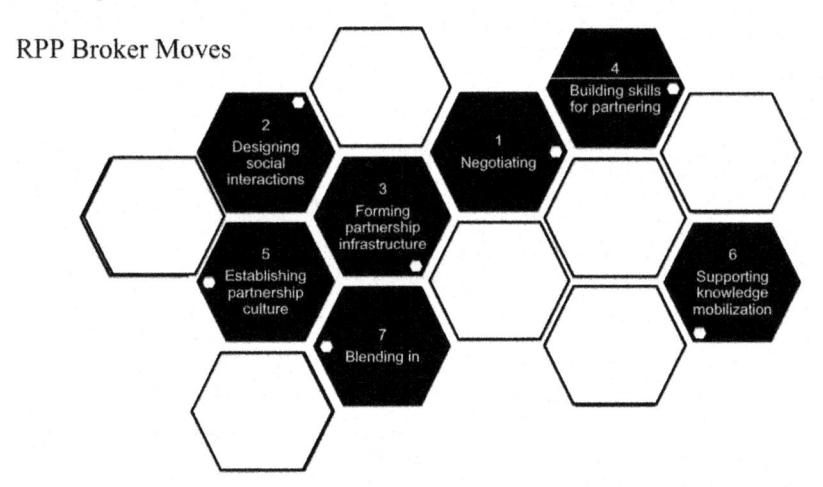

Figure 2.1 RPP Broker Handbook definition and framework, presented at the National Network of Education Research-Practice Partnerships annual forum, July 2019

15

Table 2.1 RPP broker move, definitions, and examples presented at the National Network of Education Research-Practice Partnerships annual forum, July 2019

RPP Broker Move	Definition	Example
Negotiating	The broker develops a concept for mutually beneficial research through discussions between researchers, practitioners, and their team members	• Negotiating access to data through a data use agreement
Designing interactions	The broker shapes social interactions between current or potential members of the partnership	• Using a seating chart to organize seating at an event so that certain RPP participants sit next to other potential partners
Forming partnership infrastructure	The broker operationalizes the structures, systems, and resources that make the partnership its own living ecosystem	• A template used for organizing RPP events that developed certain routines and structures within the partnership
Building skills for partnering	The broker builds the capacity of researchers and practitioners to act as brokers themselves to improve their work together in the partnership	• A tool for helping partners develop a plan for working together by defining over a timeline their planned joint activities and deliverables
Establishing partnership culture	The broker cultivates the mindset in the researchers and practitioners that they are stronger if they work together	• A list of guiding values used in one RPPs to describe the approach to work among partners
Supporting knowledge mobilization	The broker provides just-in-time coaching to partnership members while the researchers and practitioners are making key moves that support research use	• A research brief developed by an RPP broker to present research findings in a digestible manner
Blending in	The broker blends into the ecosystem of the other partnership member organizations	• Research-side brokers spending a couple days a week at a desk in the practice-side organization

PERSPECTIVES FROM OTHER BROKERS

To continue to build and expand off these initial concepts, Wentworth and Conaway held workshops focused on the role of brokers in RPPs during the 2019, 2020, and 2021 NNERPP Annual Forums.[1] During the 2019 NNERPP Annual Forum, the authors presented findings from their reflection exercise, invited attendees to break into small groups based on each of the seven themes, and asked them to explore these questions for each move:

(1) Edit the definition of this move to your liking.
- Is this a move you make as a broker?
- How would you edit the current definition?
- Are there elements you would add to the definition?
- Are there parts of this definition that should be moved?
- Are there parts that should create a new brokering move?

(2) List the tools related to that brokering move.
- Have you seen this tool before? If not, what do you like about it? What would you change?
- Do you use a variation of this tool?
- What are other tools that help brokers make this move?

Each small group generated a list of descriptors for the brokering activity and had a spokesperson present their ideas to the whole group. Wentworth and Conaway then used the themes from these data to refine the themes and their practice-based analysis. As seen in Table 2.1, after the practice-based reflection and stakeholder feedback, a second version of the framework was developed. They conceptualized the broker moves as brokering activities, actions, or behaviors. These are clustered into "brokering to strengthen partners" and "brokering to strengthen partnership." The activity named "blending in" was removed from the list based on the feedback at the 2019 meeting. Participants thought blending in was a broker action that was a means to an end – i.e., a move used to accomplish the large themes in the framework – and that the concept of negotiations was subsumed in the category of supporting research production and use. Wentworth and Conaway also enhanced the definitions of the other themes based on the input from participants.

During the NNERPP 2020 Annual Forum, Wentworth and Conaway presented the 2.0 version of the RPP Brokers Framework and collected input on the themes in the framework and potential tools and vignettes to feature in their evolving idea for a handbook (see Table 2.2). NNERPP members attending Conaway and Wentworth's session were asked to share tools or vignettes that could be used to demonstrate these RPP brokers moves. Tools were described as an object or artifact that helps RPP participants enact that part of the RPP Brokers

Table 2.2 Second version of the RPP Brokers Framework presented at the 2020 National Network of Education Research-Practice Partnership annual forum

Brokering to Strengthen Partners	
Building individuals' skills and knowledge	Building individual researchers' and practitioners' capacity to work in partnerships, and ultimately to become brokers themselves *Possible vignettes:* coaching partnership members on research skills or communication; giving difficult feedback *Possible tools:* facilitator's agenda; onboarding materials
Building relationships to weather challenges	Building individuals' skills to hold robust relationships across the partnership that can weather inevitable challenges *Possible vignettes:* having conversations that build empathy; resolving conflicts; understanding the partner's perspective; behaviors that build relationships *Possible tools:* agenda for a meeting that encourages relationship-building
Coaching to support research production and use	The broker facilitates ongoing, co-creation of useful research and use of the research in key decisions *Possible vignettes:* just-in-time conversations with practitioners or researchers about research in various stages; planned coaching sessions for practice side and research side leads to support research use *Possible tools:* synthesis of research findings into briefs, slides, and other forms of communication
Brokering to strengthen partnerships	
Developing partnership infrastructure	Creating the tangible work products necessary for conducting and learning from research across organizations *Possible vignettes:* co-developing a research agenda; co-writing a grant, negotiating legal agreements *Possible tools:* research agendas, data use agreements, data archives, grant applications
Designing social structures and routines	Shaping social structures between members of the partnership to establish common routines, larger structures for socializing, and purposeful opportunities to build trust and empathy *Possible vignettes:* creating or adjusting meeting routines; situations where trust/empathy was gained or lost; matching researchers to practitioner needs *Possible tools:* meeting agendas (for participants and facilitators); internal communications plans; seating chart for meetings

(Continued)

Table 2.2 Continued

Brokering to strengthen partnerships	
Establishing a partnership identity and culture	Developing an organizational identity and culture for the partnership independent of those of the individual partners *Possible vignettes:* co-creating a partnership vision, mission, values, and norms; new member orientation; resolving differences in authority, status, power, and culture *Possible tools:* partnership vision, mission, values, and norms statements; orientation materials

Framework and that could be used across different contexts. Vignettes were short stories that demonstrate the behaviors or enactment of a part of the framework and that would be applicable to RPPs in different contexts. Participants discussed their ideas for the tools or stories related to brokering in small groups and indicated whether they would be interested in writing up one of their ideas as a short case.

After the 2020 NNERPP Annual Forum, Conaway and Wentworth worked to collect cases from members of NNERPP who expressed interest in sharing a story or tool from their brokering work. They spent the 2020–2021 academic year collecting and curating cases from the participants in the Annual Forum. They also collected cases from other RPP brokers they knew through NNERPP, but who had not attended their 2020 session at the NNERPP Annual Forum. As the cases started to come in, Conaway and Wentworth adjusted details of the framework based on reading the cases – for example, removing the category of "establishing a partnership culture" – and included those ideas within the newly named subtheme of "developing partnership governance and administrative structures."

In fall 2020, Conaway and Wentworth also started working with Samantha Shewchuk and Paula Arce-Trigatti to conduct a structured literature review about RPP brokering. They wanted to test the framework evolving from practice to see if these concepts were backed by research and if there were any missing parts to the framework. Next, we describe the method for conducting this literature review.

STRUCTURED REVIEWS

To identify potential gaps and further refine the framework, the authors conducted a structured literature review on the qualitative and quantitative empirical evidence on the activities individuals engage in when brokering in education research-practice partnerships. First, we conducted keyword searches of research databases and search engines to identify potential peer-reviewed and gray literature, along with targeted searches of RPP-focused websites. We then scanned the reference lists of the documents identified for inclusion in the review to identify any relevant studies we had missed. Finally, we contacted the authors of documents identified for inclusion in the review, along with experts in the field, to identify additional articles to include.

In total, 531 unique citations were identified from searches of databases, search engines, and targeted websites. We excluded sources if they did not provide empirical evidence on knowledge brokering in education RPPs or if they fell outside the publication dates of January 1, 2000, to September 9, 2020. Based on the review of titles and abstracts, we selected 45 documents for full-text retrieval. We read all of these papers and, if found suitable, we included them in the review. Our searches of databases, targeted websites, and search engines yielded 18 documents. We added 14 more records through scanning references and expert elicitation, bringing the total number of documents included in the review to 32. A PRISMA flow diagram that depicts the data collection process is presented in Figure 2.2.

We extracted data from documents using a standardized data collection form. Included studies most often applied qualitative approaches, with no purely quantitative studies identified in our search. We also found that most included studies were largely descriptive in nature, using a case study approach, with interviews, document analysis, and observations being the most popular data collection techniques. In short, the authors of the included studies focused on chronicling the activities of brokers within education RPPs. Broker activities were extracted using a combination of a priori coding based on the six activities identified from the practice-based reflection, stakeholder feedback, and open coding to identify concepts from the literature that were not captured by the draft framework. (See Tables 2.4–2.9 for themes and associated literature from the review.)

The synthesis of results from the included empirical studies affirmed and expanded upon the activities identified from practice-based reflection and stakeholder engagement (see Table 2.10 for changes). Because of the review, we added one new category to the brokering skills framework, assessing and reflecting on the partnership (within the domain of "brokering to strengthen the partnership"). We expanded the original categories to include subcategories (n=19). These subcategories inherit the features of the more abstract category they belong to, but also have their own distinguishing elements. For example, when *designing social structures and routines*, brokers must establish common practices and shape social interactions between current or potential members of the partnership. Within this broader category, we identified that brokers must develop communication pathways to allow information to flow up, down, and across partnering organizations. In addition, we identified that brokers must also facilitate meetings and social opportunities so that people can share ideas and

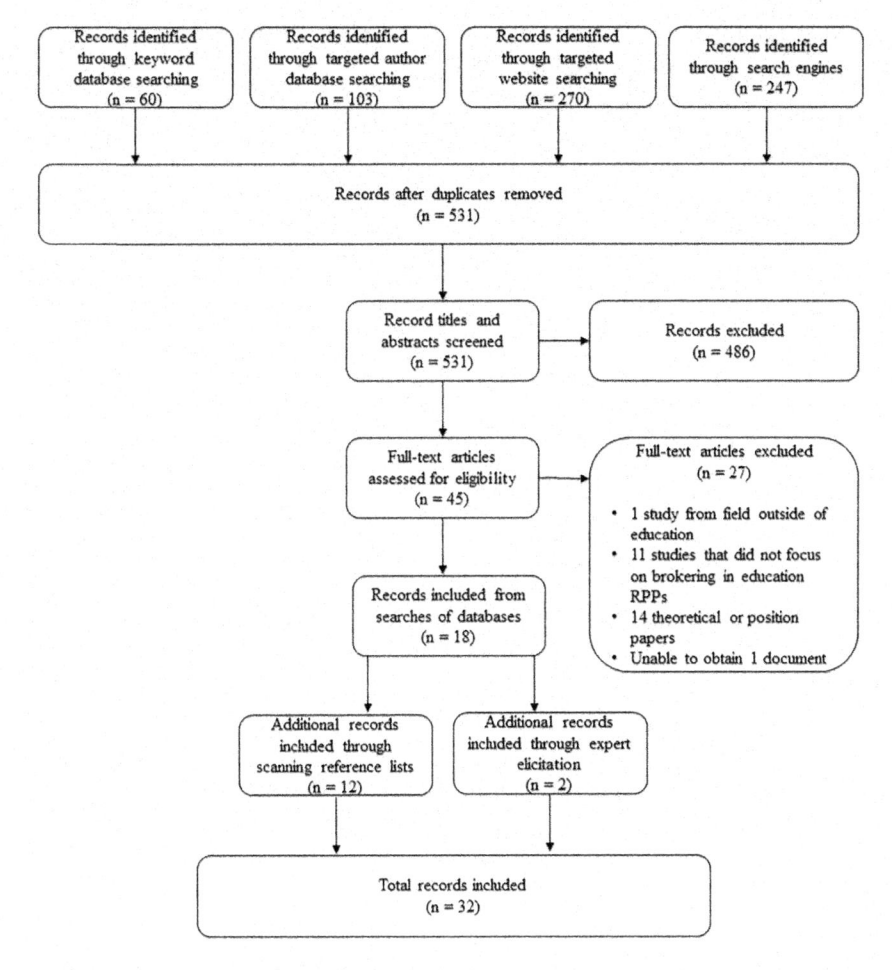

THE PRACTICE AND RESEARCH BEHIND THE RPP BROKERS FRAMEWORK

Figure 2.2 PRISMA flow diagram

solutions with one another and feel connected to the partnership and its goals. In some instances, we relegated original categories to subcategories within the final framework. Specifically, we reclassified the original categories of "developing partnership infrastructure mechanisms" and "develop a partnership identity and culture" as subcategories within the larger category of *developing partnership governance and administrative structures*. Across all subcategories, we identified 59 individual activities that brokers may engage in. We outline these activities, including relevant citations from the literature, in Tables 2.4 to 2.9. We also include in Appendix A the figure showing the association between the literature from the review and themes in our framework. In Appendix B, we list the citations collected during the structured review.

Table 2.3 Literature categorized by activity: developing partnership governance and administrative structures

Subcategory	Brokers Can:	Citation(s)
Determine whom to partner with	(1) engage decision-makers in assessment of current needs and whether a partnership is appropriate (2) facilitate discussion about which organizations are the best fit (3) build contacts, engage in conversations (4) facilitate the discussion of shared research interests, priorities, needs, and capacities (5) influence senior managers and decision-makers to endorse the project (6) facilitate discussion and generate agreement around partners' roles and responsibilities	Akkerman & Bruining, 2016; Brown, 2017; Buskey et al., 2018; Campbell et al., 2017; Coburn et al., 2008; Davidson & Penuel, 2020; Denner et al., 2019; Farrell et al., 2018, 2019; Fenwick, 2007; Firestone & Fisler, 2002; Furtak et al., 2016; Harrison et al., 2019; Klar et al., 2018; Lasater, 2018, 2019; Miller, 2007; Muñoz-Muñoz & Ocampo, 2016; Nelson et al., 2015
Create a common vision	(7) negotiate the development of common goals to guide the partnership's work (8) facilitate discussion around partners' requirements for sharing data (9) facilitate discussion around partners' expectations for sharing and disseminating findings	Akkerman & Bruining, 2016; Brown, 2017; Campbell et al., 2017; Davidson & Penuel, 2020; Denner et al., 2019; Farrell et al., 2018; Fenwick, 2004, 2007; Kronley & Handley, 2003; Lasater, 2018; Miller, 2007; Nelson et al., 2015

(Continued)

Table 2.3 Continued

Subcategory	Brokers Can:	Citation(s)
	(10) advocate for, support the development of, and manage partnership documents	
Secure funding	(11) identify potential sources of funding (12) support and manage the grant writing process	Fenwick, 2007; Firestone & Fisler, 2002; Furtak et al., 2016; Kronley & Handley, 2003; Muñoz-Muñoz & Ocampo, 2016
Implement RPP resources, processes, and procedures	(13) identify, leverage, or create organizational processes and structures to support the partnership (14) advocate for, support the development of, and manage macro-, meso-, and micro-structures to support the partnership (15) promote joint leadership on committees and research projects	Brown, 2017; Campbell et al., 2017; Farrell et al., 2018, 2019; Firestone & Fisler, 2002; Harrison et al., 2019; Hartmann & Decristan, 2018; Muñoz-Muñoz & Ocampo, 2016; Wilcox & Zuckerman, 2019
Establish a partnership identity and culture	(16) advocate for, support, and manage policies that embed the importance of the partnership (17) empower organizational staff to drive the partnership (18) create opportunities for front-line staff to take on leadership and brokering roles (19) promote and build the profile of the RPP by communicating with stakeholders	Akkerman & Bruining, 2016; Brown, 2017; Buskey et al., 2018; Campbell et al., 2017; Denner et al., 2019; Farrell et al., 2017, 2018, 2019; Fenwick, 2004; Kronley & Handley, 2003; Miller & Hafner, 2008

In addition to this structured review on RPP brokering in education, we also factored in another literature review about racism, power differences, and RPPs led by Laura Wentworth and colleagues at California Education Partners. We decided to include this review for two reasons. First, in our structured review on RPP brokering in education, we found a cluster of literature that described how RPP brokers address power differences among members of a partnership. Specifically, the subtheme of developing and nurturing relationships to weather challenges includes some literature describing brokers' efforts to build trust, mutual respect, and equitable relationships. This literature talked about helping partners resolve issues, including dealing with asymmetrical power relations (e.g., Miller et al., 2008), navigating the dynamics of authority relations, power, status, and structure (e.g., Klar et al., 2018), and establishing a shared understanding of equity (Denner et al., 2019). Second, we received some feedback from anonymous reviewers recommending we center equity and power differences in our framework as one of the most important actions brokers take to support RPPs. Consequently, we included a summary of the literature about racism and power differences in RPP, and describe here how that systematic literature review was conducted.

As described in Wentworth et al. (2022), the preliminary findings from the literature review about racism, power differences, and RPPs stemmed from a systematic survey of original research and systematic reviews published between 2000 and 2020 that cited the topic of "racism" and "RPPs." They identified related records in three search engines, which resulted in a total of 13 articles, listed in Appendix C. The analysis resulted in four key findings (see Table 2.11). RPPs reinforce racism primarily by reinforcing white, middle-class norms. Relationships among participants in RPPs are historically laden by those norms, and relationships that are interracial will inevitably deal with racism. For example, Vakil and colleagues (2016) describe relationships within partnerships between community members and researchers in design-based research partnerships as "shaped by the histories of race and differential power that set the stage of partnership formation" (p. 199).

Henderson and Laman (2020) describe how racism in RPPs reinforces power differences through organizational structures, affording status, and differences in participants' authority, often conveyed by participants' roles in their institutions. For example, Ho and colleagues (2020), in their partnerships between special education researchers and families and students, needed to address "power dynamics in hierarchical institutional culture that favor scripted white-able-middleclass cultural norms brought about tensions in building an authentic alliance with families and communities, particularly those from nondominant groups" (p. 421).

According to the literature review, RPPs may disrupt racism by using a few different strategies. RPPs can take time to build relationships and trust. Sullivan

Table 2.4 Literature categorized by activity: designing processes and communication routines

Subcategory	Brokers Can:	Citation(s)
Develop communication pathways	(20) advocate for, support the development of, and manage communication processes for sharing information within and across organizations (21) coordinate regular communication to link groups both within and across organizational boundaries	Akkerman & Bruining, 2016; Brown, 2017; Campbell et al., 2017; Davidson & Penuel, 2020; Farrell et al., 2018, 2019; Fenwick, 2004; Harrison et al., 2019; Hartmann & Decristan, 2018; Hopkins et al., 2019; Kronley & Handley, 2003; Lasater, 2018; Miller & Hafner, 2008; Miller, 2007; Muñoz-Muñoz & Ocampo, 2016; Wilcox & Zuckerman, 2019
Facilitate meetings and social opportunities	(22) synthesize information and keep records (23) facilitate and manage meetings	Akkerman & Bruining, 2016; Brown, 2017; Denner et al., 2019; Farrell et al., 2018, 2019; Firestone & Fisler, 2002; Fenwick, 2007; Hopkins et al., 2019; Klar et al., 2018; Miller & Hafner, 2008; Miller, 2007; Muñoz-Muñoz & Ocampo, 2016; Wilcox et al., 2017

and colleagues (2001) point out that researchers need to spend time prior to projects addressing community members' mistrust of researchers and to provide better understanding of the benefit of the research to the community. RPPs challenge normative or status quo practices, which Greenberg and colleagues (2019) refer to as the work together, must be "rethought, resisted, and disrupted" (p. 522). RPPs engage stakeholders in all phases of the research and align goals to practice partners' priorities. Wallerstein and Duran (2006) refer to this as a "community-driven" rather than "university-driven" research agenda (p. 314). RPPs attend to culture and values among participants and investigate interpersonal dynamics by attending to the intersectionality of different identities. Chavez (2005) describes how the language of the partnership reflects partners' culture and values. Consequently, partnership participants must examine

Table 2.5 Literature categorized by activity: assessing and continuously improving the partnership

Subcategory	Brokers Can:	Citation(s)
Involve partnership members in reflection of the partnership	(24) advocate for, support the development of, and manage feedback loops to guide partnership decisions (25) engage partners in an ongoing process of reflecting, planning, acting, and observing	Akkerman & Bruining, 2016; Davidson & Penuel, 2020; Denner et al., 2019; Farrell et al., 2018; Hartmann & Decristan, 2018; Johnson et al., 2016; Kronley & Handley, 2003; Lasater, 2018, 2019; Muñoz-Muñoz & Ocampo, 2016; Nelson et al., 2015
Design accountability systems and involve partnership members in the evaluation of the partnership	(26) engage partners in evaluation activities (27) advocate for, support the development of, and manage accountability systems	Akkerman & Bruining, 2016; Davidson & Penuel, 2020; Denner et al., 2019; Farrell et al., 2018; Hartmann & Decristan, 2018; Johnson et al., 2016; Kronley & Handley, 2003; Lasater, 2018, 2019; Muñoz-Muñoz & Ocampo, 2016; Nelson et al., 2015

their interpersonal dynamics and the influences of their differing personal and professional identities.

From this literature review, we subsequently factored into our framework the larger sociocultural context of RPPs. These brokers do not work in a vacuum and they must tend to participants' individual identities, cultures, and beliefs by finding norms that honor each participant's unique self and their collective beliefs about how partners want to work together. Brokers must design RPP practices and structures that acknowledge the historical harms of racism and other hurtful social realities like xenophobia or sexism by creating conditions through goal setting, facilitation, and specifically designed structures within the RPP that support psychological safety, healing, and disruption of status quo, white, middle-class practices. These RPP broker practices to disrupt inequities are woven in across the six parts of the RPP broker framework. The next chapter describes each element of the framework in more detail, including a case of helping researchers examine racial identity in RPPs.

Table 2.6 Literature categorized by activity: creating conditions to support research production and use

Subcategory	Brokers Can:	Citation(s)
Identify shared problems of practice	(28) source and synthesize information to better understand the problem (29) facilitate and mediate partners in identifying potential shared problems of practice	Akkerman & Bruining, 2016; Campbell et al., 2017; Coburn et al., 2008; Davidson & Penuel, 2020; Denner et al., 2019; Farrell et al., 2018, 2019; Firestone & Fisler, 2002; Hartmann & Decristan, 2018; Johnson et al., 2016; Lasater, 2018; Miller & Hafner, 2008; Miller, 2007; Nelson et al., 2015; Thompson et al., 2019; Wilcox & Zuckerman, 2019; Wilcox et al., 2017
Champion the production of actionable research	(30) negotiate the development of actionable research questions that are driven by community need (31) prioritize and support action planning (32) engage key stakeholders (including decision-makers) so project findings can be acted on (33) advocate for and support the development of a systematic approach to data collection	Akkerman & Bruining, 2016; Denner et al., 2019; Farrell et al., 2018; Lasater, 2018; Nelson et al., 2015; Thompson et al., 2019; Wilcox et al., 2017
Facilitate joint contributions to data collection and analysis	(34) facilitate collective sense-making to build shared understandings of project findings	Brown, 2017; Campbell et al., 2017; Farrell et al., 2018; Hartmann & Decristan, 2018; Hopkins et al., 2019; Johnson et al., 2016; Thompson et al., 2019

(Continued)

Table 2.6 Continued

Subcategory	Brokers Can:	Citation(s)
	(35) support the division of labor among partners	
	(36) support the creation of routines	
Build a culture of research use	(37) support and encourage vulnerability among team members (38) identify, leverage, or create institutional and individual capacity to use research	Akkerman & Bruining, 2016; Davidson & Penuel, 2020; Farrell et al., 2018, 2019; Harrison et al., 2019; Kronley & Handley, 2003; Nelson et al., 2015; Thompson et al., 2019; Wilcox & Zuckerman, 2019
Use knowledge mobilization strategies to support research production and use	(39) understand, create, and use knowledge mobilization tools for planning research projects (40) communicate and present research findings to different audiences	Benichou et al., 2019; Brown, 2017; Campbell et al., 2017; Furtak et al., 2016; Hopkins et al., 2018; Hopkins et al., 2019; Thompson et al., 2019; Wilcox et al., 2017

Table 2.7 Literature categorized by activity: developing and nurturing relationships to weather challenges

Subcategory	Brokers Can:	Citation(s)
Cultivate partnership and project relationships	(41) encourage partnerships between organizations with pre-existing relationships, where possible (42) connect campus and community assets (43) scan for and identify new partners to meet partnership needs	Akkerman & Bruining, 2016; Campbell et al., 2017; Davidson & Penuel, 2020; Denner et al., 2019; Farrell et al., 2018, 2019; Firestone & Fisler, 2002; Furtak et al., 2016; Lasater, 2018, 2019; Miller, 2007; Muñoz-Muñoz & Ocampo, 2016; Nelson et al., 2015

(Continued)

Table 2.7 Continued

Subcategory	Brokers Can:	Citation(s)
	(44) create networks or communities of practice with people relevant to a research project's focus	
Build trust, mutual respect, and equitable relationships	(45) help partners resolve issues, including dealing with asymmetrical power relations (46) navigate the dynamics of authority relations, power, status, and structure (47) establish a shared understanding of equity (48) provide dedicated time for and engage in trust-building activities with partners	Brown, 2017; Buskey et al., 2018; Campbell et al., 2017; Davidson & Penuel, 2020; Denner et al., 2019; Farrell et al., 2018; Fenwick, 2007; Firestone & Fisler, 2002; Furtak et al., 2016; Klar et al., 2018; Kronley & Handley, 2003; Lasater, 2018; Miller & Hafner, 2008; Muñoz-Muñoz & Ocampo, 2016; Nelson et al., 2015
Coordinate work within and across organizations	(49) balance schedules of partners (50) clearly communicate requirements for completing project goals (51) track partnership projects and prioritize tasks (52) facilitate data and information sharing between partners	Campbell et al., 2017; Farrell et al., 2017, 2018; Firestone & Fisler, 2002; Harrison et al., 2019; Hartmann & Decristan, 2018; Hopkins et al., 2019; Kronley and Handley, 2003; Muñoz-Muñoz & Ocampo, 2016; Nelson et al., 2015; Wilcox et al., 2017

Table 2.8 Literature categorized by activity: building individual partners' competency for engaging in an RPP

Subcategory	Brokers Can:	Citation(s)
Skills needed by partners	(53) build partners' competencies in: knowledge of self and local context; engage in work across boundaries; research evaluation and design skills; and knowledge mobilization skills	Akkerman & Bruining, 2016; Benichou et al., 2019; Brown, 2017; Campbell et al., 2017; Coburn et al., 2008; Davidson & Penuel, 2020; Denner et al., 2019; Farrell et al., 2017, 2018, 2019; Fenwick, 2004, 2007; Firestone & Fisler, 2002; Harrison et al., 2019; Hartmann & Decristan, 2018; Johnson et al., 2016; Kronley & Handley, 2003; Lasater, 2018; Lasater, 2019; Miller & Hafner, 2008; Miller, 2007; Muñoz-Muñoz & Ocampo, 2016; Nelson et al., 2015; Thompson et al., 2019; Wilcox & Zuckerman, 2019; Wilcox et al., 2017
How brokers build these skills	(54) coach partners to support and encourage certain behaviors (55) devise and deliver didactic training (56) use discursive strategies to elicit, engage, and challenge each partner's thinking (57) model behaviors that the broker wants the partners to imitate (58) engage partners in role-playing scenarios to help partners practice new skills	Akkerman & Bruining, 2016; Benichou et al., 2019; Brown, 2017; Campbell et al., 2017; Farrell et al., 2018, 2019; Harrison et al., 2019; Lasater, 2018; Lasater, 2019; Muñoz-Muñoz & Ocampo, 2016; Nelson et al., 2015; Thompson et al., 2019; Wilcox & Zuckerman, 2019; Wilcox et al., 2017

(Continued)

Table 2.8 Continued

Subcategory	Brokers Can:	Citation(s)
	(59) identify and provide opportunities for individuals to take on brokering and leadership roles	

Table 2.9 Revision of draft RPP Brokers Framework to final framework

Original Categories From 2019	Final Categories and Subcategories in 2022
	Skills to Strengthen the Partnership
Forming the partnership infrastructure	*Develop the partnership*
Establish partnership culture	• determine whom to partner with • develop a common vision • develop partnership infrastructure mechanisms • establish partnership identity and culture • secure funding • implement, maintain, and monitor RPP resources, processes, and procedures
Designing social interactions	*Designing social structures and routines*
	• develop communication pathways within and across organizations • facilitate meetings and social opportunities
	Skills to Strengthen Partnering
Knowledge mobilization	*Support research use and production*
	• identify shared problems of practice • champion actionable research • facilitate joint data collection and analysis • build a culture of research use • understand, create, and use knowledge mobilization strategies

(Continued)

Table 2.9 Continued

Original Categories From 2019	Final Categories and Subcategories in 2022
	Build relationships to weather challenges • build mutual trust and respect • cultivate project and partnership relationships
Build skills for partnering	Build individuals' knowledge and skills • the skills needed by partners • how brokers build these skills
Negotiating	
Blending in	

Table 2.10 Racism, power differences, and RPPs

Themes and subthemes from literature review and hypothesized RPP broker moves

How Do RPPs Reinforce Power Differences and Racism?		Examples of Hypothesized RPP Broker Actions Associated With This Theme
RPPs reinforce power differences	Power differences caused by organizational structures	Reflecting power asymmetries in RPP governance and administration
	Power difference influenced by status	Developing capacity of senior RPP leaders rather than all participants
	Power differences influences by authority	Allowing senior faculty to override wishes of doctoral students or practice partner
	Roles within institutions	Limiting interactions to role alike members of the partnership
RPPs reinforce racism	Centering middle-class, white norms	Discouraging norms during meetings that honor all perspectives
	Relationships that are interracial will inevitably deal with racism	Providing no space and time for acknowledging racial differences in RPP members
	Relationships are power laden by history	Ignoring the history of relationships among people from different racial groups

(Continued)

Table 2.10 Continued

Themes and subthemes from literature review and hypothesized RPP broker moves

How Do RPPs Disrupt Power Differences and Racism and Reinforce Equity?		Examples of Hypothesized RPP Broker Actions Associated With This Theme
RPPs disrupt power	Attend to power through lens in research analysis	Coaching researchers to examine sociocultural, racial, or critical lens during their analyses
	Attend to power dynamics at the start of research	Setting routines and decision-making structures that account for power differences
	Critical reflections of yourself, others, and the process	Creating space for critically examining partners' processes for working together by reflecting on how each is reinforcing or disrupting power differences
	Establish norms of behavior in community-based research	Establishing norms for how partners will work together to disrupt historical power differences
RPPs disrupt racism	Take time to build relationships and trust	Allowing time in structures to get to know the personal and professional side of each member
	Challenge normative, or status quo practices	Envisioning new institutional practices rather than status quo institutional practices (e.g., decisions are always made this way or this is the set hierarchy in institutional leadership)
	Engaging stakeholders in all phases of the research	Co-developing research questions, co-designing interventions, researchers and practitioners engaging in data collection, formatively sharing findings
	Attend to culture and values in language	Centering Afro-centric praxis rather than white, middle-class norms
	Goals aligned to practice partners' priorities	The topics of the research are based on the practice or community partners' priorities
	Attend to intersectionality of different identities	Allowing partners to present their gender and racial identities when in collaboration with each other

(Continued)

Table 2.10 Continued

Themes and subthemes from literature review and hypothesized RPP broker moves		
How Do RPPs Disrupt Power Differences and Racism and Reinforce Equity?		Examples of Hypothesized RPP Broker Actions Associated With This Theme
	Investigate interpersonal dynamics	Paying attention to silence as people usually have something to say when working together
RPPs reinforce equity	Encourage new possibilities in design and research	Centering the concepts of race and power that are often missing from certain types of research, like design-based research

CONCLUSION

Many different types of evidence factored into our development of the RPP Brokers Handbook. We included a process for collecting input and ideas from practice based on the experiences of members of the NNERPP network that identify as brokers. We conducted a systematic literature review on brokering in education. We also conducted a review of racism, power differences, and RPPs to examine the sociocultural, historical, and political contexts influencing brokering. And, we presented our process for laying together these different forms of evidence. Next, we turn to explaining the RPP Brokers Handbook through the lens of one RPP.

NOTE

1   The NNERPP Annual Forum is an annual gathering of members and friends to come together and discuss challenges, successes, and opportunities related to RPPs.

REFERENCES

Akkerman, S., & Bruining, T. (2016). Multilevel boundary crossing in a professional development school partnership. *Journal of the Learning Sciences*, 25(2), 240–284. https://doi.org/10.1080/10508406.2016.1147448

Arce-Trigatti, P., Chukhray, I., & Lopez-Turley, R. (2018). Research-practice partnerships in education. In B. Schneider (Ed.), *Handbook of the sociology in education in the 21st century* (pp. 561–579). Springer.

Benichou, M., Atias, O., Sagy, O., Kali, Y., & Baram-Tsabari, A. (2019). Citizen science in schools: Supporting implementation of innovative learning environments using design-centric research-practice partnerships. In K. Lund, G. P. Niccolai, E. Lavoue, C. Hmelo-Silver, G. Gweon, & M. Baker (Eds.), *A wide lens: Combining embodied, enactive, extended, and embedded learning in collaborative settings, 13th International Conference on Computer Supported Collaborative Learning (CSCL)* 2019, 2 (pp. 843–844). International Society of the Learning Sciences.

Brown, S. L. (2017). Negotiating position during the process of design within a researcher-developer-practitioner partnership: An activity systems analysis [Doctoral dissertation, Florida State University]. FSU Digital Library. Retrieved from http://purl.flvc.org/fsu/fd/FSU_2017SP_Brown_fsu_0071E_13753

Buskey, F. C., Klar, H. W., Huggins, K. S., & Desmangles, J. K. (2018). Spanning boundaries to enhance school leadership. Innovation and implementation in rural places: School-university-community collaboration in education, 57.

Campbell, C., Pollock, K., Briscoe, P., Carr-Harris, S., & Tuters, S. (2017). Developing a knowledge network for applied education research to mobilise evidence in and for educational practice. *Educational Research*, 59(2), 209–227. https://doi.org/10.1080/00131881.2017.1310364

Chavez, V. (2005). Silence speaks: The language of internalized oppression and privilege in community-based research. Community based research. *Metropolitan Universities Journal*, 16(1).

Coburn, C. E., Bae, S., & Turner, E. O. (2008). Authority, status, and the dynamics of insider-outsider partnerships at the district level. *Peabody Journal of Education*, 83(3), 364–399. www.jstor.org/stable/25594798

Davidson, K. L., & Penuel, W. R. (2019). The role of brokers in sustaining partnership work in education. In *The role of knowledge brokers in education* (pp. 154–167). Routledge.

Davidson, K. L., & Penuel, W. R. (2020). Chapter 11: The role of brokers in sustaining partnership work in education. In J. Malin & C. Brown (Eds.), *The role of knowledge brokers in education: Connecting the dots between research and practice*. Routledge.

Denner, J., Bean, S., Campe, S., Martinez, J., & Torres, D. (2019). Negotiating trust, power, and culture in a research – practice partnership. *AERA Open*, 5(2), 2332858419858635. https://doi.org/10.1177/23328584198586

Farrell, C. C., Davidson, K. L., Repko-Erwin, M., Penuel, W. R., Quantz, M., Wong, H., . . . Brink, Z. (2018). A descriptive study of the IES researcher-practitioner partnerships in education research program: Final report. Technical report no. 3. *National Center for Research in Policy and Practice*. https://files.eric.ed.gov/fulltext/ED599980.pdf

Farrell, C. C., Davidson, K. L., Repko-Erwin, M. E., Penuel, W. R., Herlihy, C., Potvin A. S., & Hill, H. C. (2017). A descriptive study of the IES researcher–practitioner partnerships in education research program: Final report (Technical Report No. 2). National Center for Research in Policy and Practice. Retrieved from http://ncrpp.org/assets/documents/RPP-Technical-Report_Feb-2017.pdf

Farrell, C. C., Harrison, C., & Coburn, C. E. (2019). "What the hell is this, and who the hell are you?": Role and identity negotiation in research-practice partnerships. *AERA Open*. https://doi.org/10.1177/2332858419849595

Fenwick, T. (2007). Organisational learning in the "knots": Discursive capacities emerging in a school-university collaboration. *Journal of Educational Administration*, 45(2), 138–153. https://doi-org.udel.idm.oclc.org/10.1108/09578230710732934

Fenwick, T. J. (2004). Discursive work for educational administrators: Tensions in negotiating partnerships. *Discourse: Studies in the Cultural Politics of Education*, 25(2), 171–187. https://doi.org/10.1080/01596300410001692139

Firestone, W. A., & Fisler, J. L. (2002). Politics, community, and leadership in a school-university partnership. *Educational Administration Quarterly, 38*(4), 449–493. https://doi.org/10.1177/001316102237669

Furtak, E. M., Henson, K., & Buell, J. Y. (2016, April). Negotiating goals around formative assessment in a research-practice partnership. In *Annual meeting of the national association of research in science teaching*, Baltimore, MD. Retrieved from https://www.researchgate.net/profile/Erin_Furtak/publication/301301901_Negotiating_Goals_around_Formative_Assessment_in_a_Research-Practice_Partnership/links/57113c2408aeebe07c02417c.pdf

Greenberg, M., London, R. A., & McKay, S. C. (2019). Community-initiated student-engaged research: Expanding undergraduate teaching and learning through public sociology. *Teaching Sociology, 48*(1), 13–27.

Harrison, C., Wachen, J., Brown, S., & Cohen-Vogel, L. (2019). A view from within: Lessons learned from partnering for continuous improvement. *Teachers College Record, 121*(9). https://eric.ed.gov/?id=EJ1225420

Hartmann, U., & Decristan, J. (2018). Brokering activities and learning mechanisms at the boundary of educational research and school practice. *Teaching and Teacher Education, 74*, 114–124. https://doi.org/10.1016/j.tate.2018.04.016

Henderson, J. W., & Laman, T. T. (2020). "This Ain't Gonna work for me": The role of the Afrocentric praxis of eldering in creating more equitable research partnerships. *Urban Education, 55*(6), 892–910.

Ho, D., Dawene, D., Roberts, K., & Hing, J. J. (2020). A systematic review of boundary-crossing partnerships in designing equity-oriented special education services for culturally and linguistically diverse students with disabilities. *Remedial and Special Education, 42*(6), 412–425.

Hopkins, M., Weddle, H., Gluckman, M., & Gautsch, L. (2019). Boundary crossing in a professional association: The dynamics of research use among state leaders and researchers in a research-practice partnership. *AERA Open, 5*(4), 2332858419891964. https://doi.org/10.1177/2332858419891964

Hopkins, M., Wiley, K. E., Penuel, W. R., & Farrell, C. C. (2018). Brokering research in science education policy implementation: The case of a professional association. *Evidence & Policy: A Journal of Research, Debate and Practice, 14*(3), 459–476. https://doi.org/10.1332/174426418X15299595170910

Johnson, R., Severance, S., Penuel, W. R., & Leary, H. (2016). Teachers, tasks, and tensions: Lessons from a research–practice partnership. *Journal of Mathematics Teacher Education, 19*(2/3), 169–185. https://doi.org/10.1007/s10857-015-9338-3

Klar, H. W., Huggins, K. S., Buskey, F. C., Desmangles, J. K., & Phelps-Ward, R. J. (2018). Developing social capital for collaboration in a research-practice partnership. *Journal of Professional Capital and Community, 3*(4), 287–305. https://doi.org/10.1108/JPCC-01-2018-0005

Kronley, R. A., & Handley, C. (2003). Reforming relationships: School districts, external organizations, and systemic change. *Annenberg Institute for School Reform*. https://eric.ed.gov/?id=ED479779

Lasater, K. (2018). Using the researcher–practitioner partnership to build family–school partnerships in a rural high school. In R. M. Reardon & J. Leonard (Eds.),

Innovation and implementation in rural places: School-university-community collaboration in education (pp. 233–256). Information Age Publishing.

Lasater, K. (2019). Developing authentic family-school partnerships in a rural high school: Results of a longitudinal action research study. *School Community Journal, 29*(2), 157–182. https://eric.ed.gov/?id=EJ1236596

McMahon, K., Henrick, E., & Sullivan, F. (2022). *Partnering to scale instructional improvement: A framework for organizing research-practice partnerships*. Stanford, CA: The Carnegie Foundation for the Advancement of Teaching.

Miller, P. M. (2007). "Getting on the balcony to see the patterns on the dance floor below": Considering organizational culture in a university – school – community collaboration. *Journal of School Leadership, 17*(2), 222–245. https://doi.org/10.1177/105268460701700204

Miller, P. M., & Hafner, M. M. (2008). Moving toward dialogical collaboration: A critical examination of a university-school-community partnership. *Educational Administration Quarterly, 44*(1), 66–110. https://doi.org/10.1177/0013161X07309469

Muñoz-Muñoz, E., & Ocampo, A. (2016). A three-way partnership to bridge and connect institutional perspectives on English Language Learner instruction. In J. J. Slater, R. Ravid, & R. M. Reardon (Eds.), *Building and maintaining collaborative communities: Schools, university, and community organizations* (pp. 229–240). Information Age Publishing.

Nelson, I. A., London, R. A., & Strobel, K. R. (2015). Reinventing the role of the university researcher. *Educational Researcher, 44*(1), 17–26. https://doi.org/10.3102/0013189X15570387

Penuel, W. R., Farrell, C. C., Allen, A. R., Toyama, Y., & Coburn, C. E. (2018). What research district leaders find useful. *Educational Policy, 32*(4), 540–568. https://doi.org/10.1177/0895904816673580

Sullivan, M., et al. (2001). Researchers and researched-community perspectives: Toward bridging the gap. *Health Education & Behavior, 28*(2), 130–149.

Thompson, J., Richards, J., Shim, S.-Y., Lohwasser, K., Von Esch, K. S., Chew, C., Sjoberg, B., & Morris, A. (2019). Launching networked PLCs: Footholds into creating and improving knowledge of ambitious and equitable teaching practices in an RPP. *AERA Open.* https://doi.org/10.1177/2332858419875718

Vakil, S., de Royston, M. M., Nasir, N. S., & Kirshner, B. (2016). Rethinking race and power in design-based research: Reflections from the field. *Cognition and Instruction, 34*(3), 194–209.

Wallerstein, N. B., & Duran, B. (2006). Using community-based participatory research to address health disparities. *Health Promotion Practice, 7*(3), 312–323.

Wentworth, L., Titus, R., & Kipnis, F. (2022). Racism, power differences and RPPs: A review (Unpublished manuscript).

Wilcox, K. C., Lawson, H. A., & Angelis, J. I. (2017). COMPASS-AIM: A university/P–12 partnership innovation for continuous improvement. *Peabody Journal of Education, 92*(5), 649–674.

Wilcox, K. C., & Zuckerman, S. J. (2019). Building will and capacity for improvement in a rural research-practice partnership. *The Rural Educator, 40*(1), 73–90. https://journals.library.msstate.edu/ruraled/article/view/534

Chapter 3

A Framework
What Do Brokers Do?

To illustrate the framework, we weave together a description of the different parts of the RPP Brokers Framework with a series of cases drawn primarily from the Stanford–SFUSD Partnership. We kick off this chapter with a story from this RPP, and then subsequently explain each part of the framework – brokering to strengthen partners, brokering to strengthen partnerships, and the sociocultural, historical, and political contexts of RPP brokering. We accompany each part of the framework with one or two cases from the Stanford–SFUSD Partnership to see the parts of the framework put into practice.

It is important to note we do not want to position the Stanford–SFUSD Partnership as an exemplar. Instead, our intention is to use the cases from the RPP to demonstrate what brokering might look like in action. To balance using one RPP to explain the framework in action and address the key motivation for engaging in RPPs as "shift[ing] power relations in the research endeavor" (Farrell et al., 2021), we include some reflections at the end of the chapter about the inequitable power dynamics that may emerge and opportunities to address them.

> After observing the exodus of some Black principals and assistant principals, SFUSD leader Sandra Phillips-Sved developed a hunch about why Black site leaders were leaving the district. Phillips-Sved was running a program supporting SFUSD principals to complete their administrative credential where she and a team mentored and coached most of the new site administrators. She noticed that Black administrators had exceptional leadership skills that helped them build the necessary conditions at their schools to support teacher efficacy and retention as well as student learning, especially for Black teachers and students. Despite their effectiveness, Phillips-Sved noticed Black site leaders were more likely to report

experiencing challenges due to race and leave their administrative roles, especially compared to their peers of other racial identities. For example, Black assistant principals expressed an undue burden of being placed in operational roles handling discipline where they daily had to manage the consequences for Black students being disproportionately kicked out of class or suspended from school. This took an emotional and mental toll on these leaders, as well as limited their chances to gain the instructional leadership skills necessary for advanced career opportunities. Based on these observations and reports, a desire to have a more systematic way to test these observations in hopes of changing these patterns began to brew inside Phillips-Sved.

Phillips-Sved consulted with Laura Wentworth, the director of the Stanford–SFUSD partnership, seeking a collaborator at Stanford who might be interested in examining the experiences of Black leaders in SFUSD. Wentworth was intentionally positioned to be a third-party independent broker helping Stanford and SFUSD work together. In their RPP program, California Ed Partners' goals are to help Stanford researchers work with SFUSD leaders to produce useful research and, consequently, to help SFUSD leaders use the research to improve their policies, practices, and ultimately student outcomes. Wentworth asked Phillips-Sved what types of information she wanted from the potential research, how she planned to use the research in her work, and if she had the authority to make changes based on the research findings.

Wentworth used her extensive knowledge of Stanford faculty and student expertise to find a doctoral student to work with Phillips-Sved: Crystal A. Moore. Wentworth had a one-on-one meeting with Moore to explore whether a study of Black leaders' experiences would fit into her needed experiences to complete her degree. Moore had background experience working as a coach and leader at the school and systems level in other urban districts and was gaining skills in qualitative and quantitative research methods. Moore consulted with her advisor, who encouraged her to take an initial meeting with Phillips-Sved and her supervisor Kristin Bijur, who at the time was Executive Director of Leadership Development in SFUSD. Moore applied for and received a grant from the Stanford Graduate School of Education fund supporting faculty and doctoral students to work in partnership with SFUSD on research of relevance to the district priorities. This allowed Moore to focus on the research project instead of doing other assistantship work and to attend research conferences where she could co-present findings with Phillips-Sved and Bijur, which helped refine the findings and learn with other practitioners, policymakers, and researchers.

Moore, Phillips-Sved, and Bijur attended the first meeting arranged by Wentworth in February 2021, and the trio decided they wanted to work together. The first meeting was the start of a multi-year research-practice partnership with more than one line of inquiry. From that point, Phillips-Sved and Moore met every month to co-design and operationalize the research. Their findings suggested that Black site leaders faced challenges as they tried to navigate the ways in which SFUSD operated as a racialized organization (Ray, 2019), particularly in their interactions with supervisors and district personnel. In addition, in the leader induction and credentialing program which Phillips-Sved led with a facilitating team of experienced and equity-conscious former site leaders, the curriculum provided Black school leaders with the language to be able to name, interrogate, and challenge the ways in which white supremacy culture was showing up in their daily lives (Okun & Jones, 2000). The leader program also provided individualized coaching and peer networks that seemed to buoy Black leaders and sustain them in their roles as school leaders. The research from this project and other evidence the district collected also helped Phillips-Sved and Bijur develop a call to action to expand the social justice work beyond the new leader program, so that all district stakeholders could be engaged in the work of building an anti-racist organizational culture throughout the district that would disrupt systemic inequities for students, teachers, families, and leaders in subsequent years.

WHAT DO BROKERS DO?

In this case, you can see Wentworth, the director of the Stanford–SFUSD Partnership, taking actions to build a partnership between these researchers and practitioners. She starts by centering the connections between the researchers and practitioners on the intention for how the research would be used. Why did the SFUSD leaders want research? How did they intend to use it? Did they have the authority to make changes that the research may point to? Wentworth then turns to the relationship and knowledge she has with the researchers at Stanford. Who could be interested in this topic given their expertise and current lines of research? Not described above is the time Wentworth takes to understand the capability of practitioners and researchers to work in a partnership, nor her efforts identifying existing resources that support effective partnership and finding additional resources to supplement it. Nor is the larger partnership infrastructure

A FRAMEWORK

Wentworth has established to build access to administrative data and to provide funding for Stanford research in SFUSD, nor her coordination with SFUSD's Research, Planning, and Assessment (RPA) division to adapt as they streamlined and revised their approval and support process for research. Nonetheless, those elements of her work were also essential to the project's success.

Based on Wentworth's and our other authors' experiences, and our systematic literature review, we developed a framework to describe the actions brokers take to strengthen partnering and the partnership – what we call the RPP Brokers Framework. In this chapter we define each part of the RPP Brokers Framework as seen in Figure 3.A. We use the decade-long history of the Stanford–SFUSD Partnership to demonstrate the different parts of the framework in action with a few cautions, which we shared here and discuss at the end of the chapter. While the Stanford–SFUSD Partnership has its strengths, it also has areas where it can improve. While we use these stories of broker practice as a vehicle for demonstrating the RPP Brokers Framework in action, we also share in the end the challenges the partnership has with coordinating multiple brokers across many large systems and structures. And we want to emphasize that Chapters 4, 5, and 6 demonstrate brokering tools and moves that might be suitable for partnerships in other contexts, with different types of institutions, or with different structures.

BROKERING TO STRENGTHEN PARTNERS

Half of the framework centers on the work RPP brokers do to support the individual participants in RPPs. Brokers work with the participants in educational RPPs – the researchers, teachers, principals, school district leaders, students' families, community members, and staff from community-based organizations. These individuals come with different motivations for wanting to participate in an RPP, and brokers meet each partner where they are to strengthen their participation

BROKERING TO STRENGTHEN PARTNERS

- Building individual partners' competency for engaging in an RPP
- Developing and nurturing relationships to weather partnering challenges
- Creating the conditions to support research production and use

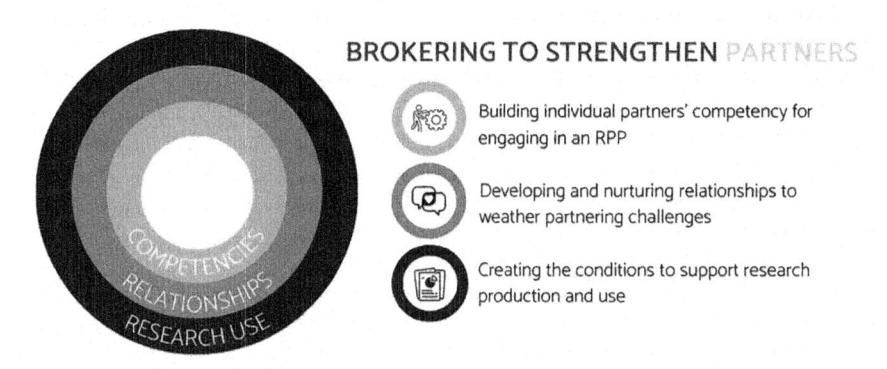

Figure 3.A Brokering Responsibilities to Strengthen Partners

41

A FRAMEWORK

in research production and use. This means developing skills, knowledge, and dispositions needed for working in RPPs, but also grappling with relationships and subsequent challenges in those relationships. Here we describe the types of moves brokers make to strengthen the partners working in RPPs. For each type of action, we first summarize the research behind the broker move. Then, we describe what those broker actions look like in practice by sharing some cases from the Stanford–SFUSD Partnership. As visualized in Figure 3.A, we start by explaining the outer circle in the figure about creating the conditions to support research production and use, and then talk about the efforts brokers make to develop relationships to weather challenges and support partners' competencies.

Creating Conditions to Support Research Production and Use

The literature on brokering in RPPs relates closely to the literature on the concept known as knowledge mobilization (KMb). To support improvement in education outcomes through RPPs, the researchers and practitioners involved must participate in deliberate planning of how research production and use relate to the design, implementation, and study of any initiative. As such, research-side partners need to be able to engage practitioners throughout the research process (e.g., research question formation, methodological approach and data collection techniques, data analysis). This includes the ability to ask practitioners questions about their needs and to be responsive to practitioners' needs. Relatedly, research-side partners also need to know how and whether research methods can be adapted to fit schools' needs. Similarly, the literature discussed in Chapter 2 suggests integration of research into decision-making is amplified when research and practice partners are able to communicate in multiple formats, such as public speaking (for presenting at researcher- and practitioner-oriented events), writing (both plain language and academic), and digital media (e.g., facilitating webinars, creating videos, posting to social media platforms).

What might this look like in practice? One of the essential roles of RPP brokers in the Stanford–SFUSD Partnership is to support research production that is useful to SFUSD. In the early stages of the RPP, most of the research produced between Stanford researchers and SFUSD leaders centered on research questions developed by Stanford researchers. One of the first moves Wentworth made as a broker was to establish a meeting agenda between researchers and practitioners that centered the priorities of the research questions, and eventually worked to align leaders' research priorities with the interests and expertise of the Stanford researchers (Wentworth et al., 2016). Here is a case of a "first date" meeting agenda that demonstrates the broker's redesign of traditional first meetings with researchers and practitioners towards centering the district priorities.

AGENDA FOR A "FIRST DATE" MEETING BETWEEN A RESEARCHER AND PRACTITIONER

Stanford–SFUSD Partnership
Laura Wentworth

Meetings between researchers and practitioners are at the heart of partnership work. In these meetings, partners build relationships, make sense of their work together, and ensure thorough communication at each stage of the research. In the beginning, these meetings are like a "first date" where partners get to know each other. The first meeting may make or break the trajectory of the relationship. Yet, how should the first meeting be organized? What should partners do during and after the meeting?

The Stanford–SFUSD Partnership has a lot of "first date" meetings. As the Partnership Director, I work to make matches between SFUSD leaders and Stanford Graduate School of Education (Stanford) researchers who could potentially work together. I keep three ideas in mind when planning first date meetings between researchers and practitioners:

- *Know your potential partner:* Research-practice partnerships are mutualistic endeavors: they meet the goals of both the researchers and practitioners. Both researchers and practitioners will have certain expectations for this meeting. To achieve mutualism, partners use these first date meetings to share the key frameworks and plans that drive the priorities of their work, like a practice partner's strategic plan or a researcher's prior research on the topic of interest to both parties.
- *Adjust for power and status:* Some partners unknowingly bring and wield status and power in practitioner and researcher relationships. The race, gender, and other identities of the individuals involved in meetings present a dynamic that can induce bias and influence the interactions between researchers and practitioners for better or worse. To address status and power issues, the agenda for the first meeting needs to be very clear about roles (who is attending and what is their role), the objectives (what does the group hope to achieve in this meeting), and the agenda (who speaks, about what, and in what order).
- *Design for a negotiation:* Ideally, the research in the partnership is seen as "joint work" or a collaborative effort where both researchers and practitioners are achieving their goals through a jointly designed project. Therefore, the first meeting needs to begin a negotiation between

all parties involved, where partners develop a concept for research that meets all needs. This negotiation will most likely take more than one meeting, but a good first meeting can set the partners on a successful trajectory.

Here is an example agenda for this type of meeting:

- **Introductions.** Who is in the room? Role in their organization?
- **Review objectives.** Why are we holding this meeting, and what do we hope to get out of it?
- **Practice priorities.** Practitioner explains priorities, programs, and their questions related to the topic.
- **Research priorities.** Researcher explains their research questions and interests based on practitioner's ideas.
- **Reactions.** Practitioners share their insights and level of interest in relation to researcher's ideas.
- **Summary.** All participants collectively summarize any synergies and next steps.

Tips for making the most of this tool:

- Send the draft agenda and a reminder about the meeting one to two days in advance. Encourage recipients to suggest changes to the draft agenda if they wish.
- In the agenda, explain the list of attendees and their affiliation, the time/date/location, meeting objectives, and agenda items.
- During the meeting, listen and ask questions more than speaking.
- Take notes during the meeting.
- When collectively summarizing at the end of the meeting, be sure to propose dates/times for a follow-up meeting if you think the meeting went well.
- Send a summary and next steps after the meeting via email.

Developing and Nurturing Relationships to Weather Challenges

According to the literature on brokering in RPPs, partners wishing to effectively work together must be able to engage with one another in productive ways that support strong relationships. To that end, brokers support *boundary spanning* efforts, defined as the transitions and interactions that occur across different sites of professional practice. These include activities such as practitioners helping to prepare a presentation for an academic conference or researchers serving as thought partners for questions that may fall outside of their core expertise. Boundary spanning requires partners to move outside of their professional responsibilities, which can be challenging on many levels. Consequently, RPP brokers need to help participants develop the skills and knowledge to successfully navigate differences that may arise due to movement beyond their organizations, cultures, and norms.

Second, brokers must have the skill and capacity to engage in regular, ongoing, and sustained *communication* between partners. This includes regularly visiting partners' home turfs to learn about partners' unique organizational contexts and being able to use specific discursive strategies to support communication across boundaries. In particular, RPP brokers help partners engage in rearticulating (summarizing and mirroring language used by partners) and "code switching" (explaining one's meanings in different partners' terms) when necessary. They may also use discursive strategies to build partners' understanding of their organizational contexts. This includes questioning (e.g., asking others about their backgrounds) and using storytelling and anecdotes to find common ground between one another and to provide context about partners' organizational settings and personal situations. Actively listening and responding to the needs of partners also plays a role in this work.

Third, RPP brokers help partners *generate agreement* with others even when conditions make their levels of authority and status different from one another. Brokers can do this in many ways, depending on their level of authority (i.e., a broker with the power or right to make decisions within the partnership or home organization) or status (i.e., a broker with a relative rank in the partnership or home organization) in the RPP. For example, brokers with authority can control the conditions that encourage certain ideas (e.g., setting the agenda in ways that privilege certain ideas). Brokers with authority can also compel partners to take a particular approach (e.g., shifting organizational policies). Brokers with status can persuade others about a course of action using their knowledge of research, organizational contexts, and their own experiences to back their arguments. Finally, brokers with less status or power can collaborate with others to amplify a message, have others with more status or authority promote their ideas, or enlist others with more status or authority to intervene on their behalf. Brokers with differing levels of authority and status may also need to find compromise in order to move the partnership forward.

What might this look like in practice? In the Stanford–SFUSD Partnership, the RPP broker matches researchers and practitioners intentionally to create a high likelihood of their developing and sustaining strong relationships. Wentworth gets to know the researchers and school district leaders in the partner organizations and understands their priorities and motivations. After consulting with the district research manager to ensure that the proposal is aligned with the district's broader portfolio of research priorities, partnerships, and projects, she then acts as a matchmaker connecting them based on their interests. As relationships develop while the partners are working together on research, the RPP broker helps partners with the boundary spanning, communication, and consensus-building moves described earlier in the literature. The RPP broker also helps the partners navigate challenges in the partnership and problem solve when the researchers and practitioners are unable to build consensus on their own. Here is one of the ways Wentworth uses the design of events to strategically sit people next to each other that either have an existing relationship or have the potential to work on future research together.

> ### CONFERENCE SEATING CHART
>
> #### Stanford–SFUSD Partnership
> #### Laura Wentworth
>
> Conferences can be a great way to build relationships across organizational boundaries, but how do you combat the tendency for people to only talk with others they already know? How do you promote discussion of research across researchers and practitioners who may or may not have existing relationships? The Stanford–SFUSD partnership uses a conference seating chart to help spark new relationships and deepen existing ones.
>
> The partnership holds an annual half-day conference on the Stanford campus for about 100 attendees from both Stanford and San Francisco Unified School District. The meeting room is filled with large round tables that seat eight to ten people. As the research-practice partnership (RPP) director, I intentionally plan the seating at each table, ensuring a mix of people from both sides of the partnership and a common thread of interest at every table. In some cases, I pair people who are already working together; in others, I pair those who might have the potential to work together on a new project. I put a list of table assignments at the registration desk and participants' name cards and materials at the table. The superintendent and dean always sit at a table up front, but otherwise I make sure to rotate so that different people are at the front or back each year. (See Figure 3.1 for details of the dating chart.)
>
> Because I use this strategy every year, regular attendees know they can request to sit near someone and often take advantage of the opportunity. Table conversations from the conference have even resulted in

A FRAMEWORK

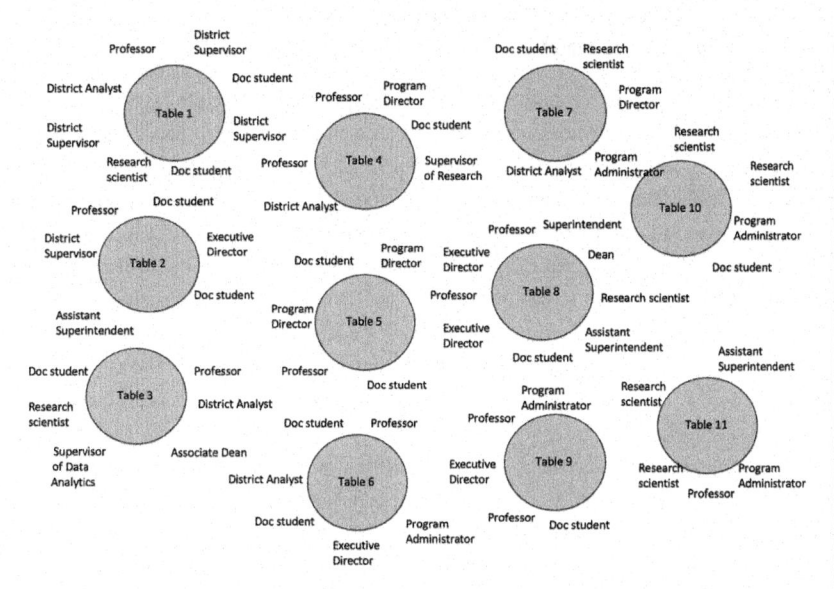

Figure 3.1 Stanford–SFUSD Partnership sample annual meeting conference seating chart with roles signified

projects that led to published papers, such as a study examining whether English learner students were over- or underrepresented in special education programming.

Tips for making the most of this tool:

- Prime people before they come by asking if they'd like to sit near someone specific.
- Make the seating arrangements shortly before the event, as registrations tend to fluctuate.
- Leave some back-up tables with extra spaces, as well as tables for people only attending part of the day.
- To balance against the more formalized interaction the seating chart creates, build in some time for more informal interaction, too (e.g., coffee breaks, transition times between sections of the agenda).
- Build in time early in the meeting for the whole table to introduce themselves to one another through a whip-around where everyone gives their name, their role, and how they are (or would like to be) connected to the partnership.

47

Building Individuals Partners' Competency for Engaging in an RPP

RPP brokers help participants build three important competencies needed for working in an RPP: knowledge of the self, knowledge of the local context, and skills and knowledge in research co-production. First, RPP brokers need to help partners build a "knowledge of self" (i.e., personal and situational factors that influence current self-representation). This can include an understanding of how one identifies by race, gender, sexual orientation, or cultural or additional characteristics of importance to the partners. Additionally, partners need knowledge of what values a person brings to the work professionally and personally, what assumptions the individual holds about the partners involved or the topics being researched, the beliefs or prejudices one holds that may influence their engagement in the work, and a person's awareness of how these characteristics influence their perspective. In addition, it also includes an understanding of one's own expertise (e.g., extensive professional experience, advanced degrees) and how this expertise can be used as a tool to support the partnership or engender certain power dynamics in collaborative work.

Second, RPP brokers need to help partners build a knowledge of the local context, including understanding of their own organizational mission, climate, and needs as well as their partners' organizational and community context. When partners start working with another organization, they need to get to know how both organizations relate to other communities. What is their organization's reputation in the community, and what is the history of their organization's work in that community? Partners also need to understand the local context in which their organizations are situated. How does each organization and its work show up and interact with the community? What is the history of their partners' organizations? What are the latest celebrations, controversies, or advancements within the partners' contexts? Understanding the local context and how the partners' organizations are tied to interacting with their communities plays a role in the priorities and work of the partnership.

Third, the literature identifies several different skills related to research co-production that RPP brokers need to support: asking researchable and actionable questions, creating data collection instruments, conducting data collection activities, analyzing data, and using research in decision-making. While some participants may already hold these competencies – for example, researchers' expertise in creating data collection instruments – others will need the help of the RPP broker to flourish. RPP brokers will need to give careful consideration to how much to build a partner organization's internal capacities to engage in research co-production themselves, versus relying on the research partner. In this next case, Wentworth described the small explicit coaching moves she uses as an RPP broker to help partners build this skill and knowledge in the moment.

What might this look like in practice? In the Stanford–SFUSD Partnership, multiple different roles in the partnership take on brokering work. For example, SFUSD has a Research, Planning, and Assessment division with a team of administrators that manage the development, review, support, and integration of research throughout the school district. They help SFUSD leaders build district capacity for engaging with research by developing learning agendas, sharing and interpreting existing research, embedding research and other forms of evidence within accessible reports and tools, providing professional learning in using evidence for improvement, and supporting their relationships with researchers across multiple institutions. In addition, many SFUSD leaders outside of the research office engage in a wide range of brokering activities, developing relationships with researchers on their own, managing projects so that the production of research may inform policy on tight timelines, and coordinating communications with research partners across multiple projects. Similarly, the director of the Stanford–SFUSD Partnership, Wentworth, supports the school district leaders, but also supports the development of Stanford researchers working to engage in partnership research. Essentially, Wentworth acts as a coach to both district leaders and researchers to help them build the skills and knowledge needed to effectively work together.

Within SFUSD, a team of administrators in the research office supports research development and use with their district colleagues as well as research partners across multiple institutions. In the following cases, Ming and colleagues describe the agendas and guidelines that their office uses to facilitate these processes.

> **AGENDAS AND GUIDELINES FOR DEVELOPING AND SUPPORTING RESEARCH**
>
> San Francisco Unified School District and Its Multiple Partnerships
> Norma Ming, Devin Corrigan, Michelle Maghes, Alec Kennedy,[1] QuynhTien Le,[2] Kathleen Bradley
>
> When school districts partner with researchers to produce useful evidence, it requires negotiating different expectations and norms across multiple stages of the research generation process. While some researchers may think of the process in terms of the legal agreements for obtaining access to data, producing high-quality research for practice settings depends on many other informal engagement and interaction processes.

49

Life Cycle of Research Projects

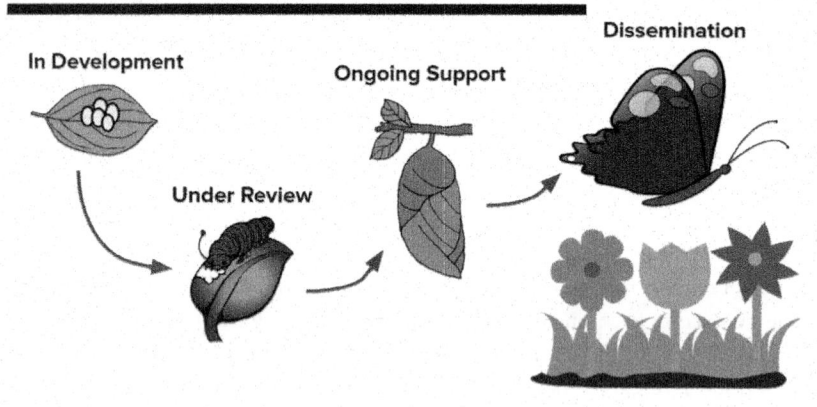

Figure 3.2 Four stages in the life cycle of research projects: in development, under review, ongoing support, and dissemination/integration

    To build shared expectations between district leaders and research partners and to guide facilitation of those processes, SFUSD's research support team uses and continually adapts a bundle of tools across these stages in the life cycle of research (Figure 3.2): developing, reviewing, supporting, and disseminating and integrating research.

    In development. Our agenda template for developing a research proposal* outlines potential meeting activities, anchored in practical priorities, knowledge, and constraints. Our accompanying internal process guidelines* delineate logistical details for drafting and sharing the agenda. They also raise questions about positionality (who has influence over the research, who is affected by it), values (which questions and methods are deemed worthy, how success is defined), and power dynamics (whose perspectives are heard and taken up) when planning and facilitating these discussions.

    Under review. We review research applications according to these ABCs (see Appendix D): *alignment* to priorities, along with practical *benefits* (validity and usefulness), which should always exceed the *costs* of conducting the research (ethical and logistical burdens). District leaders must describe* how their actions would differ if the research yielded positive findings vs. neutral/negative findings. These responses inform our internal review (see Appendix E), which may then lead to approval, requests for revisions, or a decision to decline an application.

Ongoing support. Our agenda template for supporting active research projects* lists possible discussion topics to ensure timely progress, such as refining instruments or data collection strategy, modifying analysis plans to address emerging questions, or facilitating sense-making around preliminary findings. Our accompanying internal process guidelines* address operational concerns and raise questions about unintended biases that may arise in the recruitment, measurement, and analysis processes.

Dissemination and integration. We continue to adapt and revise multiple tools* to facilitate integrating research into practice. These include templates and checklists for data visualizations, presentations, and research briefs for communicating research. Other resources include process guidelines*, agenda templates*, and various interactive tools for interpreting and applying research findings (e.g., our IDEA protocol in Chapter 5).

Roles and expectations of RPP stakeholders. Our "roles and responsibilities" matrix (see Appendix F) briefly summarizes the above expectations across these four stages of work. This clarifies the distinct roles of external researchers, who contribute expertise in relevant research literature and methods; district leaders or practitioners, who are experts in the local context and anticipated decisions; and our internal district research support team, who serve as knowledge brokers and data stewards facilitating connections between data, evidence, and action. We also maintain a longer internal version for us to explore additional nuances about specific tasks.

Tips for making the most of these tools:

- Use the process guidelines and the internal matrix as living internal documents for your team to spark discussion and calibrate on your own norms and routines, updating periodically as needed.
- Treat the agenda templates as suggestions rather than a rigid script. Encourage facilitators and participants to modify them to suit the needs of the partnership, project, context, and meeting purpose. Share the draft agendas in advance and embed the links in the calendar invitation to facilitate ready access by all participants.
- For consistency in file organization, you may prefer to have someone internal to your team start the initial copy of the template, but

A FRAMEWORK

> encourage other partners to modify or build the agendas for subsequent meetings.
> - Explore these additional resources* about issues of equity in research and discuss them with your team and with partners.
>
> *These resources can be found at San Francisco Unified School District's Research, Planning, and Assessment Department's web page, titled "Conducting External Research and Evaluation" (www.sfusd.edu/research/conducting-external-research-and-evaluation).

1 Now at the International Association for the Evaluation of Educational Achievement.
2 Now at the Los Angeles Unified School District.

Also, Wentworth describes this coaching as "mini-coaching" in that the work is informal and not pre-planned. She explains how to support research and practice negotiation, manage expectations, and integrate research findings into targeted meetings where their priority work is happening.

> **VIGNETTE: THE LONG GAME: MINI-COACHING OVER TIME**
>
> Stanford–SFUSD Partnership
> Laura Wentworth
>
> Research-practice partnerships in education are long-term commitments. This means partnerships over time will go through highs and lows, ups and downs as the partners involved negotiate their relationships. Brokers play a role in this by coaching partners about how to support partnerships for the long term.
>
> This vignette describes three types of mini-coaching sessions I often have with partners. One supports research production, and the other two support research use. These are considered mini-coaching sessions because they happen in the moment and are not planned as a formal coaching session.
>
> **Partnerships require ongoing negotiation.** In the early negotiations of a partnership, I often hear from administrators or researchers, "I'm not sure I am interested in pursuing this research question," or, "I am not sure how useful this research will be." When this happens, I ask the

practitioner or researcher, "On the topic, what question would you want to explore together?" Nine times out of ten, the person responds with a specific question, which I then encourage them to share with their potential partner. Researchers and practitioners are more accustomed to having working relationships that are more transactional, as a yes or no proposition, and less used to these relationships being a two-way street. By encouraging collaboration and negotiation even in the early phases, I help shift their thinking about what partnership looks like.

Revisit expectations and goals for the partnership. When partners are considering research findings, some partners wonder, "Now what?" I use these questions to help partners revisit their goals and motivations for the project, in hopes of linking research findings to researchers' and practitioners' questions. "What were your original research questions? Why did you want to explore those questions? Did the findings match what you expected to find? How did you anticipate using the information produced by the research in your decisions?"

Integrate findings in targeted meetings. Oftentimes practitioners need to go on a "road show," where they share findings to committees, school board commissioners, and stakeholder groups to build a shared knowledge of the findings. But they often are not sure how to communicate the research beyond their partnership. I suggest a set of tips that help integrate discussion of research findings at the right time and in the right format:

- **Start by having a small group presentation involving the practitioner who sponsored the research talking to one to two key personnel who make decisions related to the research topic.** For example, if the research is on English learner instruction at high schools, start with a meeting with the supervisor of high schools and the chief academic officer.
- **Next, host a large-scale presentation and make sure key stakeholders have the event on their calendars.** This event provides a broader network of leaders with access to the research in hopes of building their knowledge of the findings. Attendees could include teachers on special assignment, content specialists, or analysts. At this event, it is helpful to have a brief that summarizes the findings for attendees to take away and reference in other meetings and conversations.
- **Over time, the broker may help the district sponsor integrate research findings into their own presentations** as one piece of

information in a larger discussion. For example, some leaders want to reference research findings when presenting to the school board, but they may need help summarizing the findings in a digestible manner to policymakers.

This case demonstrates how brokers use mini-coaching sessions to support research production and use in real time by encouraging these strategies:

- Negotiate research questions rather than starting with a yes/no proposition.
- Revisit expectations and goals when reviewing research findings.
- Integrate findings in targeted meetings.

Secondarily, these mini-coaching sessions also build partners' skills and knowledge over time so that they can execute these moves on their own.

BROKERING TO STRENGTHEN PARTNERSHIPS

The collection of broker actions that aim to strengthen the *partnership* itself centers around building and maintaining the necessary *infrastructure* for the partnership to thrive. In essence, RPPs are a third space outside of the boundaries of the organizations engaged in the partnership. New governance, new communication channels, and new structures and systems need to be established for the

Developing partnership governance and administrative structures

Designing processes and communications routines

Assessing and continuously improving the partnership

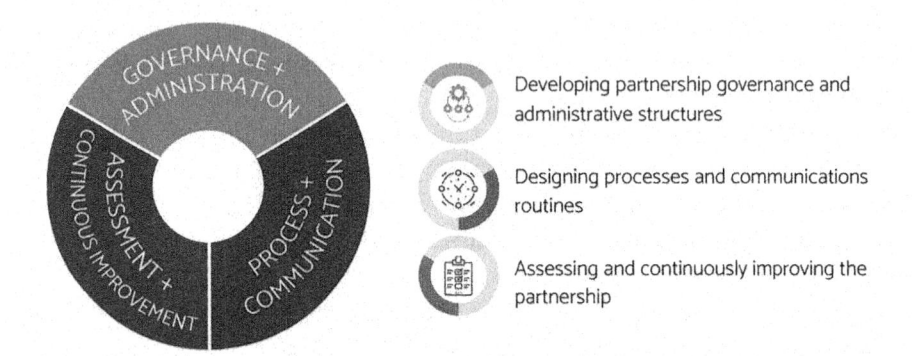

Figure 3.B Brokering Responsibilities to Strengthen Partnerships

partnership to work. As visualized in Figure 3.B, RPP brokers engage in three types of moves to develop, establish, maintain, and strengthen the partnership. They develop partnership governance and administrative structures that establish and guide the norms, values, and decision-making structures. RPP brokers also design processes and communications routines that establish and maintain the social infrastructure. We end with how RPP brokers assess and continuously improve the partnership, illustrating all of these through references to the research literature and examples from the Stanford–SFUSD partnership.

Developing partnership governance and administrative structures

Brokers play a crucial role in accelerating the various aspects of partnership development, whether they are in a supporting role or leadership position in the RPP. They are often the people tasked with "getting it done," given their central role in linking both the research and practice sides. As such, they often find themselves in a position to plan for future infrastructural needs as well. Accordingly, brokers serving at all levels will want to think through how they will facilitate the development of important governance and administrative structures to best serve partners' needs. This includes determining who is involved in partnership work; creating a common vision and related supporting documents; implementing and maintaining organizational structures; and establishing partnership identity and culture. Each of these topics is further discussed in the following.

An important task for a broker is determining who will be involved in the partnership. This may include engaging decision-makers in research, practice, and/or policy spaces in an assessment of current needs, and an evaluation of whether embarking on a partnership is appropriate. If a partnership approach is determined to be appropriate, brokers may facilitate discussions with decision-makers about which organizations have interest, resources, and capacities to support the development of a partnership. Once potential partners have been identified, brokers may engage research and practice partners in conversations to develop their interest in the partnership and to explore shared research interests, needs, and capacities. Buy-in is a key criterion for determining whom to partner with as a means for promoting sustainability. As such, brokers may also seek to influence leaders (i.e., those who are capable of amassing organizational resources, or maintaining support of the work over time) to endorse or sponsor the partnership.

Brokers facilitate negotiation of the roles individuals play in the partnership. This may include facilitating discussions of individuals' identities and culture both early in the partnership and when new partners are added. During this process, brokers can provide support and guidance to partners as they become comfortable with their new and expanded roles. Brokers must also navigate the dynamics of authority relations and status by respecting the value and power which all partners bring. Finally, brokers can play an important supportive role in facilitating shifts in identities and tasks as individual partners grow and evolve. Brokers can identify when these shifts in roles are happening and help partners manage and understand the practices and routines involved in new roles.

Creating a common vision. Lack of agreement on purposes within the whole partnership can inhibit partnership efforts. As such, brokers need to engage partner representatives in a process of creating a common vision. While RPPs can build upon existing models and approaches, they must nonetheless engage in a process of developing, adopting, and putting into practice their own partnership agreements that outline the vision and goals for the partnership. For brokers, this may include supporting the creation of a formal memorandum of understanding (MOU), data use agreements (DUA), and plans for integrating the research into each organization's work to strengthen the overall partnership. In order to form mutually beneficial partnerships, brokers can work with partners jointly to develop an MOU that outlines the basic terms (such as roles and responsibilities) for any partnership activities. Partners may also have concerns about sharing data. These concerns should be taken seriously, and brokers should work together with community partners to develop a DUA and data-sharing structures that meet partners' requirements. While partnership documents, like MOUs and DUAs, can help to formalize governance structures, they are not a panacea. Partnership documents can only work in tandem with the actions of partners, which play an equally important role (Kim et al., 2020). Brokers have to stay actively involved and build relationships between partners if success is to occur.

Evaluating readiness to engage. Finally, before an RPP is established, potential partners must first examine their own organization's readiness to engage in a partnership. This includes thinking about what organizational resources partners can offer to support the partnership. Since both organizations may already be engaged in other existing partnerships, it is important to consider what resources may already be in place and how to develop mutually beneficial arrangements to leverage them without duplicating efforts. For brokers, this might include identifying, leveraging, or creating tangible resources for these purposes. For example, brokers may identify existing organizational processes and structures (e.g., providing dedicated space, time, and technical resources) that could be leveraged to support partnership work. Brokers can also promote the development of structures that organize and preserve institutional memory for partnership work. This may include creating information and knowledge management structures that store and transmit organizational learning like a library of research reports or a partnership management tool like Salesforce for tracking interactions and meetings. It may also include cultivating structures and processes that allow for frequent communication between partners and engaging in efforts to decrease "organizational churn" and increase continuity (e.g., having practitioners who take part in partnership activities move upward in leadership structures). In addition, brokers can create processes or tools to support the partnership, such as developing partnership roadmaps, which preview tasks for each stage of the partnership. Although research-side organizations often have greater resources to build these infrastructures, RPPs need to carefully examine how they may offset these power dynamics and how they may contribute to the longer-term benefits by investing in developing these structures within practice-side organizations (Farley-Ripple et al., 2022).

Brokers will want to think through how to facilitate the development of macro-, meso-, and micro-level structures to support the partnership. At the macro level, individuals at the highest hierarchical positions (e.g., board members, superintendents) may participate in steering committees. They can act in an advisory capacity for decision-making throughout the entire partnership and take on the roles of operational management. For example, this may include priority setting, sponsoring or supporting research project proposals, and obtaining funding and resources. At the meso level, individuals at upper-organizational levels (e.g., district and school administrators with decision-making authority) may participate in committees that develop and implement mechanisms to deepen the partnership. At the micro level, on-the-ground practitioners like classroom teachers may participate in communities of practice to share and discuss educational research. The individual brokers might be embedded at any level of the system to serve as points of contact between different levels of the partnership.

In addition to structures that spread power, structures that promote shared decision-making and address issues of equity within the partnership are necessary for collaboration. For brokers, this might include helping partnering organizations to develop a shared understanding of equity (e.g., through facilitating self-reflection, leading interactive discussions, and creating action steps that lead to a more inclusive partnership). In addition, where possible, brokers can reduce hierarchy and promote joint leadership within the partnership. For example, this may include having representatives from research and practice organizations serve as co-chairs on committees or co-lead research projects. Finally, brokers must manage issues of status and power dynamics that come with the different racial, cultural, and professional identities of participants and ensure that all partners have a voice in the partnership. This can include focusing on and elevating voices from practice and other underrepresented groups during regular partnership meetings and other interactions – perhaps by providing positive recognition and credit to school partners or allowing community agencies and schools to retain control over the release of findings.

Exploring a project or partnership identity and culture. An RPP is typically composed of two or more organizations, each with their own identity. We can define organizational identities as the norms and patterns of behavior that guide how their members think and act. To be effective and sustainable, partnerships need to develop an organizational identity and culture. Partnership identity formation – moving from "we" the individuals and organizations to "we" the partnership – is likely one of the most challenging areas of partnership work, as it requires individuals in both organizations to adapt their work from their organizational, professional, and personal norms. Brokers may support partnership identity formation in a number of ways. They may advocate for policies, practices, or resources that clarify the importance of the partnership to its partner organizations. Brokers may also create opportunities for front-line educators to take on leadership and brokering roles to expand their influence. And, finally, brokers may keep partners engaged in developing the partnership identity by communicating with partners about the ways in which they want their time and efforts to lead to teaching and learning improvements.

What might this look like in practice? One example is the Stanford–SFUSD Partnership, where the administration and governance of the partnership rely on a third-party organization, California Education Partners. The third-party non-profit director relies on three important administrative and governance structures to run the partnership. First, the director hosts an annual meeting with the SFUSD Superintendent, the head of the Research, Planning, and Assessment division, the manager of research, and the Stanford University Graduate School of Education Dean. This meeting, described in the vignette below, aims to confirm the value of the partnership and monitor the progress of the partnership towards its objectives and overall vision. Second, the partnership maintains a partnership agreement. Unlike an MOU, it is not a legal agreement, but outlines the objectives of the partnership, the approach to monitoring the partnerships, and the commitments each leader is making to the partnership. The idea is that the leaders will keep wanting to work together as long as the partnership is making progress towards its shared objectives.

Lastly, the director maintains a set of three types of legally binding agreements related to research, some of which are described later in the book. For each project, there is a research proposal approved by the SFUSD research department, which provides documentation of district approval, processes for collaborating on the research and ensuring that it will contribute to practice, and informed consent procedures for collecting and sharing data. Some projects also have a DUA that allows parties to exchange administrative data for the purposes of research. Finally, the partnership also maintains an institutional-level data warehousing agreement where SFUSD houses an extract of its administrative data with Stanford University and a Stanford data manager maintains and supplies data to Stanford researchers who have a DUA with SFUSD for a research project. This warehouse is documented in a white paper (Kim et al., 2019) and a book chapter (Kim et al., 2020).

AGENDA FOR ANNUAL PARTNERSHIP COMMITMENTS AND PROGRESS MONITORING MEETING

Stanford–SFUSD Partnership
Laura Wentworth

Research-practice partnerships are formed across two or more individuals and organizations, requiring new administrative structures and governance to make them work. These structures are often carefully crafted to reinforce the goals of the partnership, while also supporting the goals of the member organizations. To work seamlessly together, leaders need to purposefully examine and review their commitments to and monitor the progress of their partnership.

As seen in Figure 3.3, we present the objectives and agenda used by the leaders in the Stanford–SFUSD Partnership in the 2018–2019 school year to support the administration and governance of the partnership during an annual meeting. In this version of the agenda, you see some accompanying materials used during a meeting to exemplify the preparation it takes for this meeting. Figure 3.4 shows a blinded chart used to judge research project impact, examining whether there is 1) no impact, 2) evidence of impact on SFUSD leaders' thinking, 3) evidence of impact on SFUSD policy, 4) evidence of impact on SFUSD system-level practices, or 5) evidence of impact on student outcomes. Figure 3.5 is a bar graph showing how many Stanford research projects each department has worked on over the prior ten years (2009 to 2019).

Tips for having a successful commitments and progress monitoring meeting:

Before the meeting:

- collect specific evidence of progress based on each partnership objective, and summarize that evidence into digestible slides

- review the objective, agenda, and accompanying materials in one-on-one meetings with each leader and prepare potential talking points for each leader
- have the meeting in person if possible
- have handouts printed rather than digital to support more face-to-face dialogue
- take notes and send a reminder after the meeting of commitments made during the meeting and other next steps
- in follow-up one-on-one meetings, revisit new commitments and discuss steps for making these commitments come to fruition

---

In attendance:
- SFUSD leaders (e.g., superintendent, head of research, manager of research, other leaders seen as leading the partnership)
- California Education Partners (e.g., director of the partnership, executive director of Ed Partners)
- Stanford leaders (e.g., Dean, Graduate School of Education)

Meeting objectives:
- monitor progress towards partnership objectives
- maintain relationships across Stanford and SFUSD leaders to support the partnership

Meeting agenda:
- introductions
- review of progress on objectives for the school year
- Figure 3.4: evidence of project impact in certain year (blinded)
- Figure 3.5: number of research projects engaged by district department per year (blinded)
- entertain the fourth objective discussed last year
- discuss commitment to future resources needed to continue partnership
- summarize commitments made in the meeting, and next steps

Figure 3.3 Draft attendance, objectives, and agenda for annual commitments and progress monitoring meeting of school district, non-profit, and university leaders

A FRAMEWORK

Degree of research impact by SFUSD department, GSE faculty
2017–2018 (13 projects)

Early Education	**SFCS** ❖ Study 1 (Faculty A, Center A) ✓ Study 2 (Faculty B, Center A)	**C&I** ☐ Study 3 (Faculty C) ✓ Study 4 (Faculty D) ✓ Study 5 (Center B) ❖ Study 6 (Faculty E) ● Study 7 (Faculty F)	**LEAD** ○ Study 8 (Faculty B, Center A)
Schools ● Student 9 (Doctoral Student A) ● Student 10 (Doctoral Student B)	**RPA** ✓ Study 11 (Doctoral Student C)	**Policy and Operations**	**iLab** ☐ Study 12 (Center C) ☐ Study 13 (Faculty G)

KEY
- ● No impact (yet) on policy, practice, or students
- ✓ Evidence of impact on SFUSD leaders thinking who is the sponsor for the research
- ☐ Evidence of impact on policy (in SFUSD or beyond)
- ○ Evidence of impact on systems level practice (more than one classroom or school)
- ❖ Evidence of impact on student outcomes

STANFORD SFUSD

Figure 3.4 Assessment of project impact in certain year (blinded)

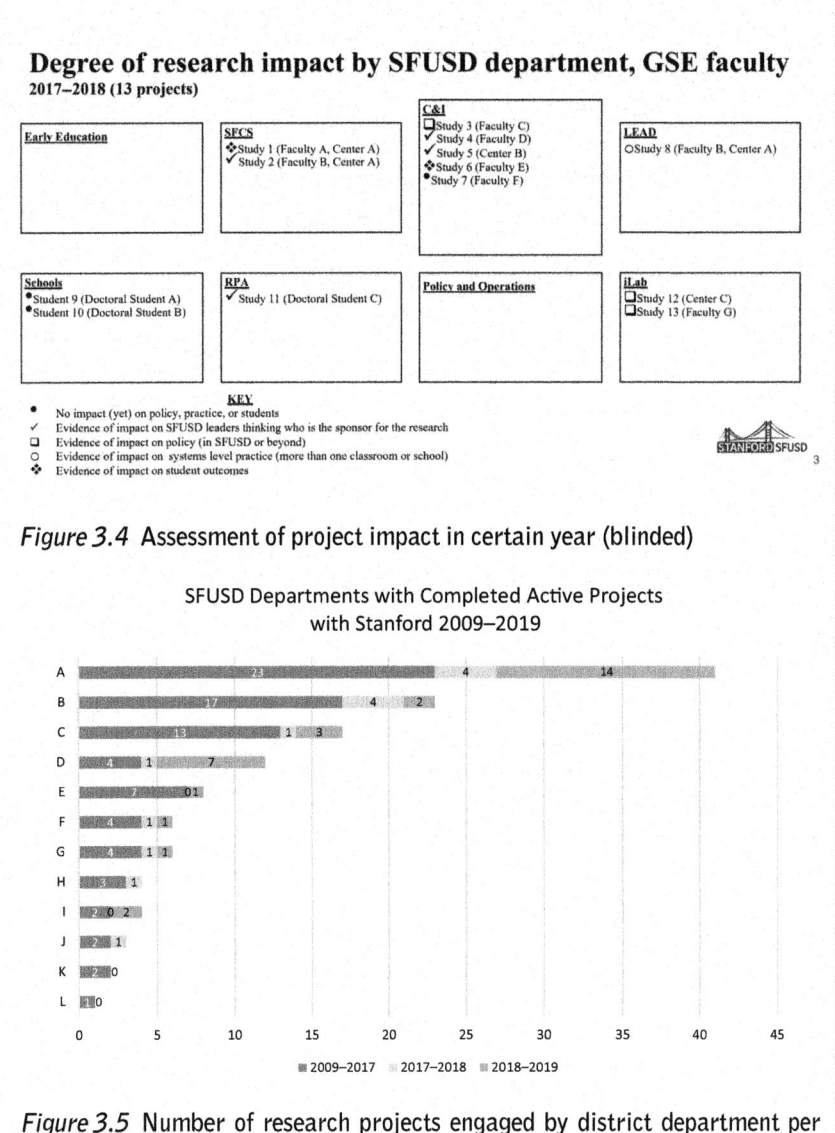

SFUSD Departments with Completed Active Projects with Stanford 2009–2019

Dept	2009–2017	2017–2018	2018–2019
A	23	4	14
B	17	4	2
C	13	1	3
D	4	1	7
E	7	0	1
F	4	1	1
G	4	1	1
H	3	1	
I	2	0	2
J	2	1	
K	2	0	
L	1	0	

Figure 3.5 Number of research projects engaged by district department per year (blinded)

Designing processes and communication routines

A second type of infrastructure that brokers develop are processes and routines related to communications among stakeholder groups. Brokers are well positioned to take on the design of such efforts, given their ability to cross boundaries at both an organizational and individual level. For example, some of the infrastructure a broker may need to consider includes opportunities that enable partners to collaboratively consider, evaluate, explore, and learn together. Brokers often shape social interactions between current, new, or future partnership members through the establishment of common routines and the development of trust and empathy. Strategies for accomplishing these aims include developing external (i.e., across partner organizations) and internal (i.e., within a partner organization) communication pathways, as well as facilitating meetings and other social interactions between partners. We elaborate on these below.

Developing communication pathways. Long pauses in communication between partners can result in confusion and stifle the progress of the RPP. As such, external communication pathways (i.e., the ways in which information flows across partner organizations) are necessary to sustain the RPP and to be responsive to partners' needs. Brokers can develop formalized communication processes, such as scheduled meetings, regular newsletters, or special events, to share information across organizations and roles. In addition, brokers can act as shepherds between systems, as they are often responsible for communicating about partnership progress to stakeholders across the organizations.

Internal communication pathways are the ways in which information is exchanged between individuals within one partner organization. Brokers can identify, leverage, or create organizational structures (e.g., dedicated departments) to act as hubs and to leverage knowledge. Moreover, brokers can support internal information exchange by ensuring that dedicated time and space is provided to make sense of new information.

Facilitating meetings and social opportunities. While the strategy described above is about the processes required to establish pathways for communicating, this strategy centers on the routines necessary for partnerships to utilize those pathways. Planning, facilitating, and documenting regular partnership meetings is a key activity for all types of RPPs; in our experience, brokers typically lead this effort. For example, they can articulate clear goals for the meeting, help develop an initial agenda, use a task-based approach (i.e., focus on definable steps that need to be taken to address the objectives of the partnership), and ensure that meetings start and stop on time. In addition, brokers may also focus on taking meeting notes and making sure that relevant information (e.g., research reports) is shared among partners.

In addition to providing an underlying structure to meetings, brokers can promote an environment of inclusion and respect for all contributions. This can be done by setting norms at the beginning of meetings that specifically foster inclusion, mediating and facilitating interactions (e.g., watching for who's talking and who's not, interjecting and redirecting with dominators and interrupters), and using sub-groups to allow for individuals to share in a less intimidating environment. Brokers should also address negative emotions (such as frustration and blame) during meetings and facilitate and allow for time for individuals to discuss and work out differences. Finally, brokers also foster an inclusive and collaborative process by paying attention to the location of meetings. For example, locating meetings at a school or community organization may help to build a sense of community ownership (instead of a sense that the meeting is university- or researcher-led).

What might this look like in practice? In the Stanford–SFUSD Partnership, participants have various skills and knowledge for working in RPPs. Some have extensive experience working in RPPs, and others have never worked in partnership. Consequently, brokers can help participants develop clear communication pathways early on in most partnership research projects to help manage expectations and set participants up for success. In this case, the author shares a model timeline of activities and deliverables that partnership participants are expected to develop within the Stanford–SFUSD Partnership and the Stanford–Sequoia K–12 Research Collaborative.

TIMELINE OF ACTIVITIES AND DELIVERABLES IN RPP PROJECTS

Stanford–SFUSD Partnership, Stanford–Sequoia K–12 Research Collaborative

Michelle Nayfack, Laura Wentworth, Norma Ming

To maintain consistent communication pathways, RPP participants need to have known routines and structures for communicating. Some RPPs use more formal structures like newsletters and research briefs, and other partnerships use more informal communication pathways like asynchronous communication via email or Slack.

We present some tools partnership participants use when they are forming to help partnership participants understand when partners will be interacting in certain activities and types of communication and what they can expect as a result of those activities and communications. These tools are referred to as a timeline of activities and specific deliverables. Here we present two examples of these timelines, Figure 3.6, used by SFUSD's research department along with their "roles and responsibilities" matrix (shared earlier), and Figure 3.7, used by California Education Partners in the Stanford–Sequoia K–12 Research Collaborative.

Part 3. Partnership and Communication Plans

Stage of Research	Involving Which SFUSD Staff/Site/ Department, If Any?	Involving Which External Audience(s), If Any?	Date(s)
Initial project ideas			
Study design			
Research approval	RPA	N/A	Allow ≥ 2 mos.
Recruitment & data collection	Primary data	N/A	___ – ___
	Secondary data*	RPA N/A	
Updates on interim progress & findings		N/A	
Internal presentation		N/A	
Drafts of reports prior to submission	RPA, ___	N/A	
Executive summary	RPA, ___	N/A	
Formal report	RPA, ___		
Submission for public circulation	N/A		

Figure 3.6 Partnership and communication plans in Part 3 of the SFUSD research department research application

Both timelines communicate:

- the development of partnership work: the activities and communication over time
- the development of research projects, and key points of communication related to this research (e.g., presentation of research)
- the expected outputs of the partnership research, what are referred to as deliverables or research products

Tips for using timelines:

- **Keep the timeline simple.** This will be shared with RPP participants in different roles, so the timeline should be one page at most and jargon-free.

- **Be sure to delineate who is doing what.** Timelines are helpful for communicating the different roles for each partner, which activities they will participate in, and who is responsible for which deliverable.
- **A timeline is only as good as how often it is referenced throughout the work of the RPP.** Some RPP projects develop this timeline at the beginning of their work together, and don't revisit the timeline. The timeline as a tool is more effective if partners revisit the timeline on a semi-annual or quarterly basis to track their progress.

STANFORD SEQUOIA K-12 RESEARCH COLLABORATIVE

Stanford | GRADUATE SCHOOL OF EDUCATION

Appendix A: Project Timeline & Deliverables

Project Timeline & Deliverables: All proposals are required to submit a project timeline with project deliverables. How will the research team and district team work together to accomplish the goals of the research project? Please use this sample project timeline or something similar to outline key project dates including project meetings, reports findings, and research activities.

Month/Year	Examples of Key Events	Example of Activity Description	Example of Deliverables
May	Research Planning Meeting/Proposal Development	e.g., project management, data collection plan, site access	• scope of work, timeline for project • communication to school sites
September	Project Kick-Off	• discuss findings from previous years • review project timeline & plans for school access, sampling or data access.	• research findings from prior school year • draft logistics, timeline for work
September–December	Data Collection Fall Collaborative Meeting	e.g., observations at a school, survey administration, interviews, etc.	• consent forms (if necessary)
February	Winter Project Meeting	• discussion of preliminary findings, progress • discussion of implications from work to date	• formative summary of research findings to date
January–April	Data Collection	e.g., observations at a school, survey administration, interviews, etc.	• consent forms (if necessary)
Ongoing	Data Analysis	e.g., code interviews, clean data set, conduct statistical analysis, conduct thematic analysis	• report of progress
April	Spring Collaborative Meeting	• discussion of more findings, progress • discussion of implications from work • discussion of next year's scope of work	• formative summary of research findings to date
June	Presentation of Summative Report	• review summative report • discuss plans for dissemination • discuss implications for policy/practice changes	• submit Stanford-Sequoia Research Brief

Figure 3.7 Timeline in the Stanford–Sequoia K–12 Research Collaborative research proposal

Assessing and continuously improving the partnership

Ongoing assessment of and reflection on a partnership's efforts are crucial if partners are to understand what's working and where further attention is needed. These aspects of the infrastructure play an important role for continuously improving the partnership over time, especially in terms of strengthening both partnership processes and initiatives. Brokers can support these efforts by designing partnership accountability systems that monitor and evaluate the RPP's progress towards its goals. They can also create feedback loops that provide partners with information about the RPP in real time so that appropriate adjustments can be made. To support the feedback process, brokers can identify, leverage, or create structures that allow for bi-directional communication. Finally, brokers can involve partnership members in an ongoing process of reflection and evaluation in order to identify and address areas of improvement.

Putting some of these ideas into practice, some partnerships have used the framework for assessing RPPs written by Henrick and colleagues (2017) to guide their evaluation efforts. In this piece, the authors identify five dimensions of RPP effectiveness: 1) building trust and cultivating partnership relationships; 2) conducting rigorous research to inform action; 3) supporting the partner practice organization to achieving its goals; 4) producing knowledge that can inform educational improvement efforts more broadly; and 5) building the capacity of the participating researchers, practitioners, practice organizations, and research organizations to engage in partnership work. The authors additionally name and describe a number of indicators that may demonstrate progress on each of the dimensions. One way in which a broker can apply some of these concepts towards assessing and continuously improving the partnership is by creating the space for partners from all sides of the partnership to collectively reflect on their work, organized by these five dimensions of effectiveness. For example, a broker might collect observational notes or informal interviews with partners that are later synthesized and shared with the whole team for reflection and discussion. Based on this, a broker might then develop a plan moving forward, focusing on the areas that partnership identified as ripe for improvement.

What might this look like in practice? As mentioned earlier, the director at California Education Partners is tasked with monitoring the progress of the Stanford–SFUSD Partnership towards its objectives. To do this, the RPP director uses Salesforce as a data platform to collect information about each line of inquiry. The RPP director works with her team at Ed Partners to create unique identifiers for each research project and all associated characteristics of the partnership: which leaders and researchers are involved, what funding did they receive, what stage of development are they in, and so on. Once a year, the RPP director and an analyst at Ed Partners analyze the data as they relate to the objectives and bring the results to partnership leaders through annual progress monitoring reports.

A FRAMEWORK

VIGNETTE: ANALYZING RPP DATA TO TRACK PROGRESS TOWARDS OBJECTIVES

Stanford–SFUSD Partnership
Fran Kipnis and Laura Wentworth

When brokers are tasked with explaining the progress their RPP has made towards its goals, they usually turn to the information they routinely collect on their work within the partnership.

In this case, we present our approach to collecting data about the Stanford–SFUSD Partnership to help assess the progress the RPP is making towards its stated objectives. We analyze these data and present findings to leaders of the RPP annually, and we also use them internally at California Education Partners to examine the progress of the partnership.

We use Salesforce to organize these data, but this type of data could also be collected on a spreadsheet. As one example, for the RPP objective, "Research is associated with advancements in policy, practices, and student outcomes," we use the data in Figure 3.8. We collect data to build cases for examining whether lines of research and published journal articles are associated with changes in school district practice, policy, and student outcomes.

Impact of RPP Lines of Research

These lines of inquiry are associated with policies and practices increasing [specific student outcomes].

Researchers	Policy	Practice	Students

Figure 3.8 Table to organize data examining impact of RPP lines of research

67

A FRAMEWORK

Tips for collecting data for progress monitoring:

- Start by thinking of the types of data that help you explain your theory of change or theory of action. Are there data that explain the inputs, activities, and associated outputs and outcomes?
- Keep the list of data you want to collect for each RPP project realistic: be careful of how many variables you collect because the list you desire can be quite long. You do not want to spend all of your time collecting data about your RPP.
- Some data are easier to find than others: for example, it might be easy to find out when a project started versus how much funding an RPP project received and how that funding is being spent.
- Pilot your data collection and analyze a small portion of data to see if it helps you answer your questions. You may learn in the process that you are not collecting the right data to understand whether you are making progress towards your RPP objectives.

POWER DIFFERENCES, EQUITY, AND RACISM

RPP brokers work to disrupt problematic power dynamics: chief among them, racialized inequities in access to and participation in RPPs. In addition to racism, partnerships experience power differences as a result of inequality related to gender, income, language, and disability, among other identities and characteristics. In Diamond's essay (2021), he explains,

> While those working in RPPs often seek to challenge such hierarchies, this aspiration and the unfolding reality are often at odds. Unfortunately, the same deficit-oriented, paternalistic, and colonial relationships can exist in RPPs that exist in other forms of research. We need to avoid assuming that racial justice will rise to the surface simply through a stated commitment to it and instead work to root out biases that lead to detrimental approaches.
>
> (p. 2)

To achieve the ideal outlined by Diamond and others, RPP brokers will need to confront these status quo, racist, sexist, xenophobic, and other undermining practices within the partner organizations. As described throughout this and other chapters, RPP brokers will need to disrupt these power differences and issues of status and authority situated in any relationship involving individuals working together. These power differences are even more pronounced in RPP work given that partnership participants need to cross institutional boundaries to work together.

RPPs have been known for wrestling with power differences and institutional hierarchies, as well as their focus on equity. The RPP community has worked to center equity in its work. Henrick et al. (2019) define equity in RPP work:

> Equity in education is allocating resources appropriately so every child has access to the supports, resources, and opportunities needed to be successful and thrive. Beyond this, equity ensures that resources are tailored to meet individual needs, build on the cultural assets of students, and are designed in such a way that all students have the opportunity to achieve their maximum potential.

Henrick, McGee and Penuel provide a description of equity in RPP goals and resources for supporting equity as a goal in RPPs. Sexton and colleagues (2020) describe equity in RPP through three concepts: 1) equity in the partnership: this type of equity sits in the power dynamics among partners used within the partnership. Sexton and colleagues encourage ongoing reflection among partners to understand whether the relationships among participants in the process support equitable relationships among participants; 2) equity in the research: this is about helping practitioners and researchers both have access to the entirety of the research process. Given the status researchers have had over practitioners in traditional research relationships, this means likely foregrounding practitioners' views in all stages of the partnership; 3) equity in practice and implementation: RPP brokers focused on equity will help their RPPs center equity in the areas of practice and implementation they are exploring and researching. To realize equity in an RPP, this also means the practice being studied or designed must itself attend to equity.

Yet, the Vetter and colleagues (2022) literature review describes how most RPPs that strive towards equity will not advance equity and social justice in their work until they realize three elements. First, RPPs must develop equitable relationships. Second, RPPs must achieve equitable outcomes. Finally, RPPs must support equitable systems. At the heart of Vetter and colleagues' findings sits one of the most important pieces of work for RPP brokers — to help themselves and the other RPP participants explore their own identity and positionality in the larger society and in relationship with one another. To achieve equity in an RPP, an RPP broker will inevitably have to facilitate these conversations about racism and equity and manage relationships and individuals address their white fragility, and understand the harms of racism that still exist today.

What might this look like in practice? The Stanford Graduate School of Education (GSE) has done some work to support their doctoral students' work in partnerships like the Stanford–SFUSD partnership that help doctoral students engage in partnership work focused on equity in process and outcome. One of the more robust efforts has been to develop a certificate in partnership research — a set of courses and experiences that help doctoral students at Stanford GSE receive explicit instruction in the research and practice for effectively working in RPPs. The course elevates partnership research in its status by being part of doctoral students' formal training program. And, the course prepares future researchers to address issues like power differences and pursuits of equity embedded in RPP work. Here we share a lesson plan from one of the courses taught in the certificate that helps students explore their own personal identities in relation to their RPP work.

> **ADDRESSING AUTHORITY, STATUS, RACISM, AND POWER DIFFERENTIALS IN PARTNERSHIPS**
>
> A Lesson Plan from EDUC 352C: Advanced Partnership Research
> Amado Padilla and Laura Wentworth
>
> Stanford University Graduate School of Education offers a certificate in partnership research to its doctoral students. Part of the certificate involves students working with their advisors in RPPs, and there are some coursework requirements. Amado Padilla and Laura Wentworth teach the third course in a three-course series related to the certificate, titled Advanced Partnership Research. Early in the course, they take a day to discuss authority, status, racism, and power differential in partnerships. Here we describe part of the lesson plan for this class.
>
> The purpose of this class session is to explore the challenges experienced within research-practice partnerships related to authority, status, racism, and power differentials. We note that some of these issues are documented by researchers and practitioners in the RPP literature. We explore these issues in partnerships by reading two influential blog posts by Angela Barton and Bronwyn Bevan and another post by John Diamond. We will discuss these types of challenges with a faculty at Stanford working in RPPs.
>
> Required Reading:
>
> > Barton, A. C., & Bevan, B. (2016). *Leveraging RPPs to address racial inequality in urban school districts.* William T. Grant Foundation.
> >
> > Diamond, J. B. (2021). *Racial equity and research-practice partnerships 2.0: A critical reflection.* William T. Grant Foundation.

Students read the two blog posts before class. Then, Padilla and Wentworth provide a short mini-lesson on the three readings using slides (see slide describing Diamond's reading in Figure 3.9). Students are asked to think about these questions when reviewing the readings:

(1) How do you think RPPs work to overcome oppressive systems stemming from the history of universities or school districts perpetuating racial injustice?
(2) How do RPPs wrestle with comprehensive solutions and power asymmetries at the same time?
(3) Is there an idea in the readings that relates to a challenge in your RPP work?

After the review of reading, students write for five minutes on their own about these questions. Then students pair with a partner and discuss these questions. Then, we have a whole-group discussion emphasizing how they responded to the last question – how do these issues show up in their own RPP work?

Then, we have a guest speaker who is one of the faculty at Stanford GSE working in an RPP, and they discuss these questions from their own experience. The students workshop the challenge the faculty is experiencing.

Diamond (2021): *Racial Equity and Research-Practice Partnerships 2.0: A Critical Reflection*

In short, RPPs must confront the *institutional histories, power asymmetries*, and *racialized organizational processes* that shape them. By taking this approach, the field will increase the likelihood that RPPs challenge oppressive systems rather than reproduce them.

Institutional histories: universities and school districts have perpetuated racial injustice.

Power asymmetries: bringing groups and institutions with unequal power together, without acknowledging that unequal power, is a recipe for continued domination.

Racialized organizations: racial oppression is reproduced through normal functioning of racialized organizations, including schools and universities (Ray, 2019). If we cannot deal honestly with the organizations that make up RPPs as they are, the quest for racial justice will remain elusive.

Figure 3.9 Slide describing Diamond's (2021) reading

EXAMINING BROKERING ACROSS ONE RPP WITH A CRITICAL LENS

While we presented a set of cases from our handbook related to RPP brokering embedded primarily within one RPP to illustrate how the cases string together, we believe it is important to be transparent about the Stanford–SFUSD Partnership's brokering challenges. Each RPP is unique, with its own strengths and flaws. In addition, all partnerships need to be attentive to the asymmetries in power and resources between research and practice communities: differential access to researchers, grants, libraries, data systems, supporting infrastructure, finances, and so on. Similar inequalities also exist between research organizations, between education agencies, and sometimes even within the same organization over time. Since they inhabit this larger ecosystem, partnerships inherit all of these inequities and must continually interrogate them so that they do not reify or amplify them.

Organizational clarity. The nature of brokering requires navigating institutional barriers and power differentials between the worlds of research and practice, particularly when people in different positions in the partnership share the brokering work. The relational nature and the fluidity of brokering create challenges when institutional affiliations become blurred. Internal brokers are positioned to offer a deeper understanding of district priorities and context, greater access to a range of decision-makers, and more timely awareness of upcoming shifts in initiatives. Sidestepping their role risks undermining their authority, autonomy, and expertise and may inadvertently exacerbate internal political dynamics. Put another way, strategic use of research (Weiss, 1979) may also translate into strategic use of research brokers. This is further complicated if external brokers assume internal roles even though they still have a vested interest in the research organization they represent. It is essential for brokers to be vigilant about transparency with regard to their institutional allegiances and the potential for competing interests.

Although all sides in an RPP wield a form of power, that power is asymmetric. Brokers with greater proximity to researchers can offer access to networks of researchers and grant money, which confers intellectual prestige as well as material power. In contrast, the power that comes from approving research agreements is more apt to elicit groans than to inspire respect or appreciation. Researchers frequently refer (incorrectly) to districts' research review committees as institutional review boards, signaling their perception of this as an inconvenient hurdle to clear rather than a meaningful process of engagement to fit the research design to its intended practical purpose. Brokers who are external to the practice agency cannot approve these agreements. Thus, they benefit from the higher-status, more intellectually and relationally rewarding aspects of developing and interpreting the research, while internal research staff bear the burden of the tedium of ensuring adherence to regulations. This can create additional friction if the time pressures on reviewing research applications may end up displacing other high-priority work that district research staff must also complete. Brokers who represent external researchers must be careful not to "cannibalize" or undermine the work of internal agency research staff; their goal should always be to build internal capacity so that ability to produce and use evidence well becomes integrated in the agency's culture and routines (Farley-Ripple et al., 2022). Partnerships need to be designed thoughtfully from the start to anticipate and minimize potential sources of friction, since once they are built, they may be very difficult to adjust.

Multiple partnerships. Like other urban districts, SFUSD has benefited from multiple long-standing, productive research partnerships. Matching projects to the unique strengths of each institution or research team requires system-level vision of district priorities and an equal appreciation for the full range of partners, to safeguard against inequities, inefficiencies, and conflicts over intellectual property. Some risks include duplicating resources when the same processes (e.g., DUAs, data transfer, research approval) are customized differently for one partner than for others (Kim et al., 2020). Other challenges may arise around protecting intellectual property if different brokers are independently cultivating overlapping projects with different research teams. Managing the inherent competition among multiple research partners for the district's most limited resources – staff time and attention – must fundamentally be done by the internal agency, who holds the responsibility to ensure the best project and does not have a vested interest in favoring one partner over the other.

Yet, balancing attention across different research organizations poses a challenge, particularly given their unequal accumulation of financial resources, institutional infrastructure, prestige, and social capital. This is further compounded when some partnerships have embedded brokers and others do not, due to the ensuing differential access to information, relationships, and power. Where brokers are embedded may also affect their relative influence, depending on the positionality and politics within the organization. Recognizing that these dynamics are likely to be continually changing across partnerships over time, partnerships and brokers should seek to address these potential inequities proactively in the design of their structures and routines and must remain ever sensitive to them throughout their work, to ensure that they are not creating additional demands that strain the capacity of the agency they seek to support.

CONCLUSION

As we saw in this chapter, there is a great deal of information contained within each component of the RPP Brokers Framework. We hope that by going into further detail with each dimension, especially in terms of providing a rich description of the research and practice that led to the naming of that particular dimension, readers are able to better understand the complexity of the activities. In addition, we also integrated a sample tool or case within each dimension in order to connect descriptions to specific broker practices. Although the examples in this chapter were primarily drawn from the Stanford–SFUSD Partnership and we examine the brokering with a critical lens, we also explore further in the next chapter approaches to these brokering activities and how some of these activities may show up differently in other partnership contexts.

REFERENCES

Diamond, J. B. (2021). *Racial equity and research practice partnerships 2.0: A critical reflection*. William T. Grant Foundation. http://wtgrantfoundation.org/wp-content/uploads/2021/07/Reflection-1__Diamond.pdf

Farley-Ripple, E., Ming, N., Goldhaber, D., Sarfo, A. O., & Arce-Trigatti, P. (2022). *Building capacity for evidence-informed improvement: Supporting state and local education agencies*. https://crue.cehd.udel.edu/wp-content/uploads/2022/10/Building-Capacity-for-Evidence-Informed-Improvement-October-2022–1.pdf

Farrell, C. C., Penuel, W. R., Coburn, C., Daniel, J., & Steup, L. (2021). *Research-practice partnerships in education: The state of the field*. William T. Grant Foundation.

Henrick, E. C., Cobb, P., Penuel, W. R., Jackson, K., & Clark, T. (2017). *Assessing research-practice partnerships: Five dimensions of effectiveness*. William T. Grant Foundation.

Henrick, E. C., McGee, S., & Penuel, W. (2019). Attending to issues of equity in evaluating research-practice partnership outcomes. *NNERPP Extra, 1*(3), 8–13.

Kim, M., Shen, J., & Wentworth, L. (2019). *Technical paper: Data infrastructure for partnership research. Structures and processes used in the Stanford–SFUSD partnership*. Stanford–SFUSD Partnership.

Kim, M., Shen, J., Wentworth, L., Ming, N. C., Reininger, M., & Bettinger, E. (2020). *The Stanford–SFUSD partnership: Development of data-sharing structures and processes*. In S. Cole, I. Dhaliwal, A. Sautmann, & L. Vilhuber (Eds.), *Handbook on using administrative data for research and evidence-based policy*. Retrieved October 8, 2022, from https://admindatahandbook.mit.edu/book/v1.0-rc4/sfusd.html

Okun, T., & Jones, K. (2000). White supremacy culture. In *Dismantling racism: A workbook for social change groups*. Change Work. www.dismantlingracism.org/

Ray, V. (2019). A theory of racialized organizations. *American Sociological Review, 84*(1), 26–53. https://doi.org/10.1177/0003122418822335

Sexton, S., Ryoo, J., Garbrecht, L., & Fall, R. (2020). Dimensions of equity in RPPs – A framework to guide partnership discussions. *NNERPP Extra, 2*(3), 12–18.

Vetter, A., Faircloth, B. S., Hewitt, K. K., Gonzalez, L. M., He, Y., & Rock, M. L. (2022). Equity and social justice in research practice partnerships in the United States. *Review of Educational Research*. https://doi.org/10.3102/00346543211070048

Weiss, C. H. (1979). The many meanings of research utilization. *Public Administration Review, 39*(5), 426–431.

Wentworth, L., Carranza, R., & Stipek, D. (May 2016). A university and district partnership closes the research-to-classroom gap. *Phi Delta Kappan, 97*(8), 66–69.

Chapter 4

RPP Brokers in Different Contexts

In the previous chapter, we went into great detail on each component of the RPP Brokers Framework, using the Stanford–SFUSD Partnership's experiences to help illustrate how the activities a broker engages in show up in practice. Based on how the chapter was presented, we likely gave the impression that the work of brokers in an RPP context encompasses all aspects of the brokering activities identified in the framework. While paying attention to all six dimensions of the RPP Brokers Framework in order to support the strengthening of both partners and partnership is surely necessary, in this chapter, we explore how variations in a partnership's context may lead to differences in which activities RPP brokers choose to emphasize.

In particular, we take a deeper dive into how a partnership's setting may vary across a number of RPP features, including its partnering organizations and the local context, and connect how these differences may alter the work of a broker. We think this additional perspective can help further describe how to more holistically approach RPP brokering activities, rather than viewing them as individual dimensions of a "to do" list. For example, the extent to which an RPP broker will need to pay close attention to building individual competency towards supporting fruitful engagement in an RPP might vary dramatically depending on prior partnership experience. Or, in other cases, an RPP might have sufficient funding to outsource the assessment of partnership health to an external evaluator. In this case, the role of the broker might focus more on supporting integration of the findings from the assessment towards improvement of RPP practice, rather than doing the assessment itself, as one might assume from a quick glance at the framework.

The examples and discussion provided in this chapter are aimed at sharing the large variation in brokering activities that may occur across partnership contexts, which is to be expected, given the large variation in RPPs. Let's dive in!

REVISITING THE DEFINITION OF RPPS AND WHAT IT MEANS FOR "TYPES" OF RPPS

We first introduced the recently released field-sourced definition of RPPs (Farrell et al., 2021) in Chapter 1, which we share here once again:

> A long-term collaboration aimed at educational improvement or equitable transformation through engagement with research. These partnerships are intentionally organized to connect diverse forms of expertise and shift power relations in the research endeavor to ensure that all partners have a say in the joint work.
>
> (p. 5)

Embedded in this definition are five key aspects of partnership work that we might consider to be "core DNA" of RPPs; that is, in order for a partnership to be considered an RPP, we might look for evidence showing the existence of these five features. They are, in order of appearance from the definition:

(1) long-term collaborations
(2) aimed at educational improvement or equitable transformation
(3) intentionally organized to connect diverse forms of expertise
(4) shift power relations in the research endeavor
(5) ensure that all partners have a say in the joint work

The beauty of this definition is that it is broad, flexible, and can apply to a wide variety of RPPs. In fact, the extent to which an RPP fully displays or commits to any of these DNA, either individually or collectively, will vary across partnership, which is to be expected given the unique settings where partnership work takes place.[1] For example, the definition of "long-term" is quite ambiguous and subject to local interpretation (e.g., is long-term measured in months, years, decades, or longer?). Or, similarly, intentionally organizing to connect "diverse forms of expertise" may mean just a handful of folks representing a couple of organizations working together in a partnership context or it may mean a large collection of individuals representing multiple organizations within a community wishing to collaborate across time and organizational space.

One special note before we explore these differences in the next section: throughout this book, you will notice that we commonly refer to the larger grouping of RPPs as that (i.e., "RPPs"). We invite readers to keep in mind that although we prefer this broader denotation throughout the book for ease of explication, this generalization ignores the underlying diversity across partnerships and implicitly assumes similarity across all five core DNA elements. The variation among these features is precisely what necessitates different brokering moves in order for the RPP broker to support the partnership's journey as it emerges and evolves. For this reason, we think this chapter holds special significance as we unpack the broader notion of "RPPs" and connect their unique features with the RPP Brokers Framework more intentionally.

MAPPING THE RPP DEFINITION ONTO THE RPP BROKERS FRAMEWORK

In this section, we map out how the core DNA of partnerships shows up in the RPP brokering framework, and then explore what that might mean for key brokering activities. We also include related cases to further illustrate how these moves have been made in practice from our community of RPP brokers. We will generally follow the order of the five strands of core DNA as presented earlier, with the exception of the second strand, "aimed at educational improvement or equitable transformation," which we will turn to last.

Long-term collaborations. First up, long-term collaborations. As mentioned previously, the definition of what qualifies as "long-term" can vary substantially between partnerships. Especially when the collaboration starts small, e.g., perhaps as a single project that involves just a few people across two organizations, the idea of establishing a "long-term" partnership may be just that – an idea. On the other hand, there are several RPPs in existence today that have been active for a decade or more (e.g., UChicago Consortium on School Research, the Houston Education Research Consortium, the Research Alliance for New York City Schools, and the Stanford–SFUSD Partnership, among others). Nonetheless, in either case, many RPPs start with an intention of being long-term, which we usually understand to mean something akin to "with no end in sight." This being the case, this particular feature of partnerships shows up in the second dimension of the RPP Brokers Framework under the "brokering to strengthen partners category": "developing and nurturing relationships to weather partnering challenges." Given the intent to work together indefinitely, wherein most RPPs embark on their collaborative journey without an expiration date, developing and nurturing relationships that can withstand any number of partnering challenges is a must. Brokering to strengthen partners in this regard will almost certainly involve continuous efforts to ensure relationships remain trustworthy, authentic, and robust, especially as various aspects of the work unfold. Partnerships that adhere less to this orientation, e.g., those that may be more time-determinant because their work is tied to a fixed grant, may end up spending less brokering time on this particular dimension and more brokering time ensuring that promised deliverables are produced. Although relationships will still need to be developed in order for the work to occur, the commitments of each partner to the project will be less than what we might expect in a multi-year effort without end.

Next we share a case from Kylie Klein, who has engaged in partnership work from both the research and practice sides across a number of organizations in the Chicago area. Kylie shares a number of strategies that may be helpful when navigating turnover at district central offices while trying to support an RPP. She additionally provides a sample email that demonstrates how to introduce yourself to new staff in hopes of cultivating the start of connections and relationships to come through the partnership.

SUSTAINING A PARTNERSHIP THROUGH PERIODS OF SCHOOL DISTRICT CENTRAL OFFICE CHURN

Northwestern-Evanston Education Research Alliance (NEERA)
Kylie Klein

One often-cited challenge that brokers on both sides of a research-practice partnership face is sustaining a partnership during periods of staff turnover at school district central offices. A district partner is a critical member of the research team. They are positioned to provide access and approvals, as well as input on research questions and study design opportunities. They also help provide contextual understandings and interpretations of research findings during and after the research is conducted. So, when your district partner suddenly leaves their role due to restructuring or other leadership changes, it can slow down your project in the best case or derail the project entirely in the worst case.

Given the importance of your relationship with district partners and the odds that at some point in your work you will face this situation, it is essential to be proactive and have strategies in place to mitigate these potential disruptions. Having worked in two school districts – one where I had six CEOs in ten years and one where I had three superintendents in three years – I have built some practical strategies for maintaining connections during turnover.

- **Make multiple points of connection.** Start by having an understanding of the district as an organization, including the explicit and implicit organization charts and internal hierarchies, so that you can identify individuals with whom you can foster an intentional connection.
- **Have a value proposition.** You need to have an engagement strategy for your multiple connections so that there is a value proposition for them to make time to connect with you. This means you should provide

them with something that is a benefit to their work, through either insights or shared learning, in order to give them a strong reason to engage.
- **Keep your connection active.** Keep your connections active by periodically reaching out with a short article or resource. District leaders try to stay current on the latest developments in their field, but sometimes things slip by. I have always appreciated when a research colleague sends me a quick note along the lines of, "Hope you're doing well. You may have already seen this, but in case you didn't, I wanted to share this recent report with you. The key takeaway of the report is _____. There is a chart on page 18 that I thought might be particularly interesting to you."
- **Make connections with support staff.** Department secretaries or office managers are essential connections that are often overlooked by research partners. Individuals in these roles are deeply knowledgeable connectors and can be tremendous resources, particularly in supporting your navigation of implicit org charts. The office manager or secretary might also remain in their position during a change in leadership and therefore can be a key support and ally in fostering new connections with new leaders. Always take an extra minute to thank them for their assistance and to be friendly and approachable.
- **Take advantage of all opportunities to engage.** District leadership turnover also has a positive side, which is that you never know who will someday wind up in a significant leadership role or leading a department that you need to engage with. I have seen teachers become department directors and principals become superintendents. Education leadership is a small world. So, when people at *any* organizational level reach out to you, do your best to be responsive and engage with them. You never know if those few minutes will make a lasting impression on someone who will someday be pivotal as a collaborator.
- **Have a strategy for making introductions.** Since we know that turnover is going to happen, it is critical to have a planned approach for fostering introductions to new leaders. When I make a new introduction, this is the general format I follow.
- Send an email to both the researcher and the new district leader.
- Introduce the researcher: name, area of work, and brief statement about work the researcher has done with the district in the past.
- Introduce the district person: name, area of work, and statement about their expertise/background.

> Example email:
> Hi Greg and Jamilla,
> Welcome Greg, it was great to meet you last week. I wanted to introduce you and Jamilla who I mentioned is one of our research partners. Jamilla Rogers is a learning design researcher. Last year she worked with our STEM schools task force to co-design and implement six professional learning workshops for principals and teachers. Jamilla, Greg Jones is our new Director of Innovation and is now overseeing STEM school support. He is joining us from Broward County where he led the creation of an accelerated pipeline for high school students to take college level science courses.
> Jamilla has been working with the school district on a research study of teacher expectations and STEM mindsets. We wrote a joint grant with Jamilla that was funded by the National Science Foundation and we are in the second year of the four-year project. Currently the project is analyzing the second round of teacher interviews.
> It would be great if we can set up a time to meet and Jamilla can bring you up to speed on what we've learned to date. We would also love to hear from you what additional areas of interest you have and if there are ways that this project can help advance some of your initial goals.
> What are some times that work for your schedules for us to meet?
> Best,
> Kylie

Figure 4.1 Sample "meet and greet" email

- Provide a short overview of the current partnership: no more than three bullets. Make it explicit that the researcher wants to hear about what new district person is interested in learning. This helps to lay the foundation that the partnership is mutually beneficial.
- Remember, new district folks might not have worked with researchers in an RPP-type relationship and may not realize the benefits of engaging with research partners.
- Set up a meet and greet. See Figure 4.1 for an example email setting up a meet and greet meeting.
  Once the meet and greet is scheduled, follow up a week before with a reminder email, and attach a short, one-page summary of the project.

> Do not attach lengthy papers, all grant materials, or a plethora of background information.
> - For the first meeting, keep the amount of information manageable. Follow up after the meeting with the relevant materials such as published papers, presentations, and data collection instruments as appropriate.

Intentionally organized to connect diverse forms of expertise. This aspect of partnership work calls on RPPs to create pathways that empower its members to work across their organizational and role-defined boundaries in order to share the diversity of their expertise within the collaboration. We see the RPP brokering activities necessary to support such involvement as primarily falling into the "designing processes and communications routines" dimension of the framework. From the RPP definition shared earlier, the phrase "intentionally organized" relates directly to the careful design of processes and routines named in the RPP Brokers Framework. How this particular feature of partnership work may differ across settings depends on the second phrase called out in the definition: "diverse forms of expertise." For example, *how diverse* are the forms of expertise? In some RPPs, the individuals working together in the collaboration may be more similar in their types of expertise than what might be assumed. A good example is a university-based PhD-trained researcher who partners with district central office-based PhD-trained researchers. Although this is a collaboration that crosses organizational and cultural boundaries, the individuals participating in the partnership likely share an underlying common language already, given their shared PhD-training. In this case, the work of the RPP broker to design processes and routines that support communications across may be more about attending to organizational factors inhibiting collaboration rather than individual factors.

Related, we could also ask, how diverse are the *organizations* represented in the RPP? In this instance we can imagine the different infrastructure necessary to enable the meaningful collaboration across partners when the RPP involves a university and district central office, as in our last example, versus a university and a single school. District central offices, especially those in large, urban settings, generally have many layers of leadership and management, which the RPP broker will need to navigate as they consider the types of processes and routines that will be necessary to support the work. In contrast, school management structures tend to be simpler, with a single principal guiding the school and fewer layers of leadership underneath. In this case, supportive infrastructure may accordingly be simpler as well.

Finally, this feature of partnerships also invites us to ask, *how much* bridge building or table setting does the RPP broker need to engage in, in order to ensure the connection of diverse forms of expertise? We have already described differences in individuals partnering and the complexity of the organizations involved. This question considers *how many*, in terms of the number of people involved in the effort. Designing processes and routines that can support the more nuanced participation and engagement of multiple partners across several organizations will require more careful bridge building or table setting than what we might see with fewer people and/or organizations. As a result, these differences will thus also shape the types of RPP brokering activities needed and may very well produce markedly different infrastructure.

The following case by Cambero and colleagues describes the development of shared values through a teacher book club in an RPP focused on the development of future STEM teachers and subsequent research examining their work together. In particular, this team highlights the importance of creating intentional social structures that will attend directly to harmful power dynamics that can show up when attempting to connect partners with diverse expertise.

DEVELOPING ANTI-RACIST FOCUSED RESEARCH AND PRACTICE AROUND SHARED VALUES

UC Irvine CalTeach and OCEAN Partnership
Socorro Cambero, Doron Zinger, and Naehee Kwun

This case highlights practices that brokers and community partners engaged in a research-practice partnership (RPP) can use to design routines attentive to social structures and remain sensitive to power dynamics.

In June 2021, an OCEAN community research fellow (UCI Orange County Educational Advancement Network, 2023) and UCI CalTeach (https://calteach.uci.edu) developed a partnership to support the social justice identity development of future STEM teachers. In 2018 the UCI School of Education's Orange County Educational Advancement Network (OCEAN) began establishing partnerships between the School of Education and K–12 schools and community organizations in Orange County, California. In each partnership, a School of Education faculty member and doctoral student, along with a research team, work in collaboration with their community partners. Together, they identify local needs and goals, and collaboratively conduct research that will inform practice. The CalTeach program is a four-year baccalaureate plus credential program at UC Irvine that aims to prepare teachers to become social change agents in high-need schools. This project was led by Socorro Cambero, a graduate student interested in improving the experiences of teachers of color, and Dr. Doron Zinger, a former science teacher and the CalTeach Director. This research project was informed by Socorro's research commitment and CalTeach's core commitment in preparing social change agents.

Their shared values grounded them in a common vision for success and put them in a position to quickly and productively move forward, building on their individual and collective strengths. To achieve their collective goal of preparing teachers committed to social justice, they developed a year-long book club series focused on issues of educational inequity that impact youth. In this case, we highlight three main brokering activities of the fellow that allowed for the development of anti-racist focused research and practice around shared values. First, the fellow positioned the partner's collective goals as a nexus to ground the work. Second, the fellow brought participants into the partnership and positioned participants as agentic and contributing. Third, the fellow committed to regularly debriefing practice with partners to iterate future collaborations. The following case provides a snapshot of the beginning and growth of the RPP in Summer 2021.

Positioning Partner's Collective Goals and Values as a Nexus to Ground the Work

To guide the design, Doron initially shared the CalTeach goals for the book club: 1) provide space for students to engage in issues pertaining to educational equity, 2) create a space that gave autonomy for students' own learning and reflecting from readings to guide book club sessions, and 3) organize a sustainable space for future teachers to create community. Socorro used these goals to guide the design and iterative changes of book club sessions. Importantly, as a research partner interested in informing CalTeach, she co-created research questions that would inform the programmatic aspects of the teacher preparation program. Research questions included 1) how a book club community informs participants' becoming socially just STEM teachers; and 2) how participants make sense of the educational inequities they are learning about as part of a community.

Given that the OCEAN fellow was new to the CalTeach space, she also simultaneously wanted to cultivate a relationship with the future teachers while facilitating book club sessions. As such, she first co-facilitated an existing summer book club that the Director of CalTeach previously facilitated. In partnership with the CalTeach Director, the OCEAN fellow enhanced the book club, including tools and processes such as critical reflection journaling. Figure 4.2 illustrates the design of the book club.

```
                    Before and After
                    Book Club Discussion:
                 Critical Reflection Journaling

                        Levels for
                 Critical Reflection Journaling

  Whole Group        ❑ K–12 Experience           Community Builder
   Reflection        ❑ Teacher Preparation Experience   (facilitated by participants)
                     ❑ Implications for In-Classroom
                        Experience


                        Small Group
                        Reflection


                   During Book Club Sessions:
                  Community Builder, Small Group
                  Reflection, Whole Group Reflection
```

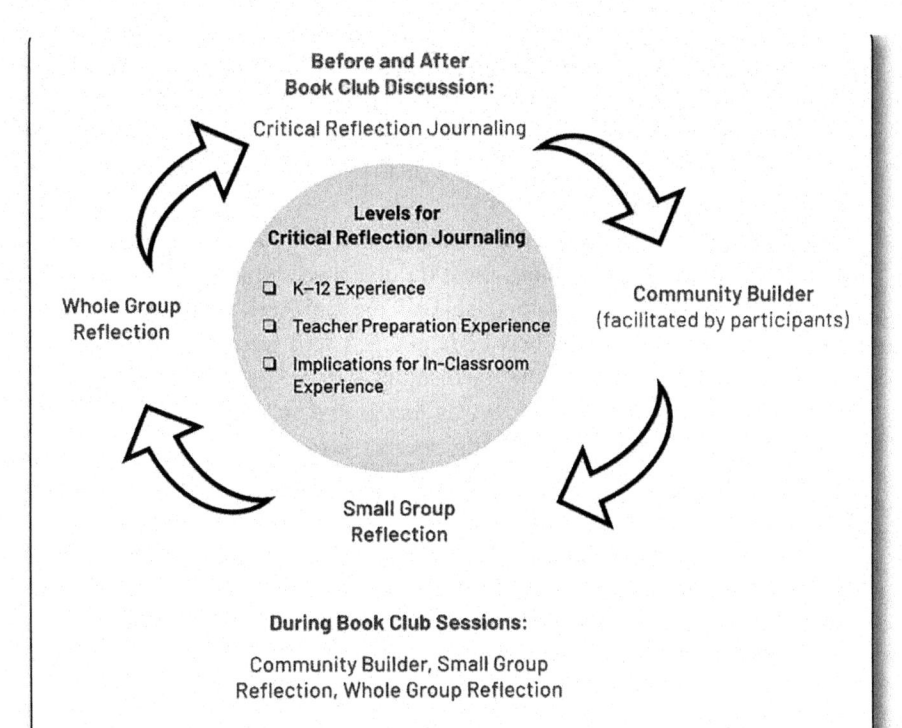

Figure 4.2 CalTeach book club critical reflection facilitation process

Tools and practices to meet collective goals. In the following sections, we highlight each goal with one tool or practice developed by the OCEAN fellow to facilitate meeting that goal, along with illustrating the process of development, implementation, and evaluation of the tool or practice.

Journaling for students to engage in issues of educational equity. To meet goal one, the partners decided to engage participants in the practice of reflective journaling with deliberate prompts designed to facilitate their anti-racist orientations. The practice emerged from participants' feedback and expressed needs, and research and analysis conducted by the OCEAN fellow. Participants requested a tangible, permanent mode of reflection that they could revisit over time. In consideration for this, the OCEAN fellow researched different approaches to support the participants, including digital modalities and paper-based reflections, ultimately deciding on physical journals that students could take them. For example, one journal prompt invited participants to reflect on their own racialized experience navigating K–12 schooling in alignment with the book they were reading, and in preparation for a discussion they would have. Ultimately, the journaling facilitated their individual reflections, as well as collectively grappling with issues of educational equity in classrooms. Participants expressed appreciation for the prompts demanding a reflection on their identities and how it informs their navigation of the material world (in alignment with our collective goals).

Developing collective agency to create a space that gave autonomy for participants' own learning. Meeting goal two required the OCEAN fellow to become a contributing part of the CalTeach community. The CalTeach Director modeled how book club sessions were facilitated during the beginning stages of the partnership, with a focus on participant agency, while the OCEAN fellow was introduced to the CalTeach community as part of the book club. The director also committed to meeting regularly to debrief and discuss the book club sessions. These activities helped the OCEAN fellow to initially connect with participating students, and equalize power in the space, where the dialogue during sessions was guided by students' own learnings and interests, often from the reflective journal prompts they responded to. The agency developed through discussions ultimately led to participants being invited to choose the books they engaged in after the first book club. A range of books was curated for the students based on their interests by the partners. This approach allowed for participants to guide their own learning and take greater ownership of it, with nearly a 100% persistence rate of participants through the three book clubs conducted during the year.

Building community to promote sustainability. To meet goal three, organize a sustainable space for future teachers to create community, each book club session began with a community builder – a tool employed to engender trust and create an inviting space for participants to bond over shared or disparate identities. As the participants did not know each other or the OCEAN fellow well, the CalTeach director and OCEAN fellow worked to deliberately select and sequence community builders to empower participants and develop their commitment to each other. The sequencing and selection of community builders was iteratively adjusted through partner meetings to create courageous and inclusive spaces while minimizing potential harm to participants. Over time, this activity was increasingly led by participants, as they were reading a separate book on developing community as part of their coursework.

Partnering iterative research and practice cycles. Critical to the development of practices and success of the book clubs was the close partnership between the CalTeach director and OCEAN fellow, as it was guided by their shared vision. They initially committed to regular planning meetings. Guided by their personal experiences as educators and students, and collective research background, they developed and refined the program in collaboration. They further committed to regular check-ins throughout the year to debrief the practices within the book club sessions, as well as between them to inform improvement. To prepare for regular meetings, the OCEAN fellow reflected after book club sessions and engaging in regular memoing. Main learnings and noticings from memoing were shared with the CalTeach Director to provide communication and perspective on the dialogue and topics that future teachers voiced.

Two key areas of discussion to support the collective goals were addressed, meeting the goals through broad program improvement and meeting the goals through improvement of the book club. For broader program improvement, the OCEAN fellow identified one regular topic discussed during book club sessions, the racialized experiences of teachers of color in the classroom. For example, book club participants referenced how building communities of resistance — such as the book club community — can help teachers like them, who are committed to just teaching practices, navigate potential resistance that arises. These important data helped inform larger programmatic changes. In this instance, the CalTeach Director committed time to discussing these tensions through regular courses in the program. As exemplified by the three practices engaged in above, participant feedback, memos, and other data analyzed by the OCEAN fellow anchored the iterative improvement of the book clubs. For example, the addition of reflective journaling and the transition for participants leading community builders and selecting their own readings. Through the ongoing collection of data, analysis, and iteration, a roadmap for book clubs for the next cohort of students was developed, which will facilitate meeting programmatic goals.

Learnings from the book club have resulted in tangible change and improvement for participants and helped develop new research, with broader implications for the social justice identity development of future STEM teachers. Future teachers' critical reflection journals were systematically coded in order to inform the field of teacher preparation. Early findings suggest that the nature of how critical reflection questions are formed and sequenced can critically inform the learning processes in the book club. Over the course of the next year, the OCEAN fellow will begin data analysis and interpreting reflection journal responses from book clubs with the participants that partake in this work.

Shift power relations in the research endeavor. This RPP core DNA strand is meant to name the explicit attention partnerships must give to addressing ever-present harmful power dynamics that show up across individual and organizational identities, positionalities, and intersectionalities. Although power dynamics should be assumed to always be present and playing a role in how individuals and organizations interact, partnerships can differ substantially in the extent to which these dynamics are indeed present as well as the degree to which the partnership works to actively address them. A few of the key ways in which power dynamics shaping the collaboration might differ across partnerships may include the makeup of the RPP (which organizations and/or individuals are involved), the historical context characterizing those relationships, and the state of current relationships among all partnership members.

Whatever the setting, the variation in the role power dynamics may play in shaping the collaboration will require a different level of attention and care from the RPP broker, especially in terms of three key brokering activities we have identified in the RPP Brokers Framework:

- building individual partners' competency for engaging in the RPP
- developing partnership governance and administrative structures
- designing processes and communications routines

For the first of these, "building individual partners' competency for engaging in the RPP," an RPP broker may need to spend considerable time helping individuals to become aware of and address their power and privilege, and how it may negatively impact the collaborative nature involved in RPPs. In other instances, some of this necessary pre-work may have already occurred among participating individuals, and thus, the activities of the broker may be more about ensuring that processes and routines established by the partnership provide the necessary support to mitigate harmful power dynamics. Similarly, depending on the existing patterns of collaboration between RPP member organizations and individuals, the RPP broker may need to spend more or less time carefully "designing processes and communications routines" that will enhance the partnership's ability to disrupt the influence of power. For some partnerships, the outsized role and reputation often assumed by university-based researchers may diminish the ways in which school-based education leaders contribute and partner, for example. For others, it may be that the participation of senior leaders on either the research or practice sides of the partnership may overshadow younger staff. RPP brokers will thus need to consider a range of potential contributing factors as they design appropriate processes and communications routines. Accordingly, this collection of brokering activities sits under the "brokering to strengthen partnership" section of the framework.

A complementary set of activities is "developing partnership governance and administrative structures," which can also be found under the "brokering to strengthen partnership" section. Because power dynamics are central to leadership-related infrastructure, we encourage all RPP brokers to spend extra time considering the various ways power can formally and informally influence RPP design decisions around governance and administration.

For example, the RPP broker can work to ensure that critical leadership and management components of the RPP are aligned with other partnership practices that foster shifts in power relations. This particular dimension of RPPs may have its own sets of challenges, especially in light of the fact that current funding opportunities typically award money mainly to research-side organizations, even for partnership grant opportunities; this can serve to reinforce existing power imbalances between the research and practice sides of the RPP, especially among the leadership of the partnership. RPP brokers can focus their work on recognizing these threats to power shifts and create infrastructure within the collaboration that lessens them. Below we share a case from a team of folks collaborating across the San Francisco Unified School District and the University of California, Berkeley, who offer insights from their experiences in formalizing partnership agreements that codify values around trust, power-sharing, and engagement.

ESTABLISHING PARTNERSHIP IDENTITY THROUGH THE CO-CREATION OF A PARTNERSHIP AGREEMENT

San Francisco Unified School District (SFUSD) and the University of California, Berkeley (Berkeley)
Devin Corrigan, Dr. Norma Ming, and Dr. Emily Ozer

Research-practice partnerships (RPPs) must define not only what they do, but who they are and what they value. A structured process for creating a partnership agreement can promote key conditions of trust, power-sharing, and engagement essential for forging an RPP's identity.

The SFUSD–Berkeley partnership valued equity in both outcomes and processes from the beginning. Dr. Ritu Khanna, SFUSD's Head of Research, Planning, and Assessment (RPA), and Dr. Norma Ming, SFUSD's Manager of Research and Evaluation, sought to integrate SFUSD's many research projects by Berkeley faculty into a formal RPP that would explicitly advance SFUSD's social justice goals through deep engagement with a range of stakeholders. Some departments, such as the African-American Achievement and Leadership Initiative, were actively seeking UC Berkeley's support in cultivating new projects to address their research needs. Beyond simply sharing data for outsiders to analyze, SFUSD wanted a partnership that emphasized co-creation of research with staff and students to build knowledge that centered their perspectives and experiences, particularly those who had been historically excluded or marginalized.

Exploratory discussions between Drs. Khanna and Ming with Prof. Prudence Carter, then-Dean of the Berkeley Graduate School of Education, revealed mutual interest in an institutional partnership, as well as the need to identify a faculty leader to spearhead its development. With over two decades' experience partnering with SFUSD on research centering youth voice, Berkeley senior faculty member Dr. Emily Ozer was a natural fit for this role. In addition to co-leading a Berkeley faculty research network on "Youth and Inequalities," she had collaborated directly with a community-based organization, San Francisco Peer Resources, which provides social justice and peer education elective classes at SFUSD to promote and study youth-led participatory action research (YPAR). These shared values set the stage for co-constructing research driven by the district's and community's interests rather than the investigator's agenda.

With support from key institutional leaders secured on both sides, the nascent RPP shifted into its next phase of development, as Drs. Carter and Khanna stepped back to allow core staff to build the partnership. This phase entailed a series of in-person strategy meetings with Dr. Ozer, Dr. Ming, and Devin Corrigan of RPA; monthly networking and partnership development meetings with eight to ten SFUSD staff, San Francisco Peer Resources staff, and Berkeley faculty and graduate students; and extensive iteration on a shared electronic draft to define the partnership's goals, values, and research agenda.

For these discussions, Drs. Ozer and Ming invited Berkeley faculty with research interests in SFUSD or from the existing Youth and Inequalities network. Continued deliberations helped clarify which faculty had the capacity to engage deeply with a co-constructed research agenda. Given the time investment necessary to forge and sustain an RPP, untenured faculty and those on "soft money" funding might need to be represented by faculty with more job security. Some faculty joined the advisory board; others maintained more peripheral connections.

Meeting agendas were decided jointly by Berkeley and SFUSD leads (see Figure 4.3 for an example), including tailored prompts ("What makes a good partnership?") and open discussions about individual and institutional research priorities. Conversations coalesced around norms of mutual respect, distributed leadership, inclusive engagement, and appreciation for diverse forms of expertise. When new members joined, the group crystallized the shared partnership identity by sharing current thinking about the RPP's vision.

Sample Agenda #1: August 15, 2018

Pre-reading: building successful research–practice–policy partnerships in child welfare

Summary of AYPF Discussion Group (American Youth Policy Forum, 2016)

Meeting purpose: discuss shared research agenda and values for SFUSD/Berkeley RPP. Generate and document ideas, discuss funding opportunities, agree on next steps for stakeholder input.

(1) Welcome + introductions
(2) Discussion of shared research agenda
(3) Discussion of shared ethics + values
(4) Discussion re: sustainable funding
(5) Stakeholder input/process
(6) Updates on pilot
(7) Next steps

Sample Agenda #2: September 13, 2018

Meeting purpose: We will discuss our proposed MOU and partnership and further explore mutual interests as aligned with SFUSD priorities. The agenda will be a combo of brainstorming ideas of mutual interest that might motivate us to connect and discussing what we would want to see in an MOU and partnership arrangement.

(1) Framing about process + motivation + goals for meeting
(2) Brief intros – name, affiliation, and discipline as relevant – 1–2 sentences about what motivates you to be here and what makes a good partnership
(3) SFUSD context and priorities – RPA and district generally
(4) What might partnership look like? What is different about this partnership?
(5) Who else should be at the table from Berkeley and from SFUSD?
(6) Next steps

Figure 4.3 Sample agenda

Based on group discussion during the first four meetings, Dr. Ozer and Berkeley graduate student Brian Villa drafted the initial version of the agreement, with Berkeley faculty and SFUSD staff contributing during and between meetings. Finalized a year later (see Appendix G), the agreement codified the partnership's shared values (trust, flexibility, diversity, shared assets, and research utility) and collaboration processes (e.g., participatory methods, co-creation with students and families, multidisciplinary research). The research agenda emerged from the intersection of equity and social justice goals with relevant research expertise, converging on interventions to support wellness, reduce absenteeism, address homelessness, and mitigate racial bias. This encompassed pre-existing research, including Prof. Susan Stone's long-standing partnership with SFUSD's school health programs, as well as Dr. Ozer's YPAR research program discussed previously.

This process of co-creating a partnership agreement helped to elucidate "who we are" and "what we do," cementing the SFUSD–Berkeley partnership identity in its early phases. Specifically, the process helped the brokers ask and answer fundamental questions about the partnership, such as:

- Among those initially interested in participating, who has the capacity to engage deeply? How might others stay connected in another role(s)?
- Whose voices were missing from the initial partnership discussions?
- Which of the partnership's goals require the most time and effort from the brokers? Which goal(s) should they focus on first? (*Example: deciding to work as a group to identify and apply for grant funding to support the other goals outlined in the agreement*)
- How can brokers negotiate roles and establish norms in a practical manner? (*Example: co-creating a process to draft and revise the partnership agreement itself*)
- What specific conditions and experiences support trust-building? (*Examples: sharing leadership, continually checking for understanding, adjusting work to align with values and concerns expressed*)

Ensure that all partners have a say in the joint work. This strand of the RPP core DNA is really about reflecting on two strands discussed earlier: (1) connecting diverse forms of expertise and (2) shifting power relations in the research endeavor. As we described previously, "connecting diverse forms of expertise" invites RPP brokers to think carefully about the tables they are setting and who is getting invited to those tables. This concept connects to the present strand through a call to action — i.e., ensuring that *all partners* are invited and supported in participating in the tables being set. In particular, a broker might need to consider carefully who is considered a partner and check to make sure that they are at said table.

As to the second part of the strand, "have a say in the joint work," the only way to make this a reality is by shifting the power relations, as we discussed earlier, so that partnerships can commit to addressing power imbalances and creating supportive spaces that encourage all partners to engage meaningfully in the work. Ensuring that this is happening is then a key message behind this dimension of RPPs. How can RPP brokers confirm this is occurring? Measuring and tracking practices over time will be necessary; these activities are very closely related to what we are calling "assessing and reflecting on the partnership" from the RPP Brokers Framework, found under the "brokering to strengthen partnership" portion.

In terms of variation across RPPs, we can think about these efforts on a continuum of available resources to the RPP. On the one hand, some RPPs might have sufficient resources to work with an external RPP evaluator that can help the team track their efforts over time related to ensuring that "all partners have a say in the joint work." The work of the RPP broker in this case might be more about identifying an evaluator with whom to work and then setting up communications pathways and routines to allow the partnership the necessary time and space to take up/act on recommendations from the evaluator. The RPP broker might also work collaboratively with the evaluator to translate findings or connect recommendations to existing initiatives, given their "insider" status to the RPP.

On the other end of the resource continuum, we might find smaller partnerships or those who have limited resources that cannot be readily allocated to initiatives outside of specific deliverables. In this instance, the RPP broker might very well have to take on all of the activities related to assessing and reflecting on partnership efforts. This may involve the implementation of quick "health checks," for example, that allow the broker to get regular temperature checks from the group regarding partnership aims. The broker might also work to set up regular reflection meetings among partners to chat through these health checks together, in addition to helping determine a plan of action. Next we share a case by Kelly McMahon, Jon Norman, and Dave Sherer of the Carnegie Foundation for the Advancement of Teaching that describes an approach for helping partnership teams create a "portrait" of their collaborative efforts describing the group's theories of how their work will catalyze change. This reflective look might then help spark meaningful conversations about how to improve the RPP itself.

DEVELOPING A PORTRAIT OF THE RPP (REFLECTIVE ACTIVITY)

The Hewlett Foundation's Deeper Learning + Diffusion of Innovation and Scaled Impact RPPs
Kelly McMahon, Jon Norman, Dave Sherer

Partnerships that embrace continuous improvement methods must learn quickly by studying their own practices, continuously adapting to changing circumstances, and incorporating what they have learned into their ongoing work. The Evidence for Improvement Framework developed by Dave Sherer and colleagues (2020) at the Carnegie Foundation for the Advancement of Teaching helps partners know what to pay attention to when reflecting on their work, including:

- the partnership's working theory of improvement, which explains how partners will realize the improvements or innovations they seek through research and/or system transformation
- the partnership's theory of partnership, or the social elements that support learning in the partnership
- the partnership's theory of scaling and the role of the environment

Using a process based on this framework (see Appendix H), partnership members can develop a written portrait of the work happening across these three areas. Portraits offer descriptive accounts of RPPs and a set of "wonderings" meant to encourage conversation among leaders. Portraits allow partnerships to better understand what is working well within the partnership, what needs adapting, and what needs more attention. The process, which can be run by RPP members by themselves or in partnership with brokers or external consultants, includes these steps:

(1) work to identify guiding questions, based on the three levels of the Evidence for Improvement Framework (Sherer et al., 2020), that will focus the development of the portrait
(2) negotiate access to interviewees and relevant documents, as needed
(3) develop a set of interview questions
(4) identify potential interviewees to inform the portrait
(5) conduct the interviews and gathering relevant artifacts
(6) analyze the interviews and artifacts
(7) draft an initial portrait
(8) share the portrait draft with key RPP members

(9) elicit feedback and iterating on the portrait until it feels accurate
(10) share the portrait with relevant parties and use it as a tool for conversation and learning, referencing the Evidence for Improvement Framework as necessary to interpret the content of the portrait

For example, this process was used with all ten of the RPPs in the Hewlett-funded Deeper Learning + Diffusion of Innovation and Scaled Impact Network (Hewlett Foundation, 2022). Each of the RPPs engaged in a six-week portrait process with three team members from the Carnegie Foundation, which we refer to as the sprint team; the sprint team facilitates the process of developing the portrait. The sprint team can consist of external staff, as was the case in this example, or could consist of brokers or other leaders internal to the RPP.

To begin the process, leaders met with Carnegie staff (the sprint team) to identify members of the RPP and people whose work was influenced by the RPP (about 15 people on average). Using a customized and expanded set of these core questions (see Appendix I), the sprint team interviewed the people identified, reviewed pertinent documents and other key artifacts, and, at times, conducted observations of key partnership activities. The Carnegie sprint team then consolidated what they learned to develop a draft portrait.

Once the portrait is complete, the sprint team can engage in other activities designed to help RPP leaders access and use the data for improvement. The leaders review the first draft of the portrait and offer feedback. After reviewing the draft, leaders meet with sprint team members, who facilitate a reflective conversation. The purpose of this conversation is to allow the RPP leaders to develop a collective understanding of what is working well and what needs to be attended to so that the partnership can make progress on its aims. The sprint team then iteratively revises the portrait until it reflects an accurate and useful image of the RPP that leaders feel comfortable sharing with others outside the RPP.

In the Hewlett Deeper Learning and Diffusion of Innovation and Impact Network, these portraits served as a way to look within and across the partnerships because they created a common framework for understanding each partnership's working theory of improvement; how the partners were learning together; and how each RPP was benefiting from enabling factors, or dealing with challenges in their broader environment as they tried to scale their interventions.

The RPPs expressed that engaging in the reflective process was beneficial. For example, after seeing the Carnegie staff "tell their story," members of one RPP realized they wanted to spend more time developing their internal narrative of their own work. By developing this improved internal narrative, the RPP was able to communicate their efforts to external audiences more easily. Another RPP that went through the portrait process identified (and corrected) a problem in their approach to measurement — they were measuring the ultimate outcomes of their work, but not the processes they were using to try to achieve these outcomes. In addition to helping these individual RPPs, the portraits were shared across the broader Hewlett RPP network. RPP members saw the portraits as valuable learning artifacts that helped them learn about other RPPs in the network.

Tips for making the most of this tool:

- Identify a team of people who will own the process and develop the portrait. Think of this as your sprint team as described in the Hewlett RPPs case. This could be an external evaluator or an internal team, but responsibility for creating the portrait should be clear.
- The sprint team and RPP leaders should discuss the purpose of engaging in the process. The purpose should be exploratory and promote learning about the current state of the RPP. Avoid making the process feel evaluative.
- Schedule the introductory meeting, review meeting, and final deadline at the beginning of the process.
- Develop wonderings based on the Evidence for Improvement Framework, privileging continuous improvement methods and mindsets. For example, a wondering might ask:
- Theory of Improvement example: Could the RPP better describe how classroom practices have changed by telling a story with data?
- Theory of Partnership example: How does the RPP develop its "social glue" that enables the collective to accomplish what individual partners could not do without the partnership?
- Theory of Scaling example: How will the work of the partnership spread to those who are not early adopters but may be more reluctant to engage?
- Try, if you can, to create visuals of the different theories depicted in the portrait. These visuals will encourage different kinds of conversations than text alone.

- The style of a final portrait is descriptive with illustrative quotes where relevant. It should not sound evaluative or prescriptive.
- The final document is typically 15–20 pages. The sections of the paper include: introduction, methods, basic overview of the RPP, a detailed description of the RPP related to each of the three levels of the Evidence for Improvement Framework with wonderings associated with each level.
- Embrace disagreement about the wonderings in the portrait because surfacing these points allows the RPP leaders to clarify, confirm, and collaborate moving forward.
- Feel free to contact Kelly McMahon (McMahon@carnegiefoundation.org) if you have more questions about how to create a portrait.

Aimed at educational improvement or equitable transformation. This component of the RPP definition relates to the outcomes partnerships may be working towards. Although there are only two categories of outcomes named here (i.e., improvement or transformation), in reality, there are an infinite number and combination of outcomes RPPs may be working towards. This is one key reason why it is quite reductive to think of RPPs as a monolithic endeavor; the considerable variation in types of goals being pursued and ways in which the resulting partnership is organized in order to meet those goals demands greater nuance. In any case, because this aspect of the definition focuses on the end result of partnership work, it involves all aspects of the RPP Brokers Framework, in terms of inputs necessary to move the partnership towards its goals. If we were to refer to an illustrative case here, we would most likely recommend all of them!

CONCLUSION

In this chapter, we explored how the five "core DNA" strands of research-practice partnerships (as defined by Farrell et al., 2021) can vary across RPPs, in addition to mapping the strands on to the different dimensions of the RPP Brokers Framework. We hope this exploration of different possible contexts that may emerge across partnerships helps illustrate the unique approaches RPP brokers will face as they engage in supporting partners and partnership. In the next two chapters, we shift our focus once again back to the RPP Brokers Framework itself and explicitly link a variety of cases shared by our community of brokers to the individual dimensions of the framework.

NOTE

1. In the previous field-sourced definition of RPPs introduced in the 2013 paper authored by Coburn, Penuel, and Geil, the authors introduced a typology of RPPs that reflected a high-level understanding of the RPPs known to exist at the time. Although many of the RPPs that were featured in that paper are still around today, the boundaries defining the three types of partnerships described in the paper are less clear today. That is, a "research alliance" (one of the categories introduced in the paper) today might very well engage in both design-based implementation research (DBIR, one of the other types) and networked improvement communities (NICs, the third type), depending on the project at hand. There are also any number of hybrid variations on the three types as well (see Arce-Trigatti, et al., 2018, for example).

REFERENCES

American Youth Policy Forum. (March 15, 2016). *Building successful research-practice-policy partnerships in child welfare*. Retrieved from: http://www.aypf.org/wp-content/uploads/2016/03/DG-brief-from-AYPF-re-RPPP-FINAL.pdf

Arce-Trigatti, P., Chukhray, I., & López Turley, R. (2018). Research-practice partnerships in education. In B. Schneider (Ed.), *Handbook of the sociology in education in the 21st century* (pp. 561–579). Springer.

Farrell, C. C., Penuel, W. R., Coburn, C., Daniel, J., & Steup, L. (2021). *Research-practice partnerships in education: The state of the field*. William T. Grant Foundation.

Hewlett Foundation. (2022). *Request for letters of interest: Deeper learning and scaled impact*. Retrieved November 10, 2022, from https://hewlett.org/request-letters-interest-deeper-learning-scaled-impact/

Sherer, D., Norman, J., Bryk, A. S., Peurach, D. J., Vasudeva, A., & McMahon, K. (2020). *Evidence for improvement: An integrated analytic approach for supporting networks*. Carnegie Foundation for the Advancement of Teaching.

Chapter 5

Cases Describing Brokering to Strengthen Partners

Partnerships exist to serve their individual partners. This is why we often see brokers onboarding new partnership members, helping researchers learn how to write for practice audiences, or helping practice members learn how to build a research agenda – all tasks that benefit individual partners more directly than the partnership itself. But if those individuals can then engage more effectively in the partnership, the brokers' work is a smart investment in their partnership's long-run success.

In this chapter, we present a set of cases written by brokers in the field that relate to each of the components of brokering to strengthen individual partners. They are organized by theme: developing partners' competency with partnering, developing and nurturing relationships to weather partnering challenges, and creating the conditions to support research use.

Within each theme and as seen in Figure 5.1, we organize the cases according to more specific headings that relate to the actions brokers take, such as brokering through explicit teaching of skills and brokering by using tools and processes to develop skills. Then, we provide a short description of each case so readers can understand the content of the case and how the case relates back to practical actions brokers take to strengthen the partnership. We use text boxes to call out the cases, including a title, author names, and their partnership(s).

DEVELOPING PARTNERS' COMPETENCY WITH PARTNERING

It's rare for people participating in RPPs, whether researchers or practitioners, to have had prior training in how to work effectively in a research partnership. Researchers typically know little about the types of activities or decision-making that practitioners routinely engage in, and practitioners typically know little about the priorities of the ivory tower or the intricacies of research methodology.

- Building individual partners' competency for engaging in an RPP
- Developing and nurturing relationships to weather partnering challenges
- Creating the conditions to support research production and use

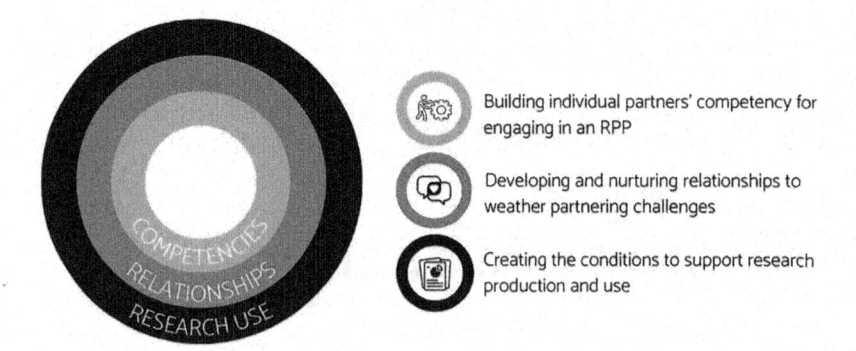

Figure 5.1 Brokering to strengthen partners

No one goes to "partner school" – which makes it that much harder for researchers and practitioners to work together.

Here we provide cases describing an array of strategies brokers have used to tackle this challenge. Some partnerships take the approach of directly teaching the necessary skills, while others create systems and structures that facilitate skill-building.

Brokering through explicit teaching of partnering skills: Certain types of skills lend themselves to teaching through workshops, especially if the partners themselves identify the skills as ones they're invested in learning. Research-side partners may also have access to faculty or other resources outside the partnership that can help deliver content and build skills among partnership members. Tyler Rogers from the Georgia Policy Labs illustrates this approach through a summer training program for practice-side partnership members.

INCREASING PRACTICE PARTNERS' SKILLS THROUGH FREE WORKSHOPS

Multiple Partnerships
Tyler Rogers, Georgia Policy Labs

In research-practice partnerships (RPPs), it takes constantly evolving skills and knowledge among all involved to maintain the capacity for working together. At the Georgia Policy Labs (GPL) in the Andrew Young School of Policy Studies at Georgia State University, we believe that our government, school district, and non-profit partners are catalysts and brokers for creating evidence-based policies and programs. We work alongside our partners – using the data and context they share with us – to produce evidence and actionable insights. These insights lead to policies and programs that realize the safety, capability, and economic security of every child, young adult, and family in Georgia. Professional development is a key component of our theory of action, ensuring our partner researchers and programmatic leaders have the relevant skills to analyze data and rigorous research results to inform decision-making. Time, budgetary, and other constraints, however, can make attending professional development challenging. RPPs can play a unique role in connecting the resources of a university to communities to strengthen capacities, encourage the use of rigorous research, and enhance evidence-based policymaking.

To build these capacities, our RPP offers free professional development to our partners and the broader policy community (e.g., non-partnering non-profit organizations, university researchers) each summer that teaches skills that participants can implement quickly. To date, we have hosted 12 training sessions focused on data visualization, causal research methods, program evaluation, graphic design, and data analysis using different coding languages, attended by over 500 participants from school districts, non-profit community partners, university partners, and state agencies in Georgia and across the country.

Our process begins early in the year by contacting our partners to determine their skill-building needs and desires. Based on their feedback, we contact faculty and staff across campus to see if they offer a resource that addresses these needs and would be willing to facilitate a workshop on the use of the resource. We also rely on the university's professional networks if we are unable to identify relevant resources from within the university or if there is no university-based facilitator available. After identifying a facilitator, we work with them to develop workshop descriptions, confirm workshop dates, and discuss what data would be relevant to workshop participants (i.e., provide facilitators an overview of who will be in attendance).

For example, in 2020, we began the year by asking our partners what workshops or resources would be most helpful. Our partners noted how data visualization was an important part of their work and how they wanted to learn more about how to turn large data sets into meaningful visual insights. After sharing this feedback with our university networks and assessing the available resources, we were connected to a professor in our school that had extensive experience teaching R – a free statistical software – to students, and we decided to offer three three-hour workshops in July and August. Due to the COVID-19 pandemic, however, we offered these workshops virtually. As part of these workshops, we organized the logistics, shared workshop descriptions, hosted the virtual workshop platform, and sent calendar invitations. We also worked with the facilitator to use data and examples in the workshops that would be relevant to participants, which made the workshops more engaging and impactful. The usefulness of these workshops, coupled with additional partner feedback, led us to offer three additional training sessions in 2020 centered on using Python for data analysis.

In 2021, over 110 individuals attended at least one of the three virtual workshops – an over 24% percent increase in attendance compared to the in-person professional development we held in 2019. We also recorded the workshops for registrants who could not attend, which gave us an opportunity to post these and subsequent workshops on our website through an external video hosting platform for asynchronous and on-demand learning. The workshops from 2020 to 2022 have over 3,300 views. Additionally, the lessons we learned offering these virtual workshops have equipped us to facilitate virtual and hybrid meetings and events better in 2022, and we were excited to have offered virtual professional development in the summer that had over 140 total participants.

GPL's Summer Training series has become a vital component of our service to the community and part of the fabric of our organization. Developing our partners' skills in these areas helps them better conduct rigorous research, helps all members of the RPP to better communicate these results, and allows our partners to engage even more thoughtfully on research methods and communications strategies. Moreover, our partners and friends look forward to these workshops, which have led to connections between people at different agencies in different states across the country. These workshops grow the skill and will of our practice partners for engaging with research. They also allow us to grow our policy ecosystem and begin forming new partnerships; we invite informal partners and interested agencies who want to move towards an evidence-based culture but are not currently interested in the full RPP relationship. Their existence underscores our RPP's desire to be a convenor that works collaboratively on research that is valued in the eyes of our practice partners and ultimately drives policy and programmatic decisions that lift children, students, and families – especially those experiencing vulnerabilities.

Here are a few suggestions for other organizations wanting to organize these types of capacity-building endeavors:

- Begin asking for partner feedback on what professional development would be most helpful as early as possible.
- Use the expertise found within the university and the university's professional networks and partner feedback to design engaging workshops that utilize relevant content and content-specific data sets.
- Consider offering your workshops in a virtual format to expand the potential audience.
- Some virtual meeting platforms can create customized registration pages that will automatically generate and email a calendar invitation to people who register to attend.
- If possible, record your workshops and post them online to encourage asynchronous and on-demand learning opportunities for those who cannot attend.

Brokering through creating systems and routines that support using research in practice. A central task of RPPs is making meaning from data collected through research activities. Although practitioners and researchers may have many ways of discussing data in their work, guiding discussions of data and research evidence that also lead to valid implications for action may be challenging. If so, a data discussion protocol such as the IDEA protocol shared by Norma Ming at the San Francisco Unified School District can create structure that allows partners to communicate effectively and make meaning together.

IDEA DATA DISCUSSION PROTOCOL

San Francisco Unified School District
Dr. Norma Ming

Practice organizations routinely consult data and evidence from a variety of sources to guide planning, analysis, and improvement efforts. Yet, making sense of the rich, complex data available can be challenging, not just to identify what's most relevant, but especially to formulate valid and useful inferences and implications for action. Within research-practice partnerships (RPPs), navigating multiple differences in institutions, roles, and experiences alongside nuanced research findings adds another layer of complexity.

One tool that SFUSD uses to guide data discussions is the IDEA protocol, which I adapted from the Carnegie Foundation for the Advancement of Teaching (2016) for use in SFUSD's continuous improvement initiatives. As seen in Figure 5.2, the tool reflects features from tools familiar to educators, such as "KWL (Know–Want to know–Learned) charts" (Ogle, 1986) and the ladder of inference (Argyris, 1982). The tool helps facilitators and participants structure their discussions of data and evidence to guide action by:

- focusing conversations on the relevant questions to inform policy and practice
- anchoring implications for action in clear evidence
- designating opportunities for partners to contribute based on the stage of discussion and their expertise

The IDEA protocol highlights four stages of discussion with guiding questions listed here and also described in Figure 5.3:

(1) **Intention:** What do we want to learn from the data?

Anchoring the discussion in the *intention* helps focus attention on what is most relevant, not merely what is interesting. It situates the conversation at the boundary between what is known and what is not yet known, with an eye towards how the new knowledge may help disambiguate between potential future actions.

(2) **Description:** What do we observe in the data?

The *description* captures trends and variation in the data, illuminating multiple possible dimensions that might otherwise remain hidden. It establishes shared understanding of the key findings before advancing the discussion to more divergent inquiry.

(3) **Explanation:** How might we explain our observations?

The *explanation* connects evidence to theory, exploring questions about confidence in the findings, alternate explanations, underlying causes, likelihood of predicting future results, and applicability to different contexts.[1]

(4) **Action:** How might we act on what we've learned?

Moving from knowledge to *action* weighs the strength of the evidence alongside cost–benefit tradeoffs and other priorities. It also considers who should take what action, with whom, when, where, and why.

Staff in SFUSD's Research, Planning, and Assessment division tailor their use of this protocol for different audiences and purposes, incorporating it into meeting agendas, presentation slide templates, and visual organizers for shared note-taking. Cases include exploring data, reviewing research articles, testing improvement theories, or interpreting emergent findings from a research-practice partnership. Other SFUSD staff have continued to adapt this protocol when reviewing data in their own staff meetings as well as community presentations.

For an RPP setting, the guiding questions elicit complementary perspectives from research and practice. Practice-side partners are experts in their local context, bringing knowledge of institutional values, other important initiatives and influential actors across the system, relevant environmental factors, and the feasibility of proposed actions. Research partners are experts in methods for reviewing related research literature, collecting and analyzing evidence, and testing and revising theories.

In a collaborative discussion of WestEd's evaluation of SFUSD's middle-school math and computer science initiatives, curriculum and instruction leaders mentioned a range of the findings' implications such as examining curricular tasks, supporting higher quality questioning, strengthening teacher coaching and collaboration, and encouraging more

IDEA Data Protocol

- **Intention**: What do we want to learn (affirm, confirm, or explore) from inspecting these data? What do we envision we may see?
- **Description**: What do we see in the data?
- **Explanation**: How might we explain what we notice? What alternate explanations exist? What is *not* explained? How does this compare to expectations?
- **Action**: What else do we want to learn? What actions might we take next?

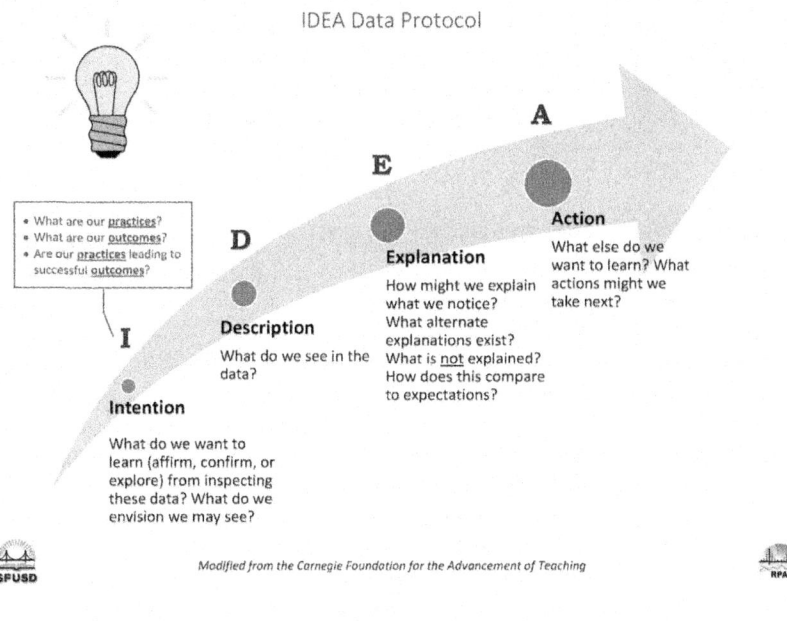

Questions to consider:
- What are our *practices*?
- What are our *outcomes*?
- Are our *practices* leading to successful *outcomes*?

Modified from the Carnegie Foundation for the Advancement of Teaching

SFUSD — RPA

Figure 5.2 Visual representation of the protocol

reciprocal student talk. When I invited the researchers to comment on the connections between the research and those implications, they affirmed that the strategy of questioning was well supported by data, observing that the structures were in place and that the time could be used more strategically. This signaled where the evidence was stronger and suggested a direction for focus.

IDEA Data Protocol: Possible Use Cases and Guiding Questions

	Consulting Existing Research	Improvement Cycles: Testing Theory	RPP*: Interpreting / Integrating Findings
	Intention		
I	What do we want to learn from consulting this research? (e.g., common challenges, promising practices, alternate approaches)	What theory are we testing? What results might we observe if the theory is correct? If it's incorrect?	P: What is our problem of practice? Why do we believe research will help address it? R: What are the questions motivating the research?
	Description		
D	What are the key claims or findings? Which populations, interventions, outcomes, and contexts are represented?	What does the evidence show about our implementation and impact?	R: What are the findings? How do they compare to other contexts? P: What else did we observe?
	Explanation		
E	What is the theoretical explanation for these findings? How does that compare to alternate explanations? How robust is the evidence supporting these claims?	Are the results consistent with the theory? Should we revise the theory? If so, how?	R+P: What do we think caused these results? What level of confidence and caveats apply? R+P: To what other contexts, settings, and/or populations might these findings apply (or not)? Why or why not?
	Action		
A	Which research recommendations are most relevant for us? How might we improve the alignment between those recommendations and our practices? What else do we want to learn?	Which practices should we adopt, adapt, or abandon? What other questions do we want to explore?	P: Given the likely applicability of these findings to our target context(s), what actions might be worth doing? When, where, by whom? R: What is the likely leverage (effect) of those actions, given what is known from research? P: What is the feasibility of these actions?

* RPP = Research-Practice Partnership; R = research team; P = policy / practice partners

Figure 5.3 Possible use cases and guiding questions

Tips for making the most of this tool:

Possible Challenges	*Recommendations*
Researchers might feel constrained by a structured discussion, since traditional academic routines follow a "lecture, then Q&A" format.	Introduce the protocol by its purpose: to maximize learning from research through a more focused, equitable, interactive, and productive discussion.

(Continued)

Continued

Possible Challenges	Recommendations
The richness of the conversation may be limited by the absence of critical voices.	Before scheduling the meeting, identify key stakeholders and decision-makers and anticipate how power dynamics might influence the openness of dialogue.
Asking the audience to discover patterns in the data may take time away from exploring possible explanations and implications.	Have researchers first highlight key patterns from their analysis of the data, then encourage the audience to inquire or elaborate further.
Practice-side partners might feel compelled to describe a broad range of next steps, rather than focusing narrowly on what the study findings support.	Acknowledge that there are many promising ideas beyond the scope of this study. Consider designating a "parking lot" for topics that could be addressed through other research.
Researchers might feel inhibited from offering an honest critique of practices that are not supported by the evidence out of a desire to maintain positive relationships.	Frame the conversation with the shared belief in using evidence to learn how to improve practice, while also noting the limitations of the evidence.

Practice-side partners often have relatively little experience in specifying a research agenda that would help them improve their work and in embedding reflection on research into their planning. When this is the case, building this work into a broader strategic planning effort can make this task easier, as Carrie Conaway illustrates through her approach in the Massachusetts Department of Elementary and Secondary Education.

TYING RESEARCH REFLECTION AND PLANNING TO STRATEGIC PLANNING

Massachusetts Department of Elementary and Secondary Education
Carrie Conaway

Practice organizations often run annual strategic planning and review cycles. These routines present an opportunity for brokers to coach partners on research use by connecting research planning to strategic planning.

At the Massachusetts Department of Elementary and Secondary Education, the research and planning office led an annual strategic planning cycle. The Department's commissioner would determine the broad goals for the organization, and its leadership team would work with their staff to build out a plan for reaching those goals. Using an adapted version of the Deliverology planning framework (Barber et al., 2010), the planning team ran meetings to help the program staff:

(1) examine what they learned from their work in the prior year by reviewing existing evidence
(2) brainstorm ideas for what initiatives they should continue, change, or drop
(3) narrow the list of ideas to land on a set of initiatives
(4) develop a learning agenda: a list of research questions the program staff would like to explore to support the strategic plan

Typically, they held one meeting on each of these four topics, though sometimes it took an extra meeting or two to bring the whole plan together.

The research and planning office embedded their coaching on research production and use within the strategic planning sessions, relying on the first session to elevate prior research and the fourth to build the learning agenda for the coming year. By repeating the process annually, the program staff improved at articulating research questions and interpreting findings, and the research team improved at anticipating what questions the program staff might ask. The research team could then use the learning agendas generated in these meetings to drive both their internal work on research development and their responses to requests from external researchers.

This planning process also surfaced emerging work, giving both program and research staff more lead time to integrate research into new initiatives. For example, one year the planning meetings with the educator effectiveness team revealed that the team would soon embark on an ambitious plan to improve teacher preparation statewide. The advance notice allowed the research team to coach the educator effectiveness team on articulating their research needs as they designed their initiative, and it also signaled to the research team to look for opportunities to advance research production and use in this area. Ultimately this new line of inquiry led to building a research-practice partnership on teacher preparation policy with the Center for the Analysis of Longitudinal Data in Education Research, which has generated papers on the teacher preparation

CASES DESCRIBING BROKERING TO STRENGTHEN PARTNERS

> and licensure landscape (Cowan et al., 2017) in Massachusetts, a descriptive analysis of a performance review model for teacher licensure (Cowan et al., 2018), and a study of the predictive validity (Chen et al., 2019) of a performance review process for teacher candidates, among others.

DEVELOPING AND NURTURING RELATIONSHIPS TO WEATHER PARTNERING CHALLENGES

While RPPs might begin with just one small project, they build towards sustained collaboration over time. As with any long-term relationship, challenges will inevitably arise where the partnership is tested. Key staff may turn over; a district might need to say no to a research request; a project may generate an unexpected finding; and so on. RPPs will only survive those challenges if the individual relationships that make up the partnership are deep and trusting. These cases illustrate how to create and sustain those relationships.

Brokering to build strong relationships from the beginning. Even in partnerships that have a formally designated broker role, everyone in the partnership needs to contribute to building strong relationships. Beth Polito and Tammy Moriarty of the Stanford–Sequoia Collaborative for Leadership show how to do this in the early phases of a partnership through a multi-layered approach.

MULTI-LAYERED BROKERING TO DEVELOP NEW LINES OF RESEARCH AND PROGRAMMING

Stanford–Sequoia Collaborative for Leadership
Dr. Beth Polito, Las Lomitas Elementary School District, and
Dr. Tammy Moriarty, Center to Support Excellence in Teaching

When partnerships are just getting started, they need a lot of brokering work to build relationships and avoid pitfalls. This often involves multiple people in different roles employing brokering skills, rather than a single broker.

Multiple members of our RPP engaged in brokering activities to support the development of our partnership. They

- connected partners to address a need from the school district
- met with partners as they built their working relationships

- supported partners throughout the research proposal process and formation of an advisory committee

Connect partners to address a need from the school district. During a strategic planning process, Las Lomitas school district leaders identified leadership development as an area that needed greater attention because of its importance and impact on the quality of the school experience for students and staff. The school district did not have the resources to offer a full leadership development program on its own. It needed thought partners that were experts in the field and could help them build the capacity of school and district leaders to implement research-based leadership practices.

The superintendent began searching for a partner who had expertise in leadership development and could help strengthen both existing and aspiring leaders in her district. The superintendent reached out to the director of the Stanford–Sequoia K–12 Research Collaborative (the Collaborative), a research-practice partnership between the Stanford GSE and nine local school districts, to help connect the district with Stanford researchers that had expertise in leadership development.

Meet with partners as they build their working relationships. The Collaborative's director connected the superintendent with two researchers from Stanford University GSE's Center to Support Excellence in Teaching (CSET) who had been doing work in leadership development for teachers, school leaders, and district leaders. The Collaborative director coordinated an initial meeting with both partners to discuss what the superintendent was looking for and for the superintendent to learn more about CSET's leadership work. After the initial meeting, both the superintendent and the researchers from CSET felt invigorated by the conversation and felt like the potential partnership would be a good fit. The two parties met several more times, with the director being a part of these conversations, to make decisions about the program design, district and participant recruitment, research design, and a timeline that would make the shared ideas into a reality.

Support partners throughout the research proposal process and formation of an advisory committee. The superintendent and the CSET researchers worked together to design a new program called the Stanford–Sequoia Collaborative for Leadership. The goal of this program is to build the leadership capacity of leading teachers, site leaders, and district leaders who feel ready to address persistent problems of practice within their systems that will change the learning experiences for their historically marginalized and underserved students. The program aims to support the growth and development of participants' leadership identity and stance, strengthen their ability to practice leadership, and build a strong community of leaders within and across participating districts. See the program description (Center to Support Excellence in Teaching, n.d.). A total of five neighboring small school districts, who are all a part of the broader Sequoia Collaborative, agreed to participate in the new leadership program. Both the superintendent and the Collaborative director helped to foster the district relationships and build interest for district participation.

In addition to the creation of the SSCL Program, the Collaborative director encouraged the partners to apply for a grant from the university to study the development of leadership at multiple levels within the participating school districts. The partners put together a proposal that was accepted. The research study will inform the partner school districts about how best to promote leadership development within and across their districts. An advisory committee consisting of the five superintendents meets periodically to discuss the progress of both the program and research and to provide feedback as it develops.

Here are a few tips for supporting partnership with multiple brokers engaging in brokering activities:

- If there are multiple brokers, they need to make sure to work in concert with each other as a means to bolster mutually beneficial relationships and work towards common goals.
- One key role of brokers is to leverage their access to resources (e.g., grant funds, strong relationships with other superintendents) to help strengthen the partnership.
- Brokering activities take time to develop; a single meeting is rarely sufficient to identify and build shared goals.

In early phases of partnership, existing offices that do related work may have questions about the value of the partnership or not see themselves in the work, and RPP members may have difficulty engaging with them. Finding common ground between these groups can be crucial to the partnership's success. Beth Vaade, Brianne Monahan, and Amanda Kruger tackled this challenge in the Madison Education Partnership by creating a "first date" meeting between the RPP and the district's institutional research and evaluation team, building from the first date meeting agenda from the Stanford/SFUSD partnership shared in Chapter 3.

111

"FIRST DATE" MEETING AGENDA TO BUILD COMMUNITY AND FIND COMMON GROUND

Madison Education Partnership
Beth Vaade, Brianne Monahan, and Amanda Kruger

Meetings are a key strategy for connection in research-practice partnerships. In these spaces, RPP members not only report on and continue progress towards their goals, but also build trust and relationships between people. First meetings are especially important to gauge the interest between the potential partners, establish norms and expectations, and inherently either address or play into a power dynamic in the group. Even working with an established partnership, introductions and reintroductions continue to build a community within both organizations and expand the partnership's reach.

The Madison Education Partnership (MEP) has brought the Madison Metropolitan School District (MMSD) and the Wisconsin Center for Education Research (WCER) at the University of Wisconsin–Madison together in a research-practice partnership since 2016. Entering its sixth year, MEP was led by a core team of three co-directors (two from WCER, one from MMSD) who facilitated, led, and brokered many lines of research. As seen in the organizational chart for our RPP in Figure 5.4, one of our primary partner departments in MMSD was the Institutional Research and Evaluation (IRE) team. In addition to leading the research efforts for MMSD, this team also oversaw all external research work in the district. The MMSD co-director oversees this team in her role as Executive Director of Research and Innovation.

Wisconsin Center for Education Research (WCER)
Madison Education Partnership (MEP)

- MEP Co-Director #1/Exec. Director of R&I
- MEP Co-Director #2
- MEP Co-Director #3
- MEP Project Manager
- MEP Research Assistant

Madison Metropolitan School District (MMSD)
Institutional Research & Evaluation (IRE)

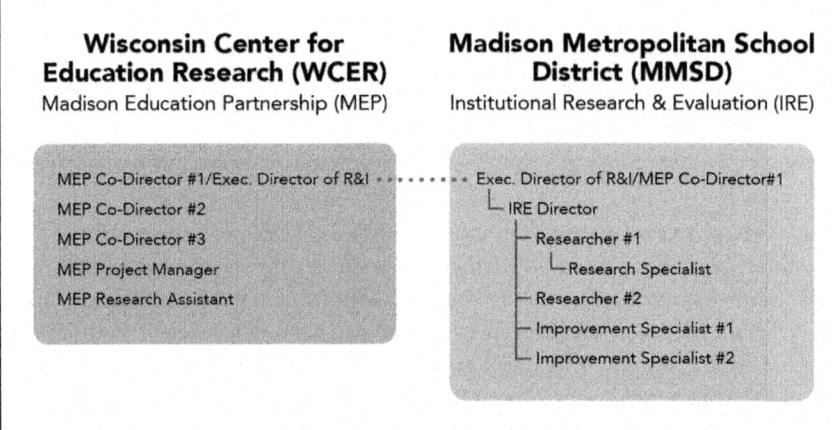

- Exec. Director of R&I/MEP Co-Director #1
  - IRE Director
    - Researcher #1
      - Research Specialist
    - Researcher #2
    - Improvement Specialist #1
    - Improvement Specialist #2

Figure 5.4 Organizational chart for the Madison Education Partnership

Since the start, MEP and IRE have wanted to cultivate strong, collaborative relationships with one another, but faced some challenges. While the two teams shared similar interests and training, differing incentives, expectations, and ways of working made it difficult for the IRE team (an office historically focused on accountability and quick-turnaround requests for district leaders) to engage in MEP research projects. Opportunities where MEP and IRE team members did collaborate with one another were not always positive. MEP team members found it difficult to engage IRE team members in their projects, and IRE team members felt as if they didn't always fit in with academics and that their contributions were not needed or appreciated.

To address these challenges, our team decided to host a "first date" meeting between the MEP and the IRE teams to reinvigorate the relationship. We wanted the meeting to serve as a chance to build community and identify areas of potential collaboration going forward. We also wanted to create a durable meeting format that could be reused during other introductions and transitions over time. The 60-minute meeting took place in person and covered four major topics:

- introducing ourselves and defining our shared purpose
- getting to know each other
- finding common ground, in both our shared and unique sets of skills and interests
- identifying next steps for the work this year

Building from the tool shared in Chapter 3 by the Stanford–SFUSD Partnership and Laura Wentworth's Tool: Agenda for a "First Date" Meeting Between a Researcher and Practitioner (see Chapter 3, p. 64), MEP's MMSD co-director and the IRE director developed an agenda with the focus of finding common ground between UW MEP staff and MMSD IRE staff with equal power and influence. Placing our MMSD co-director (who serves on both the UW MEP and MMSD IRE teams) as the broker between the two groups, she ran the meeting and facilitated debriefs with both groups after the meeting.

Tips for making the most of this tool:
Create a fast-paced and fun agenda:

- multiple activities, no more than 20 minutes per activity
- all participants have a prescribed and active role in every activity
- make it fun! Build in humor and playfulness to keep the mood light

CASES DESCRIBING BROKERING TO STRENGTHEN PARTNERS

Make it about more than the meeting:

- create pre-work for each team and post-meeting follow-up so that the work lives beyond those 60 minutes
- allow times for more candid conversations in smaller teams before and after the meeting

Vary your design:

- layer in activities that involve individual, small, and large group work
- vary between times for discussion and times for creation and be explicit about which you are doing when

Pay attention to the logistics:

- if possible, have a dedicated facilitator who can keep the meeting on track, on time and help find common ground
- set meeting norms in advance, laying ground rules for how we will interact in this space

Researchers often worry about the implications for their relationships and their partnership if they find negative results from their research. While negative findings certainly can damage a partnership, they're not nearly so common as a problem that researchers rarely plan for: turnover. Many practitioners change roles every few years, hampering sustainability if brokers don't plan for early investments in deep relationship-building throughout the partnership. Kylie Klein with the Northwestern-Evanston Education Research Alliance supported sustainability by making multiple points of connection and keeping all those connections active through repeated, purposeful contacts. She found that even just forwarding a recent piece of research or sharing a summary of a recent initiative can help. (This case can be found in full on pp. 94–96 of Chapter 4.)

Sustaining relationships is challenging enough in RPPs that involve just one district and one research team. When a partnership spans multiple districts or researchers, the challenge multiplies. Michelle Nayfack from the Stanford–Sequoia K–12 Research Collaborative uses an annual superintendent dinner to reinforce relationships in her RPP and build investment in their shared work.

SUPERINTENDENT DINNERS

Stanford–Sequoia K–12 Research Collaborative
Dr. Michelle Nayfack

When partnerships include many leaders and researchers, all with unique priorities and contexts, it is critical to find ways to build and strengthen trusting relationships so that the research-practice partnership can weather different kinds of challenges. The Stanford–Sequoia K–12 Research Collaborative (Sequoia Collaborative) uses annual superintendent dinners as one strategy to support relationship-building and strategic planning.

The Sequoia Collaborative is a research-practice partnership that brings together researchers from Stanford's GSE and district leaders from eight independent elementary school districts and the high school district that they all feed into. Each fall, the nine superintendents are invited to have dinner at an off-site location (e.g., a local restaurant) with the dean of the GSE and one or two faculty leaders who have a strong investment in the Sequoia Collaborative's success. The dinner is primarily a social event. Attendees enjoy a glass of wine and a nice meal together. To provide some structure to the evening and to ensure that everyone views the event as productive and worthwhile, the broker works with the GSE dean to develop some conversation starters that create periods of focused conversation throughout the meal.

As the broker, I use a few different tools to provide organization and structure to the dinner. The first, a facilitator's agenda, helps get everyone who has a role in the event on the same page. It maps out how each portion of the evening will unfold and provides talking points for anyone who is being asked to contribute. The second, dinner discussion questions, is provided in hard copy on the tables to get everyone thinking ahead of the discussion. These questions are designed to push the group forward and to encourage conversation about topics that have been raised in other meetings that did not include the full group of leaders. Example discussion questions include:

- Does it feel important that we communicate research findings to all partner districts in the Collaborative? If so, what could that look like?
- Are you communicating with your board and other district stakeholders about your partnership research with Stanford? If so, how? If not, what would it look like if you did?

CASES DESCRIBING BROKERING TO STRENGTHEN PARTNERS

- What's one thing you've learned from participating in a Stanford research study this past year, and how are you using that information moving forward?

During organized discussions, it is useful to identify a small set of leaders who are willing to help drive the conversation. For example, at the Sequoia Collaborative dinner outlined in this sample facilitator's agenda, I asked Mary Streshly (former superintendent in the Sequoia Union High School District) to discuss her idea for more regular meetings with the superintendents in order to increase communication and support joint decision-making.

Tips for Planning Superintendent Dinners

- Meet ahead of time with specific leaders who are willing to provide leadership and can help drive the conversation. Give these leaders well-defined roles.
- Meet ahead of time with any VIPs (e.g., the Stanford GSE dean) so that they feel comfortable with their own role and talking points.
- Let guests mingle for the first 30 minutes of the evening, but pre-assign seats for the meal. Use name placards to identify each person's seat. This encourages leaders to interact with new colleagues and supports relationship-building.
- Resist the urge to maximize productivity and pack the agenda. Superintendents rarely get to relax and unwind with each other. Make sure that they feel like they are "off the clock" and can have a little fun.
- Record any key comments, thoughts, or next steps that come out of the dinner discussion and organize these into an email communication back to the group to keep momentum from this dinner going.

A challenge many partnerships struggle with is that the research and practice partners work from physically separated spaces, making it harder to build and sustain relationships. Moonhawk Kim with the Oakland Unified School District–UC Berkeley RPP took the strategy of embedding himself in his partner district at least one full day each week. This creates opportunities for chance encounters where he can understand the district context and uncover partnering needs, which then allows him to provide the right support for individual partners.

EMBEDDING IN THE PARTNER SCHOOL DISTRICT

Oakland Unified School District–UC Berkeley
Research-Practice Partnership
Moonhawk Kim

Brokers work to establish, maintain, and strengthen productive relationships with collaborators across partnering institutions. However, differences in organizations, identities, and cultures make such efforts challenging. While various approaches exist to cultivate frequent, sustained, and deep interactions, one way to address this challenge is to *embed brokers* in a partner organization.

The OUSD–UC Berkeley Partnership was established in 2018. From our earliest days, the partnership wanted to foster close collaboration between the district team coordinating research activities and the director of RPP from the university. Thus, I, as the director, arranged to be embedded at the district's Research, Assessment, and Data (RAD) Department, where I work at least one full day a week.

I spend the majority of my time at RAD in scheduled meetings with RAD and non-RAD staff. I meet weekly with RAD's research leadership to discuss current and prospective projects. I introduce the partnership to any district leaders I have not yet met. During unscheduled time, I coordinate collaborations in progress while remaining available to interact with other OUSD staff when appropriate. In the future, I plan to join internal RAD projects related to research (e.g., curating research and evaluation carried out at OUSD to feature on their website). These activities benefit the partnership by increasing its visibility and helping me better learn the context in and the needs of the district, which I can then discuss with RAD's research leadership.

Embedding in the district provides further concrete benefits, namely a district Google account. My district email address helps establish credibility with OUSD staff members who might be wary of collaborating with unknown entities. My access to district staff calendars expedites finding a common meeting time among university researchers and OUSD staff, who have highly constrained schedules.

My time spent embedded in the district also enables chance meetings. I have "watercooler" conversations with administrators and staff members from different teams and departments. I meet staff members with whom I would otherwise not have arranged a meeting. I use these opportunities to publicize the partnership as well as to learn about the district's work, culture, and personnel. These encounters can foster more natural conversations than what formally scheduled meetings might afford. All these opportunities help me observe and understand the district's needs more closely. That, in turn, better prepares me to strategize with the RAD team on how to support those needs through partnership collaboration.

One issue to be careful of is that embedding university staff in a school district may reinforce the power asymmetry in favor of the university, wherein the embedded broker uses the connections they develop in the district to advance the university's research agenda. We have safeguarded against that in two ways. First, our partnership focuses on public impact rather than scholarly production, making it less likely that we would prioritize work of academic but not practical interest. Second, my own prior experience working in a school district's research office gives me insight into some of the considerations internal research offices must contend with that aren't obvious to external researchers (e.g., district priorities, other research partners, competing demands, and staff workload).

To guard against these pitfalls more generally, two principles should underlie any broker embedding arrangements. First, the practice organization's research team should always retain control over shepherding the organization's engagement in research; the embedded partner is there to learn from and support them, not to replace or supplant their work. This cautions against investing in infrastructure that may inadvertently undermine the autonomy, work, or capacity of the district, particularly since what may seem like short-term convenience may unintentionally hinder the longer-term development of the organization (Farley-Ripple et al., 2022; Kim et al., 2020). Second, the arrangement should prioritize goal alignment, organizational clarity, and transparent communication across institutions so that the embedded partner and the district work in concert rather than at cross purposes.

Tips for Embedding Brokers in Practice-Side Settings

- Clearly lay out the expected roles and responsibilities for the embedded broker and the practice-side partners, as well as the processes and communication channels for everyone to use.

- Design embedding arrangements in ways that continuously promote the research coordination between the research organization and practice organization's research office.
- Coordinate with the internal research leaders to develop the terms of the embedding and help build relationships with other practice-side leaders.

Brokering to address differences across partners. Working across multiple organizations inevitably results in differences of opinion within the partnership – from big decisions such as which projects to prioritize to small decisions such as how to word questions on a survey. Forging consensus among individual partners with different perspectives on the work is central to brokers' work. The cases in this section illustrate how formal and informal brokering moves can promote collaboration. First, Daniel Potter from the Houston Education Research Consortium describes a multi-layered approach to building agreement among partner members who are independent from and sometimes even in competition with one another.

BUILDING CONSENSUS AND TRUST AMONG COMPETITORS

Houston Education Research Consortium (HERC), Kinder Institute for Urban Research

Daniel Potter

Some partnerships involve practice-side partners from multiple organizations that have previous relationships with each other. Sometimes these relationships are helpful, and other times they pose a challenge for the research-practice partnership (RPP) broker to manage. What strategies could brokers use to support the relationships across these practice partners?

Starting in summer 2017, the HERC expanded its number of public school district partners from a single district to 11 districts, serving nearly 715,000 pre-K to grade 12 students in the Houston area. HERC faced a pivotal challenge in creating a regional RPP that joined together entities (i.e., independent school districts in the Houston area) that operate independent of and sometimes in competition with one another.

HERC implemented two key strategies to directly confront and successfully overcome this challenge: first, a biannual meeting with all of HERC's public school partners; and second, monthly one-on-one meetings between HERC and each partner public school district.

The biannual meetings, which HERC calls its Regional Working Board, are scheduled so that representatives (e.g., superintendents, assistant/associate/deputy superintendents, directors) from each practice partner can attend. An agenda is shared in advance of the meeting, and the meeting is typically structured to serve several purposes: share updates from ongoing projects; get feedback on work that is being done; and brainstorm, plan, and come to consensus on future research projects.

This final point, "come to consensus," is a core component for how HERC has created cooperation among competitors. HERC does not vote on its regional research projects. Instead, as the HERC broker, I develop consensus among our practice partners by following this process:

- First, I hold one-on-one meetings with key members of each school district to begin the conversation about their high-priority, actionable topics that HERC could research. These one-on-one meetings take place in advance of the biannual meeting, and ideas generated from these conversations are shared across districts.
- Second, during Regional Working Board meetings, which can consist of up to 30 people, small group breakouts are used, where I sort representatives from each district into different groups to discuss the ideas shared from the earlier one-on-one meetings. Small group breakouts allow for more conversation and sharing of perspectives.
- Third, after a limited amount of time (normally 10 to 15 minutes), each of the small groups is combined with one of the other small groups to create larger groups, but not yet return to the full group setting. I incrementally combine groups to look for similarities in what was discussed in the smaller groups and to prune which topics get shared with the full group.
- Fourth, after spending time in these combined groups (normally 15 to 20 minutes), the full group reconvenes to share what has been discussed. A representative from each group shares with the full group, and I emphasize having a district representative be the person speaking. Once ideas have been shared, I start the process of consensus-building

towards the next research topic by summarizing the key ideas, leading group discussion of each idea's pros and cons, and challenging the practice partners to think about how they would use the results of a potential study.

The biannual meeting is typically scheduled for two hours to allow for the time necessary to accomplish these tasks.

The one-on-one meetings, which HERC calls check-in meetings, are standing once-a-month meetings where I connect with a district liaison (typically not the superintendent). The check-in meetings are much more informal and are intended to serve as a venue to discuss ongoing projects, but more importantly to build and develop relationships between HERC and district leaders. There is not a formalized agenda for these meetings, which provides flexibility for discussion across a range of topics. Importantly, the one-on-one meetings provide districts with the opportunity to bring to HERC's attention any questions, topics, or issues that are specific to them (in contrast to the biannual meeting, which challenges districts to think about issues that extend to neighboring districts as well). From these conversations, HERC is able to identify opportunities for district-specific analyses, while also centering the regional aspect of the partnership. The one-on-one meetings are typically scheduled for 30 to 60 minutes.

Tips for Using Meetings to Promote Relationship-Building

- In planning a large-scale meeting with multiple partners, send an agenda ahead of the meeting so that each partner knows what to expect.
- Focus less on establishing a research question during large meetings with your partners. Instead, set out to identify a topic of interest; specific questions can be developed later.
- Hold the one-on-one check-in meeting even if there is nothing to check-in about. Yes, partners are busy, but those are the occasions to build and nurture relationships between researchers and partners.

Katherine Hayes from the Los Angeles Education Research Institute took a different tack, using informal moves in and out of meetings to find common ground and meet partners' varying needs in the context of a contentious survey design process.

INFORMAL BROKERING MOVES TO OVERCOME DIFFERENCES IN A PARTNERSHIP

Los Angeles Educational Research Institute (LAERI)
Dr. Katherine Hayes

In a partnership, researchers and practitioners work together even though their cultures and priorities often differ. To overcome these differences, brokers make specific moves to build relationships to weather any challenges based on these divides.

One way I have attempted to strengthen relationships as a broker between Los Angeles Unified School District (LAUSD) leaders and LAERI researchers is through my work on the LAUSD School Experience Survey (SES). This climate survey asks questions of students, parents, and staff regarding their perceptions of their school experiences. The survey has undergone numerous iterations and formats during its tenure and continues to change every year, hopefully for the better. At LAUSD's invitation, LAERI eagerly joined our efforts, demonstrating its expertise and willingness to support the district. Training in survey methodology from LAERI provided a ripe context for building relationships that could overcome differences.

Yet, the survey development process can be very challenging. For example, the SES has had four managers since its inception, and their differing perceptions of survey content and design made the survey somewhat disjointed. Program administrators provided items designed to meet their specific information needs; however, we had limited or no information on item validity. In addition, some program leaders wanted additional survey items, while district leaders insisted that we shorten the survey.

When we asked LAERI to help us revise the survey so that it would yield more reliable and valid findings, the process created a perfect illustration of the researcher-practitioner mismatch. When LAERI and LAUSD leaders focused on joint item selection, the setting presented the greatest opportunity for using brokering moves to overcome differences. These meetings typically involved staff from LAUSD's Office of Data and Accountability (ODA) and relevant Department of Instruction divisions and lasted two to three hours, often with multiple follow-up meetings. Not everyone in the room came to the meeting with the same understanding of their role and voice, but all came with the desire to contribute to an improved survey. LAERI researchers clearly had experience and expertise in surveys and a range of content areas to bring to the discussion, while district partners had their own priorities, areas of expertise, and interests at heart.

- First, I honored a deep respect for the potential contribution of each person in the room by repeatedly recognizing the expertise and enthusiasm brought by LAERI staff and District practitioners.
- Second, as the broker, I had the responsibility to help translate between the two cultures when there was confusion. For example, LAERI often offered insights on the impact of analyses used in survey research (e.g., response rates, drop-off rates). I attempted to address those issues with practitioners so that, even if the implications of these analyses weren't necessarily immediately apparent or accepted, they could still inform practice over time.
- Third, I convinced both LAUSD leaders and LAERI researchers to be willing to sacrifice some degree of methodological perfection for practicality. In one example of negotiating, LAERI stated that in some cases presenting an item as a question instead of a statement yielded more valid results, but ODA leads argued for consistency, since all the other questions were already presented as statements.
- Finally, I encouraged the group to place our collective goal above that of the individual need. The parties around the table might disagree on survey length (ODA leaders), the need to answer specific research questions (program leaders), and the use of sound survey principles in SES (research leaders), but we all wanted the survey to be successful. I attempted to balance the tensions of these demands by arguing that we eliminate certain items, while also advocating for LAERI's recommendations regarding the importance of systematic item presentation and the inclusion of key items related to ongoing research or trends of interest.

Some of the conversations were difficult, but the goodwill and flexibility on the part of researchers and practitioners with the help of a broker has built trust and built relationships, thereby strengthening the partnership and supporting its success.

Creating the conditions to support research use. The point of a research-practice partnership is to generate research that is used in practice. This is a straightforward goal, but it's easy to stumble along the path to this outcome, particularly when key conditions that support research use aren't in place. Two conditions that brokers can directly influence are production of research that is likely to prove useful to practice partners and communication of research findings.

Brokering to support research use through strategic research production. Practice partners may struggle to know which type of inquiry will be most valuable to them: research (a systematic investigation designed to contribute to generalizable knowledge) or a program evaluation (assessments of whether programs are doing what they are intended to). In the next case, Lila K. S. Goldstein describes a tool that her partnership, the NEERA, created to guide practitioners and highlight the important data confidentiality issues that may be associated with each approach.

AM I SUPPOSED TO BE DOING A PROGRAM EVALUATION? A QUIZ TO NAVIGATE WHETHER TO CONDUCT RESEARCH OR AN EVALUATION

Northwestern-Evanston Education Research Alliance (NEERA)
Lila K. S. Goldstein

Partnerships between universities and K–12 educational providers are rife with events, programs, and other activities. While many are specifically associated with research activities, others arise for additional purposes such as service or mutual learning opportunities. Research-practice partnership (RPP) brokers are often asked to help both research- and practice-side partners navigate decisions on whether to pursue research on the various activities that link the research and practice organizations.

The NEERA operates within Northwestern's Office of Community Education Partnerships (OCEP), which facilitates a wide swath of programming connecting Northwestern and the Evanston school districts. The Northwestern student groups, faculty, and staff who create programs that bridge Northwestern and its district partners are often left wondering, "Am I supposed to be doing a program evaluation?" The answers to this question can vary greatly.

Some Northwestern affiliates may need to do a full research project: a systematic investigation designed to develop or contribute to generalizable knowledge around their programs and the people they serve. Some may only need to specifically evaluate, assure, or improve performance. Some may not need to systematically examine their program in a formal way at all.

CASES DESCRIBING BROKERING TO STRENGTHEN PARTNERS

Those who do need to evaluate their programs can also do so within a broader research project, and less formal evaluations and reflections can live alongside more formal investigations, as well. Defining whether the work is in the realm of research, program evaluation, or neither helps point people in the right direction.

To this end, we developed the following BuzzFeed-style quiz, where the answers add together in the background to direct users to the right resources (Figure 5.5).

This quiz can be used in a couple of ways. It can be posted on the RPP's website, where it explains what kinds of projects it covers to provide direction on where to seek guidance, or it can be used to frame discussions and direct advice between brokers and program providers.

(1) IRB: Do you have capacity for working through the Internal Review Board process for research approval? Capacity includes expertise, time, etc.
   (a) Yes. I am or my team is prepared to write an IRB proposal.
   (b) Maybe. I or my team could make the time or learn the skills necessary to do this if need be.
   (c) No. Not applicable for my event or program, or I do not have the capacity for this.

(2) Time frame: Is there a clear beginning and end to this event or program or is it rolling/open-ended?
   (a) Yes, there is a single event or series of events with clear beginning and end points.
   (b) No. While there may be a clear beginning, there is no projected end date/time.

If yes to question 2, follow with: Recurrence: How likely is it that this event or program or something based on it will happen again in the future?
   (a) This is definitely happening again as planned.
   (b) This is definitely happening again, possibly with substantive changes.
   (c) If this goes well, it or something similar will happen again.

Figure 5.5 A quiz to navigate whether to conduct research or something else

> (d) This is unlikely to happen again in its current form, but we hope to learn from this for other programs or events.
> (e) This is unlikely to happen again.
> (3) Funding: Does your funder request study, evaluation, or reporting?
>   (a) Funder requires generalizable or publishable research based on this event or program.
>   (b) Funder requires data-driven evaluation or report.
>   (c) Funder requests data-driven evaluation and requires at least some kind of report.
>   (d) Funder does not request data-driven evaluation but requests at least some kind of report.
>   (e) Funder does not request any kind of report.
>   (f) There is no funder.
> (4) Learnings: How do you hope to learn from investigating this event or program? Select any that apply.
>   (a) I do not hope to investigate this program or event in any way.
>   (b) I don't know.
>   (c) We are trying to determine or demonstrate whether this is feasible or possible.
>   (d) We are hoping to improve this program or learn how to improve similar programs that will happen in the future.
>   (e) We are hoping to learn about how this kind of program works for the kinds of people who are involved in it, maybe for publication.
>
> **Answers**
> - **Research**
>
> Brief definition: Systematic investigations designed to contribute to generalizable knowledge using private or identifiable information
>
> Important detail: Can also be used for program evaluation
>
> Need IRB approval: Yes
>
> Resource: Email ed_partnerships@northwestern.edu to learn more about doing research with community partners
>
> - **Evaluation**
>
> Brief definition: Assessments of whether programs are doing what they are intended to
>
> Important detail: Generally, not collecting private data

Figure 5.5 A quiz to navigate whether to conduct research or something else

> Need IRB approval: Unlikely, but email ed_partnerships@northwestern.edu if you are unsure
> Resource: See this website (https://ocep.northwestern.edu/data-partnerships.html) for resources to get you started
> - **No Investigation**
> Brief definition: No systematic investigation needed
> Important detail: N/A
> Need IRB approval: No
> Resource: Email ocep@northwestern.edu for questions about conducting programs with community partners
> - **Consult**
> Are you in a pickle? Are you not sure what to do next? Maybe your funder requires research, but you do not have the capacity for writing an IRB proposal. Maybe you do not have funding to accomplish the evaluation needed to get funding. Maybe you are just a little lost. But cheer up! We're here to help. Email us at ed_partnerships@northwestern.edu.

Figure 5.5 (Continued)

- **Research.** To complete research, users need funding and capacity to apply for IRB approval. If they have those two resources and either an expectation or desire to do research, we point them in the research direction.
- **Program evaluation or no formal investigation.** If users' funders do not need research and the users do not want to or have capacity to do research, they will be directed either to program evaluation or to no formal investigation based on other factors.
- **Program evaluation.** A program evaluation is only feasible if there is a clear time frame and supportive funding. Program evaluation will only be worthwhile if there is room to apply their learnings to that or similar programs. With those in place, reasons to do a program evaluation include a desire to improve or learn about feasibility of it or similar programs, a requirement from funders for data-driven reporting, or a program recurrence that depends on documented success.
- **No formal investigation.** If neither research nor formal program evaluation are feasible or worthwhile, or they are feasible but there is no driving reason to do either, we will direct users to no formal investigation.

CASES DESCRIBING BROKERING TO STRENGTHEN PARTNERS

- **Consultation.** Users who have reason to do a formal investigation but not the capacity, users who are required to investigate but have no idea what they might try to learn, or users who are otherwise in a pickle are directed to NEERA for help.

Whether and how to try to learn from activities conducted across learning institutions, such as universities and K–12 educational providers, are questions that will arise again and again. Brokers can use a quiz like this to help advise and direct the people who hope to bridge these organizations. Tips for making the most of this tool:

- Use or revise it to serve as a framework for explaining what you need to have in place to conduct research or program evaluations and what the benefits can be. It does not have to be used as a quiz.
- Determine ahead of time where you would direct people or what resources you will use to help people.
- Many people will come to you thinking they know that they need to be doing research or program evaluation. Keep the factors this quiz asks about in mind as you advise them, because they may need redirection.

Brokering to support research use through communication of research findings. Research that practitioners don't know about by definition won't be used. One way to promote awareness, and therefore use, of research is to host a research roadshow, as Erin Baumgartner and Jessica Vasan from the Houston Education Research Consortium did throughout the Houston Independent School District. This took the form of a series of meetings to help staff understand why research might be useful for decision-making and to build awareness about specific projects and the research partnership as a whole.

RESEARCH ROAD SHOWS

Houston Education Research Consortium (HERC)
Erin Baumgartner and Jessica Vasan

Many research-practice partnerships (RPPs) face the challenge of inconsistent awareness and knowledge about the partnership's work on the practice side, especially when the practice partner is a large organization. The Houston Education Research Consortium (HERC) addressed this challenge by offering a research roadshow to academic departments throughout the Houston Independent School District (HISD). The goals of the roadshow meetings were simple:

- to help staff in departments across the district have a better understanding of research, including how, when, and why to use it in decision-making
- to share information about existing work being conducted by the district's own research office
- to make staff aware of the HERC partnership and the past and current research HERC has conducted with the district
- to ensure departments were aware of how to request research support

The meetings typically had eight to ten participants: a HERC associate director, an HISD/HERC research manager, the HISD director of the Research and Accountability office, and five to seven HISD staff members from a given department, including the department's director. We structured the meeting agenda as follows:

(1) a "do now" exercise for participants as they entered the session ("As we get settled, please jot down some responses to either or both of these questions: in the planning you do and the decisions you make in your work on behalf of HISD's students, how do you use research? And/or: what does it mean to ensure your work is evidence-based?")
(2) introductions
(3) a review of the desired outcomes or goals of the session
(4) a review of participants' "do now" responses
(5) an overview of the work that HERC has conducted in partnership with HISD, the research conducted by the HISD Research and Accountability office, and the process for requesting a study or program evaluation
(6) wrap-up and questions from participants

HERC partnership members also collaborated to create a facilitator's agenda based on the above six sections of the agenda, which we used to help presenters clarify meeting goals, track meeting preparation tasks, and record participant input, confusion or concerns, and follow-up items. It also included relevant talking points and key takeaways for each section of the agenda to ensure consistency across meetings and facilitators.

> One key learning for facilitators from the roadshow was that participants define "research" quite broadly. In the "do now" exercise, we heard participants cite anecdotal evidence, raw data outputs, and quantitative and qualitative analyses included in published research literature. Another challenge that facilitators foresaw but did not explicitly address was the variation in levels of familiarity with the research department's work, the partnership, and research in general. We plan to differentiate for levels of knowledge and experience within and across groups in future roadshow sessions.

A condition limiting research use is that researchers often struggle to write summaries of their work in an accessible format and style. In collaboration with Jeff Archer of Knowledge Design Partners, Jessica Holter from the Tennessee Education Research Alliance looked to solve this problem by creating a guided interview process that helps the researcher articulate the key takeaways from their work and why the topic is important, as well as how the study might be misinterpreted and what it *can't* tell us.

> ## AN INITIAL INTERVIEW GUIDE FOR WRITING POLICY BRIEFS
>
> ### Tennessee Education Research Alliance (TERA)
> ### Jessica Holter
>
> Education researchers and those in the practice and policy space often do not speak the same language, making it challenging to build a shared understanding around the findings and implications of important research studies. Researchers tend to focus on how a particular study advances the field, while practitioners and policymakers often want to know how research can inform specific actions to solve pressing problems. This disconnect is one reason why writing a useful research brief is so difficult. In collaboration with Jeff Archer of Knowledge Design Partners, the TERA developed a series of brief-writing tools designed to help make sense of the research early on in the writing process. On our team, these tools are used by those who serve as a brief's primary author when the author is

not the researcher (typically a graduate assistant or a research analyst). As TERA's Communications Director, I also use these tools when I edit briefs written directly by a researcher.

One of these tools is the Initial Interview (Tennessee Education Research Alliance, n.d.), a structured conversation with a researcher about the key takeaways from a specific study, guided by a set of questions designed to prompt the researcher to formulate explanations meant for a policymaker or practitioner audience. We structured the line of inquiry around the key takeaways that policymakers or practitioners should understand from a particular study or set of studies. The guiding questions we use in these initial interviews are aimed at clarifying and supporting these key takeaways. For example, the interviewer will ask how the researcher would explain both the research process and the findings to a non-research audience. We ask them to explain how big or small a difference is in non-statistical terms, focusing not only on how a result should be interpreted but also on how it might be misinterpreted. At this early point, the interviewer also hones in on what kind of visual representation might best convey a finding to someone who is unfamiliar with statistics.

Though still a work in progress, our Initial Interview process has helped ensure that by the time we share the briefs in draft form with our partners at the state education department, we have already wrestled with how to communicate the brief's key findings to non-research audiences. This enables TERA's partners to focus their reactions and feedback on possible implications from the research instead of trying to also sort out its meaning.

Tips for Conducting Initial Interviews (Appendix P)

- Schedule a 45- to 60-minute interview with the researcher to make sure you have ample time to really dig into the important questions without feeling rushed.
- Prepare in advance for the interview by reading each study carefully with the guiding questions in mind and adjusting questions as needed to get the most out of the one-on-one time with the researcher.
- Share the interview questions ahead of time with researchers so they know what is coming and can start to think about their work in terms of its key takeaways.

- During the interview, repeat back what you heard the researcher say to check your own understanding and interpretation.
- If possible, record the interview so you have a full record of the conversation for your reference later. Taking notes, facilitating a conversation, and interviewing is tough! (It can also help to have a note-taker in the room.)
- Let the questions guide the conversation, but don't use them as a script that you follow verbatim. Dig in deeper with probing questions where you need to and skip questions that may not be as relevant.

Confronted with the same problem of how to translate existing academic work, Beth Vaade, Brianne Monahan, and Amanda Kruger of the MEP took a similar approach to TERA's Initial Interview process but added in collaboration with the district's research office and with practitioners as a double-check on clarity and utility.

CREATING AN ACCESSIBLE PRACTITIONER BRIEF FROM AN ACADEMIC RESEARCH PAPER

Madison Education Partnership
Beth Vaade, Brianne Monahan, and Amanda Kruger

The MEP has brought together the MMSD and the WCER at the University of Wisconsin–Madison in a research-practice partnership since 2016. As an established RPP, MEP staff and researchers have produced over 20 reports, briefs, and other communications, all posted to its website. All MEP directed-work has a district author and sponsored work has a MMSD contact point who reviews any outgoing research publications or briefs in addition to the work being reviewed by the MEP governance bodies, WCER director, and MMSD superintendent. While all MEP reports, summaries, and memos are written with the goal of being understood by a lay audience, MEP also has supported formal research papers following academic writing conventions.

Recently, one of our supported researchers from the University of Wisconsin–Madison shared a new academic publication she authored about the relationship between family engagement strategies in 4-year-old kindergarten (4K) and student outcomes in literacy and social-emotional skill development. Upon review, we knew the findings would be of interest to the MMSD community, but they would struggle to read the academic article and understand how the findings apply to their classroom communities. And if they never read it, they could not use the findings.

Our solution was to employ an existing method — a practitioner-targeted research product — but create it collaboratively using a new process for our partnership through a brokering role. We enlisted the help of two members of the district's research and innovation (R&I) team to create a practitioner-facing research brief, "How Does Family Engagement Influence Outcomes for 4K Students?" (Madison Education Partnership, n.d.). As frequent MEP collaborators, two of our R&I team members were uniquely positioned to help the researcher and MEP communicate this work in MMSD.

To create this brief, R&I team members employed the following steps:

(1) First, the R&I team members met with the UW researcher to confirm their understanding of the key findings and most important implications for district practitioners.
(2) Then, the R&I team drafted a three-page brief, including a high-level summary of study research questions, methods, and findings, plus two sections geared at elevating practitioner agency when explaining the research.
(3) MEP then paid teachers and a school principal small incentives ($25 checks) to review the new brief over a two-week time span and provide feedback about the brief's utility for a practitioner audience. The R&I team sent a list of specific questions for teachers and a principal to respond to and guide their review (see Figure 5.6). MEP's project manager selected several members of MMSD's 4K from different roles and spaces who had participated in prior MEP research projects and who were target users of the research findings.
(4) The feedback from respondents enabled the R&I team to clarify the brief and was particularly helpful in understanding how practitioners viewed the reflection and "extra credit" portions of the brief.

The brief ran in the MMSD Administrator Bulletin and Board of Education weekly newsletter, which could be accessed by school-based leaders to share with their staff members. While the same barriers to access may still be present due to the dissemination strategies available to the team at the time of publication, the involvement of 4K practitioners throughout the brief development process resulted in a product that was clearly

133

> - Does the format and language used in this brief strike the right level for practitioners — accessible, while also pushing thinking about research and 4K practices?
> - From your perspective, is there a clear story being told about the research rationale and its findings?
> - What about the research and brief, if anything, either resonates or seems surprising based on your experience?
> - Does the "How Can I Think About This Research" section help you reflect and consider your own practice in light of this research?
> - Is the "Extra Credit" section on statistics and standard deviations interesting? Helpful or confusing? Unnecessary or a value-add?

Figure 5.6 Guiding questions for practitioner review of 4K brief

focused on the study findings most germane to the practice environment, avoided jargon, and emphasized readers' agency in drawing implications from the research for their own understanding and application. In addition, the process of collaboratively developing the brief between R&I staff, the researcher, the MEP project manager, and 4K teachers created additional connections within the partnership to build on in future work.

Tips for making the most of the tool:

- **Leverage the expertise of your practice-side partners.** Having the R&I team lead the research brief-writing process led to not only a better brief, but also a stronger relationship between UW and MMSD staff.
- **Engage with practitioners outside of the partnership.** Our best feedback came from teachers and principals who weren't familiar with the research and engaged an audience outside of the administration.
- **Know your audience.** Be realistic about what engages your audience. How much time do they have to read the work? What would they take away from it? Test your assumptions by integrating members of your target audience into your review process to ensure your finished product reflects their expertise, needs, and perspectives.
- **Create a clear plan with intermediate steps and due dates.** Lay out what you need to do and by when early on, and communicate clearly throughout the process to stay on track.

Another challenge with research use is that research products often don't make clear what an initiative looks like when done well, and how that's different from typical implementation. Laura Booker and Nate Schwartz from the Tennessee Department of Education developed a strategy that helps with this: contrasting case studies that are selected specifically to illustrate these differences, creating concrete examples that resonate with practitioners.

CONTRASTING CASE STUDIES

Tennessee Department of Education
Dr. Laura Booker and Dr. Nate Schwartz

State and district staff value deliverables that they can immediately put to use. In Tennessee, after struggling for several years with the right approach to illustrative case studies, we found that our partners particularly liked research reports that featured contrasting cases that could be adapted as tools for staff professional development.

For example, one of our team's projects focused on understanding and evaluating district implementation plans for our state Response to Instruction and Intervention (RTI²) initiative. After conducting interviews with leaders in schools where there had been more and less progress in shifting student learning trajectories, the team wrote four short case studies – two from the "big movers" and two from the "small movers" – illustrating key themes that emerged. These contrasting case studies were used by the department's staff in professional development sessions with hundreds of district and school administrators across the state. Administrators read the studies and reflected on key differences in the four stories. The two "big mover" cases were also included in a public report (Tennessee Department of Education, 2016a) that was printed and widely distributed.

We used a similar strategy to bring to life the nuances of a research report on elementary literacy. After conducting observations of early grades reading classrooms, the team wrote "A Tale of Two Classrooms" (Tennessee Department of Education, 2016b), which was included in a broader report released by the state. This piece describes two different first-grade classrooms using different instructional strategies to teach the same concepts. Immediately, we heard from instructional coaches across the state that they were using this section of the report in professional development sessions with teachers to help them think through their own instructional practices. The cases were so popular that the team also created an additional more specific set of contrasting vignettes (Tennessee Department of Education, 2017) in another literacy report two years later. The stories were grounded in actual observations of specific classrooms, but they incorporated details from a wide range of observations to better illustrate the main research findings.

As this strategy developed, our team improved at building the development of contrasting vignettes and case studies into our project timelines. In some instances, our case studies were developed for internal use, and at other times, they were developed once the partnerships decided to publish research findings more widely. We kept a number of guidelines in mind:

- Plan research with case studies/vignettes in mind so that you can allow time for data collection activities that will capture the kinds of details about the program or topic of interest that make the illustration real. Many "cases" included in research reports tend to feel generic, and they lose the journalistic quality that makes readers want to know more.
- Focus on key differences across cases. The intent here is to highlight the possible choices available to your audience and to highlight justifications for making particular choices.
- Avoid obvious conclusions. If the things you are describing feel like common sense, then a vignette is unnecessary. Instead, highlight the areas where subjects were forced into difficult choices and illustrate stronger and weaker ways of dealing with these choices.
- Think about whether and how you will preserve anonymity (especially important for the non-ideal cases).
- Consider your key audience and the practices you are hoping the research might influence. Look for dissemination opportunities (professional development workshops, etc.) that will provide this audience with time to thoughtfully engage with your findings. Think about activities during these events to promote the kinds of engagement that leads to meaningful change.
- In written materials, provide guiding questions for educators that allow for thoughtful engagement with case studies.

NOTE

1 A deeper examination of what constitutes high-quality evidence for educational decision-making is presented in Ming & and Goldenberg's (2021) "Research Worth Using" framework.

REFERENCES

Argyris, C. (1982). The executive mind and double-loop learning. *Organizational Dynamics, 11*(2), 5–22.

Barber, M., Kihn, P., & Moffit, A. (2010). *Deliverology 101: A field guide for educational leaders*. Corwin.

Chen, B., Cowan, J., Goldhaber, D., & Theobald, R. (2019). *From the clinical experience to the classroom: Assessing the predictive validity of the Massachusetts candidate assessment of performance*. CALDER Working Paper No. 223–1019–2. https://caldercenter.org/publications/clinical-experience-classroom-assessing-predictive-validity-massachusetts-candidate

Cowan, J., Goldhaber, D., & Theobald, R. (2017). *Massachusetts education preparation and licensure. Year 1 report. American institutes of research (AIR)*. www.doe.mass.edu/research/reports/2017/05EdPrep-Year1Report.pdf

Cowan, J., Goldhaber, D., & Theobald, R. (2018). *Massachusetts teacher preparation and licensure: Performance review program for initial licensure study. American institutes of research (AIR)*. www.doe.mass.edu/research/reports/2018/01prpil-analysis.docx

Farley-Ripple, E., Ming, N., Goldhaber, D., Sarfo, A. O., & Arce-Trigatti, P. (2022). *Building capacity for evidence-informed improvement: Supporting state and local education agencies*. Retrieved from https://crue.cehd.udel.edu/wp-content/uploads/2022/10/Building-Capacity-for-Evidence-Informed-Improvement-October-2022–1.pdf

Kim, M., Shen, J., Wentworth, L., Ming, N. C., Reininger, M., & Bettinger, E. (2020). The Stanford–SFUSD partnership: Development of data-sharing structures and processes. In S. Cole, I. Dhaliwal, A. Sautmann, & L. Vilhuber (Eds.), *Handbook on using administrative data for research and evidence-based policy*. Retrieved October 8, 2022, from https://admindatahandbook.mit.edu/book/v1.0-rc4/sfusd.html

Ming, N. C., & Goldenberg, L. (2021). Research worth using: (Re)Framing research evidence quality for educational policymaking and practice. *Review of Research in Education, 45*(1), 129–169. https://doi.org/10.3102/0091732X21990620

Ogle, D. M. (1986). K-W-L: A teaching model that develops active reading of expository text. *The Reading Teacher, 39*(6), 564–570.

Tennessee Department of Education. (2016a). *Supporting early grades student achievement: An exploration of RTI2 practices*. Division of Data and Research. www.tn.gov/content/dam/tn/education/reports/rpt_an_exploration_of_rti2_practices.pdf

Tennessee Department of Education. (2016b). *Setting the foundation: A report on elementary grades reading in Tennessee*. Office of Research and Strategy. www.tn.gov/content/dam/tn/education/reports/rpt_setting_the_foundation.pdf

Tennessee Department of Education. (2017). *Building the framework: A report on elementary grades reading in Tennessee*. Office of Research and Strategy. www.tn.gov/content/dam/tn/education/reports/rpt_bldg_the_framework.pdf

Education Research Alliance. (n.d.). *TERA research brief process: Initial interview guide*. https://peabody.vanderbilt.edu/TERA/files/NNERPP2019_TERA_Initial_Interview_Guide.pdf

Chapter 6

Cases Describing Brokering to Strengthen Partnerships

The crux of RPP brokers' work sits in their efforts to build and strengthen their partnerships. As described in Chapter 5, RPP brokers spend a good amount of time brokering to support the partners or the individuals working in these partnerships. But much of the work RPP brokers do relates to strengthening the partnership itself, given that these partnerships occur in an organizational space that none of the participants in and of themselves structure and lead. Consequently, brokers spend the bulk of their time bridging the organizational differences through boundary spanning practices (Penuel et al., 2015; Farrell et al., 2022) and creating what Farrell and colleagues (2022) refer to as "boundary infrastructure" (pp. 198–200). Brokers spend a lot of time building, maintaining, and strengthening RPPs as a third space where partners can work together on research production and use.

When we asked leaders in the RPP field to build cases about the tools and actions they take to support RPP work, many of the cases sat within the category of brokering to strengthen the partnership. As we described in Chapter 3, we think of this type of brokering as 1) developing partnership governance and administrative structure, 2) designing processes and communication routines, and 3) assessing and continuously improving the partnership. We also see all the work RPP brokers do, including the work to strengthen the partnership, as making room for equity in both process and outcome, which inherently means managing power dynamics in partnerships (e.g., potentially giving more resources to perspectives and priorities that historically have been sidelined) and interrupting racism and other systemic injustices (e.g., challenging normative or status quo partnership structures and systems that reinforce racism like having RPPs teams who are not representative of the student groups they are trying to support with their research).

In this chapter, we present a set of cases written by brokers in the field that relate to each of the components of brokering to strengthen the partnership. As seen in Figure 6.1, we present each subtheme under brokering to strengthen

DOI: 10.4324/9781003334385-6
This chapter has been made available under a CC-BY-NC-ND license.

CASES DESCRIBING BROKERING TO STRENGTHEN PARTNERSHIPS

- Developing partnership governance and administrative structures
- Designing processes and communications routines
- Assessing and continuously improving the partnership

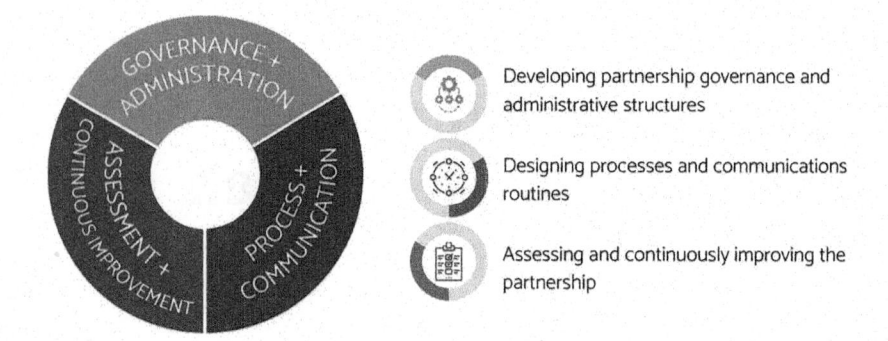

Figure 6.1 Brokering to strengthen partnerships

partnerships: governance and administrative structures, processes and communication routines, and assessment and continuous improvement. Under each subtheme we organize the cases according to more specific headings that relate to broker actions like creating DUAs or meeting routines. Then, we provide a short description of each case so readers can understand the content of the case and how it relates to practical actions brokers take to strengthen partnerships. The cases are signified by larger text boxes and title, author names, and their respective RPPs are acknowledged.

CASES ABOUT BROKERS DEVELOPING PARTNERSHIP GOVERNANCE AND ADMINISTRATIVE STRUCTURES

Partnership governance and administrative structures involve brokers taking action to develop data infrastructure and agreements, establish research agendas, and create partnership agreements (often involving vision statements). Here we present cases addressing each, exemplifying these broker actions.

Data Infrastructure and Agreements. A DUA specifies the conditions under which data are being shared and the requirements researchers must follow around data confidentiality and privacy. They are an essential legal backbone behind any project where data, whether qualitative or quantitative, are being shared for research purposes. Jorge Ruiz de Velasco provided an example from the Youth Data Archive at the John Gardner Center at Stanford University.

DATA USE AGREEMENTS

Youth Data Archive, John Gardner Center at Stanford University[1]
Jorge Ruiz de Velasco, PhD, JD

The DUA is a formal agreement that memorializes how researchers will obtain access to, transfer, and safeguard data protected by state and federal privacy laws. Beyond the legal formalities, a DUA can also be the "first handshake" that builds trust and lays the groundwork with partners about what *they* might want to learn, who you are, and how seriously you will protect their data and observe ethical standards for research.[2]

A DUA is also a good place to put into words the central purpose of the collaborative and may often include a specification of the research question(s). This elaboration of purpose can suggest the new knowledge and program improvement benefits that may justify any inherent risks to protected subjects. Consequently, the DUA can serve as a foundation for an IRB application, where necessary.

Some tips for writing DUAs:

- **Which projects require DUAs?** It is prudent, if not always a legal requirement, to have a DUA in any case where researchers plan to acquire data with a student or teacher name, number, or any other information that can be traced back to a specific person.
- **Who "owns" the data?** This question can be settled in the DUA and generally relates to the authority the researcher/research organization seeks with respect to the acquired data. In some cases, data may be transferred to researchers in order to create a database for a long-term, open-ended research or evaluation agenda that is not time-delimited but otherwise approved by IRB. In those cases, the researcher will co-own the data, and the DUA should make plain that the legal requirement to protect the privacy of human subjects will outlive any time-limited DUA or research-practice partnership.

In most cases, however, researchers act as agents for their partners and in the service of a specific, time-delimited and negotiated set of research questions; practice partners always own their data. As such, the DUA makes clear that the practice partner has the right to demand the destruction/erasure of administrative (raw) data previously transferred and that authority to use the data be terminated under terms spelled out in the DUA. Clarifying the practice partner's data ownership provides reassurance that researchers will not use legally protected

administrative data to pursue an independent research agenda without prior written approval.
- **Ongoing Training.** It is important to train new staff on DUA procedures. One way to operationalize this is to develop and to regularly update DUA templates (Appendix J) and partner communication protocols for the DUA development process, including a one-page overview (Appendix K) and correspondence templates (Appendix L). These templates can be used to onboard new researchers, educate stakeholders, standardize communications, and update team members.
- **Periodically align DUA language with IT security developments.** With rapid changes in how organizations manage and secure data electronically, periodic review of internal data use protocols by IT experts is critical. Improved encryption for laptops and greater control over the security procedures of third-party data storage providers like Google Drive and Box Drive have enabled organizations to approve those methods/devices for transfer and, in some cases, for long-term data archiving. But that is not true in all cases, so it is important to check with IT!
- **The DUA template.** The DUA template (Appendix J) focuses on quantitative (administrative records) data but can be adapted to describe how researchers will protect qualitative data (e.g., digital recordings and written records of interviews, focus groups, direct observation notes, and surveys).

Another case demonstrating efforts to administratively manage RPP data infrastructure is Adam Corson's description of a Chicago Public Schools data dictionary to be used across multiple RPPs, which helped the partnership to develop common understandings about data definitions.

CHICAGO PUBLIC SCHOOLS DATA DICTIONARY WIKI

University of Chicago (Consortium on School Research, Chapin Hall, Education Labs, Inclusive Economy Lab, National Opinion Research Center), Northwestern University (School of Education and Social Policy), American Institute for Research, The Learning Partnership.

Adam Corson

When multiple research partners and district departments work with the same data, how can you ensure that everyone uses consistent data definitions? The Chicago Public Schools Data Liaison created a data dictionary (data wiki), with support from the University of Chicago Consortium on School Research, to record and maintain key information. Most data questions can be answered by looking at the data dictionary first, saving valuable time for researchers and practitioners alike.

Overall, the wiki details roughly 30 data sets frequently used by researchers. The level of detail in the data dictionary varies depending on the respective data set; district information will be much more detailed compared to data sets from state or charter sources (including information on state-administered assessments). For example, the wiki page for the Illinois Assessment of Readiness (IAR) only contains a list of variables, a link to the IAR section of the Illinois State Board of Education

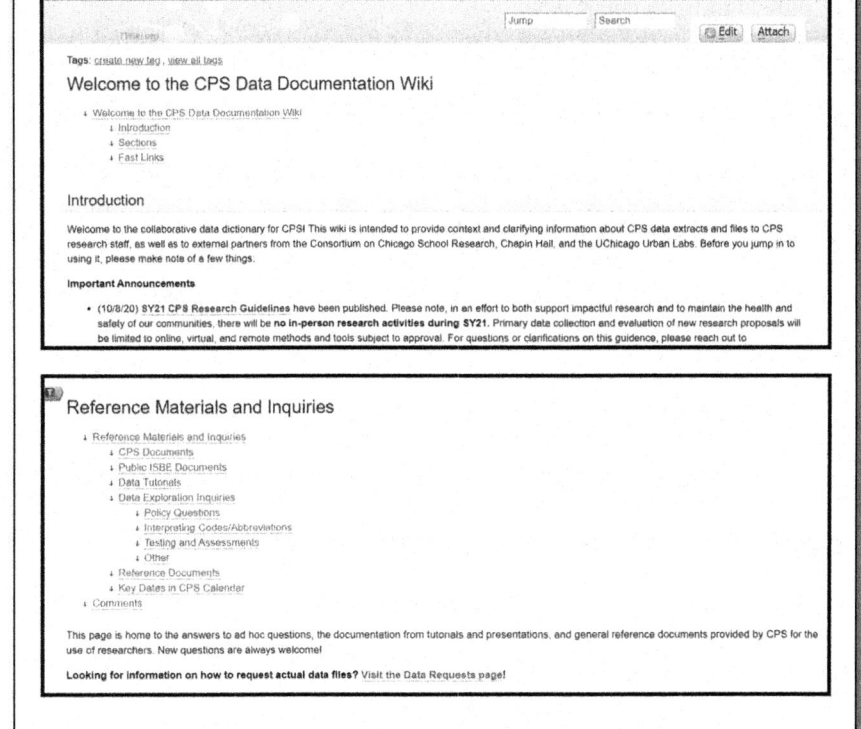

Figure 6.2 Screenshots of the Chicago Public School Data Wiki

website, and links to previous assessments used by the state that are recorded in the wiki.

The Chicago Public Schools (CPS) data dictionary has become a valuable trove of institutional knowledge since the district does not keep its own central data dictionary. As seen in Figure 6.2, the wiki provides a number of resources, including:

- information about data sets such as changes in data sets across years or variable descriptions – the type of information often lost when key employees depart – and information about data origin, usage, and format
- templates for both scopes of work and amendments to data-sharing agreements with the district
- tutorials on a range of district tools (like the annual Student Voice survey or the implementation of a new postsecondary planning tool) and links to guidance documents from CPS, the Illinois State Board of Education, and State/Federal Student Privacy Laws (i.e., FERPA and ISSRA)
- slide decks and notes from training sessions for partner organizations' researchers regarding CPS data and systems (i.e., how data gets from the classroom to the central office to the external researcher)

The wiki has helped researchers and practitioners involved in partnership work in a number of ways. First, the data dictionary mitigates the loss of institutional knowledge about the data set. Second, the data dictionary assists researchers seeking to understand data sets more quickly so they can produce informed and timely analysis. As researchers are co-developing research questions with district partners, the wiki is frequently referenced, especially when drafting scopes of work with the district. Lastly, most data questions can be answered by looking at the data dictionary first, saving valuable time for researchers and practitioners alike.

Partnership Agreements. Virtually all research-practice partnerships that have developed beyond the early phase have agreed on two documents that are central to codifying their governance structures: a DUA (described earlier) and partnership agreement that includes their vision, approach to working together, and sometimes their research agenda. The partnership vision spells out the intentions behind the partnership: what work they plan to do together and why. This often includes a detailed research agenda: a formal codification of the question-generating process described in earlier sections, or some agreement about the structures for decision-making and working together. Similar to an MOU, but different from a DUA, partnership agreements are usually non-binding but are useful as a reference for making daily decisions about the work of the RPP. Co-creation of a partnership agreement like this can help strengthen the partnership as well, as Devin Corrigan, Dr. Norma Ming, and Dr. Emily Ozer found by doing this work with the San Francisco Unified–UC Berkeley partnership (please see full case included in Chapter 4).

Some RPPs refer to their partnership agreements as a commitment document outlining the norms and routines participants need to adhere to when working in an RPP. Brokers use commitment documents to develop understanding with new participants they are onboarding or when making decisions about who receives funding and resources from the RPP given their level of commitment to the RPP.

The Northwestern-Evanston Education Research Alliance (NEERA) created a commitment agreement that new researchers must sign upon starting a project with the partner districts. Rather than focusing on legal documentation, it instead focuses on the intents and commitments the partnership has around how the partners work together. They use the agreement to build a shared identity and culture, as well as to reduce the onboarding work when new researchers begin.

CAN I GET THAT IN WRITING? CODIFYING RESEARCHER COMMITMENTS

Northwestern-Evanston Education Research Alliance (NEERA)
Lila K. S. Goldstein

Researchers' and practitioners' expectations about research partnerships are often out of sync. Relationships between researchers and practitioners too easily default to researchers pitching their ideas to practitioners, and practitioners feeling like the research is a yes or no proposition. To set clear expectations for all partners and support a mutually beneficial partnership, the NEERA created a partnership agreement (see Appendix M) that each new set of researchers must sign upon embarking on a research project with our partner districts.

NEERA began in 2017 after years of less formal relationships among Northwestern University and the school districts in Evanston, Illinois. Those forming the partnership early on had experience working in research-practice partnerships (RPPs) and research alliances. While many RPPs house a specific and largely unchanging set of researchers working with community partners on individual problems of practice, our research alliance sets up an infrastructure for a variety of researchers to work with community partners on a series of issues. Because our structure meant that we would frequently be onboarding new researchers who may be less familiar with partnership work, we decided to develop a partnership agreement to define, formalize, and make transparent our expectations of what it means for any researcher who does work as part of this partnership.

While memorandum of understanding (MOUs), data-sharing agreements, and other legal documents set forth expectations for partnership, a partnership agreement may be more or less detailed than those other sorts of documents. It does not carry any legal weight, so it can be less detailed, taking a more conversational tone and allowing more flexibility for change. What it contains more of, however, is concrete detail on how to conduct a partnership relationship and the reasoning behind that.

Our partnership agreement begins with the mission of our organization. It then details what we expect researchers to commit to doing both broadly, like ensuring reliability of research through appropriate supervision of inexperienced researchers, and more specifically, like collaborating with practitioners from design through publication. For the latter, we include specific examples such as soliciting feedback from districts on feasible randomization levels or selecting representative cohorts. The thread through all of these commitments is collaboration and open communication with practitioners, NEERA staff, and other researchers. This is the core of the partnership agreement. Subsequent pages detail the steps for applying to conduct specific research projects, where we keep data and how data are transferred and accessed, suggestions for collaboration and partnership (e.g., sample check-in timelines and feedback solicitation processes), and more details on the district's Office of Community Education Partnerships (OECP).

This partnership agreement is available through the NEERA and OCEP websites to all Northwestern affiliates. We regard it as a living document and strive to update it as needed to best reflect our partners' needs and best communicate our expectations for researchers.

Tips for using this tool:

- Share this agreement in a one-on-one meeting between you as a broker and the researcher, ideally before or after the first meeting with school district leaders.

- Refer to the principles of the agreement in larger partnership meetings so researchers are aware of these principles beyond just reading and signing the agreement.
- Use the principles in the agreement for coaching, and refer to the agreement when you are coaching the researchers about their work in partnership.

Research Agendas. We included two more cases describing the development of a research agenda, as this is a part of RPP governance that is revisited and revised often as the RPP develops maturity. A research agenda outlines the priorities of the RPP members for conducting research and historically has centered research aligned to the outcome the RPP is focused on improving in the practice partners context. Here we present Joy Lesnick and Alyn Turner's approach within the Philadelphia Education Research Consortium for developing a research agenda.

DEVELOPING A RESEARCH AGENDA

Philadelphia Education Research Consortium (PERC)
Joy Lesnick and Alyn Turner

One of the key balancing acts for RPP brokers is helping partners develop a mutually beneficial research agenda that all partners are interested in and committed to pursuing together. How can RPPs create a research agenda that balances internal interests and needs with external expertise and capacity?

At the Philadelphia Education Research Consortium, we develop a research agenda by beginning with two separate brainstorming meetings: one with staff from the district's Office of Research and Evaluation and one with staff from Research for Action, the district's research partner. The district staff use the information we have to identify possible projects that fulfill three conditions: 1) the results will be of interest or use to program offices and district leadership (whether they know it yet or not); 2) there is available data that can be easily shared with our partners; and 3) the results of a research project will still be useful when they are available. It is important to us that all three conditions are met when identifying possible projects, as it is essential to the success of the project. Meanwhile, the Research for Action team reviews the previous work conducted by the partnership, alongside available research from external sources, to develop a list of possible projects. The team then splits into groups to create a list of possible projects with a brief description of the rationale/utility for each project. The team ensures that these possible projects build on the research team's prior interests and that the partnership has the capacity to support this work.

Next, staff from the district's Office of Research and Evaluation and staff from Research for Action meet together to discuss which projects to take on for the year. We put all of the ideas together and identify the top tier, second tier, and save-for-later priorities. The practice-side research team is largely responsible for identifying the priorities based on their knowledge of the district and program office needs. We also start to sketch out who from the partnership will lead and work on each project, what additional buy-in is needed from internal and external stakeholders and funders, what the timeline is for project completion, and how the results will be shared and incorporated into existing district processes. This process usually takes two hours.

After that meeting, Research for Action creates a summary of their understanding of the discussion and priorities for district review with the goal of aligning the expectations of the district and Research for Action. Once an attempt is made to impose more structure to the topics – operationalizing questions into projects details like what research questions will we pursue, using which methods and data sources, in what time frame – a round of revisions is usually needed to clarify nuances in the research topics and confirm how they intersect with the district's information needs and RFA researchers' interests. Once we settle on an agreed set of projects for the year (usually two or three), project leads begin working through the details, typically on a staggered basis.

This case demonstrates how brokers support the development of partnership infrastructure by:

- using inside district information, access to school district partners, and knowledge of available data to identify partnership projects that are both important and feasible
- creating shared buy-in for the annual partnership research agenda.

CASES DESCRIBING BROKERING TO STRENGTHEN PARTNERSHIPS

Here is another case describing a process used for developing a research agenda involving a state education agency, from an RPP where they prefer to blind their RPP name. It demonstrates how researchers' skills can be used to facilitate the process by analyzing state agency plans, and it also describes a process of using voting to prioritize research in the agenda.

ESTABLISHING A PARTNERSHIP IDENTITY AND CULTURE

[Name of RPP blinded]
Ashley Pierson, Maria Cristina Limlingan, Tim Speth, Molly Branson-Thayer, and Gail Joseph

When forming a research-practice partnership (RPP), the process of developing a research agenda or learning agenda provides opportunities to build partnership identity and culture. Researchers and practitioners work together to co-create a research agenda and establish norms for the partnership.

Part of a nationally funded strategy focused on preschool program improvement, this partnership began in 2018 between two research organizations and a practice organization at the state level. The overarching goal of this RPP was for researchers to provide key information and facilitate continuous quality improvement with practice partners to improve the quality of preschool education in the state. The research agenda for this RPP was co-constructed by state agency staff and research staff in the fall of 2018 and refined throughout 2019 with input from state agency staff and other stakeholders.

A research agenda or learning agenda is a set of prioritized research questions that guides the work of the research-practice partnership over a set time frame, typically a year or more. Ideally, the research agenda will be co-constructed by practice and research partners working together. In this partnership, the researchers developed a six-step process (see Figure 6.3) to engage practice partners in co-constructing the research agenda. During this process, the partnership identity and culture began to be formed, and norms, roles, and expectations were established between and among researchers and practitioners. The process sought and included input from staff within the practice agency who worked across the state and had varied amounts of decision-making power. This was intentional

149

to help create buy-in both from agency leadership as well as agency staff responsible for the day-to-day work related to the research agenda.

First, researchers reviewed and translated relevant state agency documents (such as a strategic plan) to develop a list of 23 potential research questions. After feedback from key practice partners, the list was narrowed down to ten questions to ensure there was no duplication with other ongoing state efforts.

Second, researchers facilitated a collective discussion with a core group of state agency staff and external partners to determine the criteria for prioritizing these research questions. The criteria decided upon through a voting process were feasibility (the research question can be answered in the timeframe of the project), impact (how much the research question will help inform the initiative), and political will (the research will be supported by and inform the work of the legislative body).

Third, state agency staff rated the ten potential research questions using the selected criteria through an online survey to practice partners (see Figure 6.4). This step could also be done in person during a meeting, though the online format in this case allowed additional state agency staff to participate, creating more buy-in across the agency.

Fourth, researchers developed study plans to address the research questions. Then, both practice and research partners met to finalize the research agenda questions by sharing the results of the voting and discussing the research plans for each of the selected questions. Based on feedback at this step, the research partners then revised and finalized the research agenda and shared it back to the group.

The formalized voting and rating processes used in developing the research agenda, as well as the clear documentation of the process and the steps, helped to establish clear expectations and participation norms. These processes also helped begin to form the identity of the partnership as one that is inclusive, where practitioners from multiple levels and departments of an agency make clear decisions about research priorities with guidance from researchers.

This case demonstrates how brokers help establish a partnership identity and culture through:

- following a clear and inclusive process that gives agency and voice to practice partners
- establishing meeting norms and decision-making processes

Learning Agenda Process Steps
September 20, 2018

July 2018

1 Translate self-assessment, workplans, strategic priorities into potential research topics and questions
Research partner takes workplan and self-assessment information, strategic plans/initiative overview, and the draft learning agenda created from discussion at the conference and translates into potential research topics and questions

August 2018

2 Select criteria (Meeting 1 – Aug. 9)
Group reviews criteria suggested by research partner, adds additional criteria if desired, and ranks criteria that will be used to help prioritize research questions (criteria could include feasibility, data availability, resources needed, impact level, timeframe, etc.)

September 2018

3 Prioritize research topics/questions (Online – Sept. 12–19)
Group ranks topics/questions based on selected criteria, with an online survey option to allow for participation in decision-making by those unable to attend

4 Develop study plans for learning agenda
Research partner reviews and consolidates prioritized research questions, reviews data availability, and develops study plans to address prioritized research questions

5 Review and confirm learning agenda (Meeting 2 – Sept. 24)
Group reviews the potential studies that can address prioritized research questions, prioritizes studies to pursue, and confirms learning agenda

October 2018

6 Finalize learning agenda
Research partner finalizes the learning agenda document and disseminates agenda back to the group

Icon credits: translate by luca fruzza; selection by Ben Davis; prioritization list by Vytautas Alech; Research by Aneeque Ahmed; group by Rakesh; Document by Satisfactory (all from the Noun Project)

Figure 6.3 Document shared with practice partners that outlines process

- generating a record of the research agenda process that serves as a foundation for the partnership and a reference to orient new partnership staff

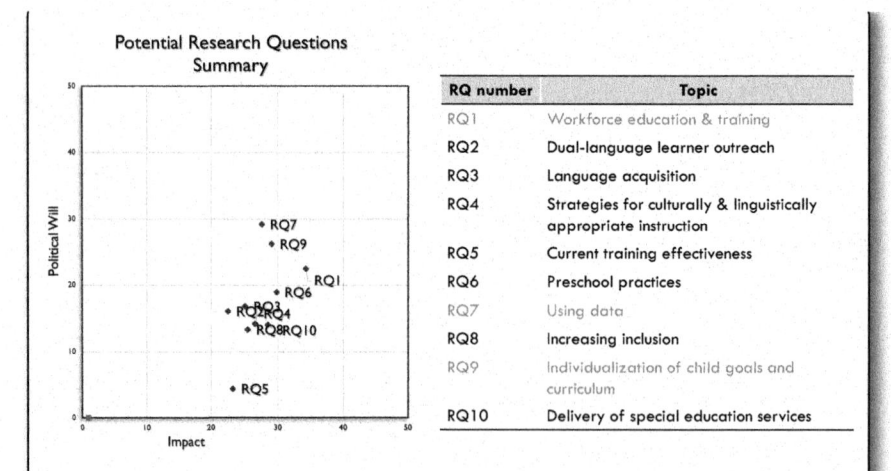

CASES DESCRIBING BROKERING TO STRENGTHEN PARTNERSHIPS

RQ number	Topic
RQ1	Workforce education & training
RQ2	Dual-language learner outreach
RQ3	Language acquisition
RQ4	Strategies for culturally & linguistically appropriate instruction
RQ5	Current training effectiveness
RQ6	Preschool practices
RQ7	Using data
RQ8	Increasing inclusion
RQ9	Individualization of child goals and curriculum
RQ10	Delivery of special education services

Figure 6.4 Voting information from step 3 ranked on criteria selected in step 2

Secondarily, the case exemplifies how brokers can build relationships through trust-building meetings guided by a clear process for co-creation of a research agenda, as well as how brokers can develop partnership infrastructure in the co-created research agenda and the documented process of generating the agenda.

DESIGNING PROCESSES AND COMMUNICATIONS ROUTINES

Partnership processes and communication routines involve brokers taking action to establish meeting routines, conference and event designs, norms and values, and channels for internal and external communications. Here we present cases addressing each exemplifying these broker actions.

Meeting Routines. Meeting routines can span from weekly to annual. The Boston P-3 Partnership conducts weekly check-ins with a standard agenda to keep work moving on all elements of their partnership, including data collection, coding, and interpretation. They found that the weekly cadence helped keep the work top of mind even during the shift to fully virtual work during the pandemic.

WEEKLY PROJECT CHECK-INS WITH STANDARD AGENDAS

Boston P-3 Partnership
Annie Taylor

Regular, transparent communication between research and practice partners is key to supporting research, especially lengthy studies or studies with implementation as a key research focus.

The Boston P-3 Partnership meets weekly to discuss its universal pre-K study. The meetings include all members of the research and practice partners, with two or three participants from the district and three or four from each research partner organization. The meeting agendas are sent out ahead of time by the practice-side Evaluation and Data Manager and include both status updates for ongoing work and time to discuss deeper issues at length (e.g., survey development or review of data presentations). Action items are assigned to appropriate members of the group and sent as follow-up after the meeting. All notes during the meeting are captured by a rotating member of the study team within the set agenda and saved in a rolling document shared with all partners. The tool provides an example of this format. The Evaluation and Data Manager on the practice side plays a critical role in ensuring this process is completed as they are the bridge between the academic researchers and the practitioners at the district. Importantly, this role does not dictate the topic of all meetings but rather ensures the processes and initial topics of meetings are set.

Consistency in expectations around meeting agendas and follow-up can be key in addressing future research changes or unforeseen circumstances. Our set, consistent meetings were particularly helpful when the team had to adjust to Boston Public Schools school closures in March 2020. The group paused all in-person data collection and instead seamlessly refocused on virtual coach interviews and surveys. Because meetings were already set each week, the study team was able to stay connected about the ever-changing COVID situation, therefore enabling this nimble refocusing. District staff were incredibly pressed for time and responsibilities at the beginning of the pandemic and without this existing structure in place, this project easily could have been de-prioritized instead of adapted.

The meetings have also helped with data interpretation. For example, the group used meeting time to develop a new coaching log survey and create a clear coding scheme that aligned with both the qualitative coding from coach interviews and the practical application of coaching within the district. Finally, consistent meetings have also helped bridge the knowledge gap between what happens in the district and how data are being analyzed by the research partners. For example, the group realized the need to re-categorize types of coaching support captured in the coaching log to better fit the actual work of the coaches. After discussing directly with coaches, the study team was able to re-analyze the data to align with the different classroom, leadership, licensing, and professional development support coaches provide, as opposed to grouping all coaching sessions together.

Tips for Making the Most of This Tool:

- Ensure team members are clear on who is gathering agenda ideas, sending agendas, and sharing action items. Ideally this is one consistent person.
- Share the agenda a day ahead of time so team members can add items if needed.
- Embed connecting or team-building time in the beginning or end of agendas.
- Write action items that are specific, timebound, and pertinent to the immediate work of the group.
- Always share agendas and action items with all team members shortly after each meeting, regardless of whether they are actually attending the next meeting. This is an easy way to ensure all members stay in the loop.

Example of Tool:

Below is a blank template for one of the set agendas used by the Boston P-3 team.

Date: MM/DD/YYYY	Participants:
Agenda	Set beforehand and send to all participants – including 5–7 minutes of connecting (either with a specific ice-breaker question or informal discussion)
Update on previous action items	Previous action items copied here, and progress is reported prior to the meeting

CASES DESCRIBING BROKERING TO STRENGTHEN PARTNERSHIPS

Date: MM/DD/YYYY	Participants:
Notes	Notes from the current meeting collected by one team member
Parking lot items	Items that are important for future agendas but not pertinent to this meeting or requiring an immediate next step
Action items	List of immediate "to-dos" for team members organized by each responsible member to be sent out via email after the meeting

Norms and Values. When RPPs form and sustain, RPP brokers work to establish norms and values earlier guide the social interaction among participants. Similar to the meeting routine described above in the Boston P-3 Partnership case, processes for establishing and using norms and values need to be intentional and revisited over time. We refer the reader to an additional case from Cambero, Zinger, and Kwun that was shared previously in Chapter 4, where the group describes their process for developing anti-racist focused research and practice around shared values.

Conferences and Events Design. One of the ways RPPs make their work visible to their members and others in their organizations is by hosting research conferences and large-scale events. These events involve intentional planning by brokers to make sure all the details are right. The brokers need event planning skills, as well as skills in architecting the social network of the event. Blekic and Thompson describe the design of their annual symposium for stakeholders in their partnership with Oregon Department of Education and Oregon State University.

ANNUAL SYMPOSIUM WITH STAKEHOLDERS: REFLECTING, CONNECTING, PLANNING

Oregon Department of Education and Oregon State University English Language Learner Partnership (ODE/OSU ELL Partnership)
Mirela Blekic and Karen Thompson

Annual research-practice partnership (RPP) gatherings are opportunities to reflect on the past year, meet with existing partners, create new connections, and consider plans for the future. These gatherings build a social infrastructure that brokers can leverage to support many different aspects of a partnership throughout the year.

Since its inception, the ODE/OSU ELL Partnership has held an annual partnership review meeting, open to a broad range of stakeholders and intended to set the direction for future work. The attendance at the meetings ranges from 30 to 40 participants and includes partnership members, other researchers and practitioners not regularly involved in the partnership, legislators, and community members. The half-day annual meetings are held in fall and include time for lunch and informal socializing, in addition to facilitated activities and discussions. While each annual meeting has a slightly different focus, every meeting follows a general agenda:

- brief overview of accomplishments and milestones of the partnership
- sharing of findings from partnership research (Partnership Research and Publications – Oregon State University, n.d.a)
- reflecting on ways partnership research has influenced policy and practice and discussing additional policy and practice implications (Ever EL Infographic – Oregon State University, n.d.b)
- consideration of future work and ways to collaborate
- reflection on the day's conversation and action steps each participant can take in their current roles

As part of the general agenda, partnership leaders facilitate a special session with topics ranging from an in-depth discussion of solving a problem of practice to a partnership visioning session. For example, one special session focused on research about multilingual students conducted by researchers in the region who were not involved in the partnership, covering topics such as American Indian and Alaska Native language learners, credit recovery for newcomer students, equity and the seal of biliteracy, and Latinx parent leadership. This special session helped sustain existing relationships and explore developing new ones, creating the possibility of developing a broader research coalition or network for future collaborations. It also reflected the partnership's effort to be mindful about what is being studied and how, who is missing from the conversations, and how the knowledge and evidence the partnership produces can support decision-making, all in the service of advancing equitable outcomes for English learners.

Each year, facilitators of the partnership review meeting conduct a short reflective evaluation of the event, which helps assess the day's learning and aids in planning future activities. When asked about their view of the partnership, these words emerged frequently in participants' responses: collaboration, learning, responsive, support, data, and evolving. In the words of one participant, "One of the key principles of a research-practitioner partnership is that the university does *not* bring the research expertise, and the schools/districts/state does *not* bring the practice expertise; but rather that both groups bring a range of both types of expertise. This RPP does a great job of embodying that principle."

This case demonstrates how annual review meetings can serve as a vehicle to build social structures and routines in a number of ways:

- **Facilitating relationship-building.** While participants consider priorities and needs of multiple stakeholders by engaging in the meeting, they build relationships with each other.
- **Building trust.** During the meeting, partners develop trust for their work together by having an opportunity to influence what is being studied.
- **Broadening participation and emphasizing equity.** The meeting allows participants to reflect on whose voices are missing in the research conversation and develop approaches to engage more stakeholders.
- **Connecting research to practice.** Partners reflect during the meeting on whether they are making a difference (2019 Symposium Policy Briefs – Oregon State University, n.d.c).

In addition, this case illustrates how sharing research findings and discussing implications for practice and policy can build individuals' skills and knowledge by:

- helping participants to increase individual and organizational capacity to transform the way partnerships conduct research
- improving the use of research results to inform policy and practice

Managing Internal and External Communications. A large portion of RPP brokers' role is managing internal communications for the RPP and external communications about the work of the RPP to the larger community. Here we describe five types of communication processes, from maintaining quarterly memos, to establishing a RPP newsletter, to having a communication strategy brief, to developing "no-surprises" research release processes, and to representing your partnership through visual communications.

In the first case, Dr. Callie Edwards from the Friday Institute explains her process for using quarterly memos as a way to maintain internal documentation of the communication across partners.

QUARTERLY RPP FACILITATION MEMOS

The Reedy Creek Magnet Middle School Center for the Digital Sciences/Friday Institute for Educational Innovation (RCMMS/FI) Research-Practice Partnership

Dr. Callie Edwards

With so many people, strategies, and activities involved, RPPs need a streamlined way to communicate progress and next steps. RPPs require social processes often guided by specific artifacts (e.g., briefs, memos, agenda) that help all people involved stay abreast of the RPP's developments.

When I joined the RCMMS/FI RPP, it had made great strides as an early stage partnership, but I noticed a need to document just-in-time updates, activities, and action items across research and practice partners. In an effort to cultivate consistent communication and collaboration across the RPP, I started writing detailed quarterly RPP facilitation memos to monitor work and share progress over time. I maintain a standard structure to the quarterly memos, with five fundamental sections:

- **Introduction.** A general overview of the contents of the memo.
- **Updates.** A high-level status update on the previous quarter's action items (i.e., are the items in progress or complete? Have the objectives shifted?)
- **RPP facilitation activities.** An in-depth discussion of what RPP facilitation activities were conducted each month. Some examples include:
  - coordinating and facilitating biweekly one-on-one meetings with specific partners (i.e., research team member, magnet coordinator), monthly meetings with research team, and biannual RPP leadership meetings with principal investigator, co-principal investigator, principal, and magnet coordinator
  - organizing and implementing the logistics for partnership events, such as teacher professional development sessions, conference presentations, and school open houses/magnet fairs

CASES DESCRIBING BROKERING TO STRENGTHEN PARTNERSHIPS

- surveying RPP partners, distilling data, and recommending decisions based on those data
- creating and revising scopes of work for every role in the RPP leadership team to enhance sustainability

- **Action items.** An identification of three to five action items slated for the next quarter.
- **Future considerations.** An exploration of any larger-scale implications for the partnership to consider moving forward.

My memos are typically between four and eight pages, and I include tables, hyperlinks, and bookmarks to make the page more engaging and accessible to the readers. Since implementation, the quarterly RPP facilitation memos have been highly praised by both the Friday Institute and Reedy Creek partners as an effective documentation strategy for tracking the partnership's progress over time and next steps. For example, in one email reply, Reedy Creek's principal commented,

> This is a great write up! Thank you for sharing and documenting the work that is being done. I have one request. Would you mind also sharing this document with my Area Superintendent? I would love for her to see all the work that has gone into our partnership and our plans for the future.

An additional benefit of the memos is that they showcase the often invisible but necessary work of relationship development, facilitation, and maintenance activities provided by the broker to the partnership. For instance, in another email, the project's principal investigator also commended my work, stating, "Thanks for the detailed memo of the team's activities with Reedy Creek. You've been busy!"

Moreover, the memos assist partners with completing mutually beneficial reporting requirements such as the researchers' funding agency end-of-year reports and practitioners' school and magnet award applications. This advantage was summarized succinctly in an email from the principal investigator as follows, "Thanks so much for putting this together. Among other things, these memos make our reporting to the National Science Foundation so much easier."

Simultaneously, Reedy Creek's magnet coordinator expressed, "By providing a timeline and specific examples, these memos help us to convey a clear picture of our RPP work for those seeking to understand the impact our partnership has on students and the school community."

Tips for making the most out of this tool:

- **During each quarter, maintain comprehensive notes of RPP meetings, activities, and decisions.** I do this by creating an RPP log, or a running table that delineates each RPP facilitation activity I engage in, the date/time for the activity, the participants involved in the activity, and any notes or links to supplemental documents.
- **Determine how you will send and save the memos.** I email my memos to the RPP leaders, including the research team's principal investigator, the school's principal, and the school's magnet coordinator as an FI Branded Google document. A FI Branded Google document is a bit more polished than a general Google document because it contains our organizational header, logo, and mission statement (see Appendix N for the template), yet retains the versatile functionality of Google. For example, this type of document allows the recipients to make comments if necessary, which would not be possible if the document was a PDF. The memos are also saved in a shared Google drive, enabling team members to access them throughout the year.
- **Use the quarterly time frame as a guide, not a mandate.** While I have typically sent memos at the end of quarter, due to the rapid changes associated with COVID-19/remote learning, in 2020 I also began developing interim memos to promptly share updates between quarterly memos. These interim memos included just two sections: 1) background/purpose, and 2) updates.

Another case describing internal communications is Erin Baumgartner and Christy Dafonte's approach to using a newsletter to communicate across their teams in the HERC at Rice University and the HISD.

SUPPORTING COMMUNICATION ABOUT THE PARTNERSHIP WITH A NEWSLETTER

Houston Education Research Consortium-Houston Independent School District (HERC-HISD)
Erin Baumgartner and Christy Dafonte

Building channels of communication can be difficult when research-practice partnerships (RPPs) engage directly with many departments and individuals across a district. Partnerships may use a newsletter as a tool for regularly communicating partnership activities and the research produced by the partnership to a variety of partners across the school district.

Throughout the ten-year history of the partnership between HERC and HISD, we have always felt the need to improve communication. Each year, in hindsight and experience, we recognize new opportunities to grow our relationship and connections. Our bimonthly newsletter allows us to share our work widely across the district and to deepen those connections.

The primary goal of creating the newsletter is to ensure HISD departments that are not actively involved in a particular project have an idea of the research occurring in other areas within the district. It's quite common that a department could benefit from the findings of a study but were not the primary department with whom the study was developed, and the newsletter allows us to narrow those communication gaps.

As seen in the sample newsletter in Figure 6.5, we highlight updates or statuses on many of the projects we have going on and share information about upcoming findings meetings on projects (in case folks in other departments are interested in joining), a reminder of contact information for the internal liaison to HERC, other upcoming events/talks, and summaries of/links to recently published HERC research briefs.

The feedback we have received on this newsletter from departments across the district has been largely positive. For example, we have seen occasions where individuals who weren't directly involved in a project request to be invited to a meeting where HERC is sharing out findings, because they see the potential for the research to help their departments as well.

Brokers can develop newsletters for their RPPs for numerous reasons. While everyone's context and rationale for creating a newsletter may be different, we have produced some tips for creating a newsletter we thinking may be more universal in nature and hopefully helpful for other RPP brokers:

- Identify the purpose: For our partnership, our purpose is to expand the number of departments across the district who know what types of HERC research projects are currently in progress.
- Determine the right cadence: At first, we started trying to do monthly newsletters, but realized the lift was too heavy and sometimes there weren't many changes in project statuses to justify doing it that frequently and switched to every other month.

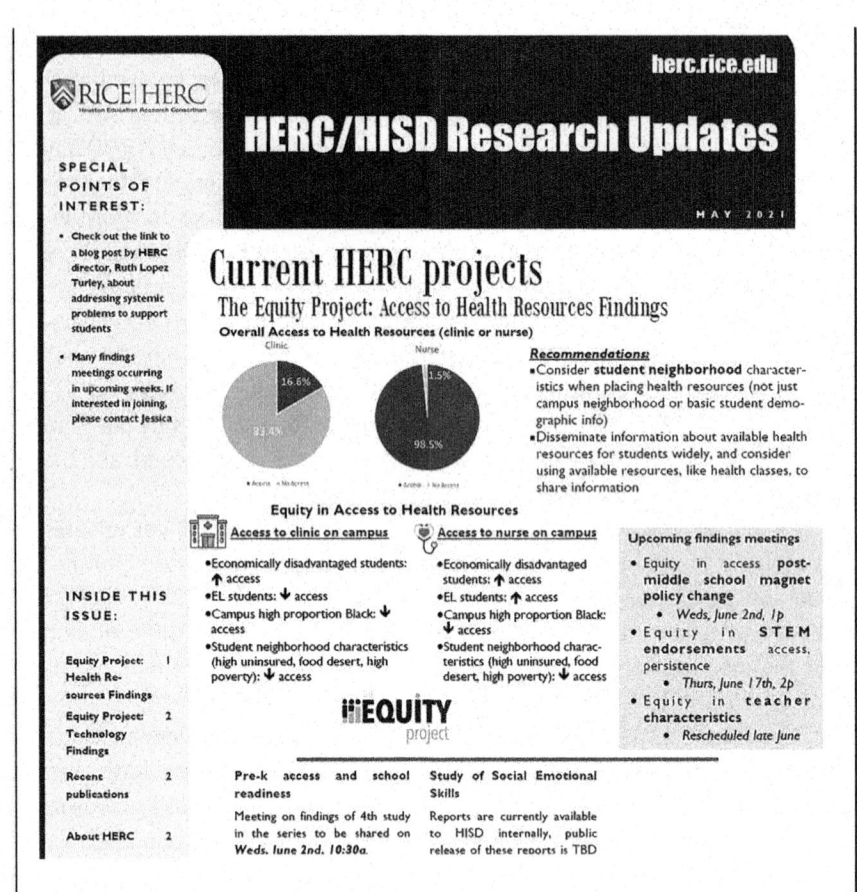

CASES DESCRIBING BROKERING TO STRENGTHEN PARTNERSHIPS

Figure 6.5 Example of Newsletter

- Choose a primary author: In the HERC/HISD instance, the associate director for HISD research at HERC creates the first draft of the newsletter, then shares it with the HISD liaison. Before writing the draft, we often discuss what content might be helpful to include for the upcoming newsletter. A week or two before distribution, the HERC associate director and HISD liaison meet to review and make any last-minute changes to the content.
- Select your audience: We want this newsletter to reach across departments at the school district, from the superintendent's office to specific programmatic departments. Our internal liaison has built a large mailing list of people we have worked with over the years and updates it frequently.

- Keep it short: As you can see in the example document, our newsletter is only a one-page, two-sided document. This is very intentional. We want to increase the chances that someone will take the time to glance at it without it feeling like a burden. A few strategies for creating a streamlined newsletter include using bulleted lists rather than paragraphs to increase the likelihood of the recipients reading everything, ensuring font size is appropriate to facilitate easy reading, and embedding text hyperlinks to additional resources or copies of full reports. If you are decreasing font size to accommodate the wording, then you are using too many words.
- Keep it visually interesting: Colorful pictures, logos, and other images are good ways to help draw the eye and bring attention to any major topics or deadlines more effectively than simple text and font changes.
- Dates are important: Make sure to include dates for any upcoming events, meetings, or presentations, or releases of results. If dates cannot be shared with the general audience, then provide the contact information for the person who can answer any additional questions.

On the external communications side, we offer three useful cases that demonstrate how brokers do this work. First, Beth Vaade, Brianne Monahan, and Amanda Kruger from the MEP describe the "no-surprises" research release process they developed, based off of the UChicago Consortium on School Research who originated the practice (Roderick et al., 2009).

A "NO-SURPRISES" RESEARCH RELEASE PROCESS

Madison Education Partnership
Beth Vaade, Brianne Monahan, and Amanda Kruger

Releasing research briefs and findings is a critical process that communicates findings to a broader audience and exhibits trust between partners. A major goal of a partnership is having all research conducted being published to support accessibility of the findings and legitimacy of the partnership. How do partnerships ensure all research will see the light of day while maintaining trust in the relationship?

The Madison Education Partnership (MEP) has brought the Madison Metropolitan School District (MMSD) and the WCER at the University

of Wisconsin–Madison together in a research-practice partnership since 2016. As an established RPP, MEP had a research release process since its inception, formally written into our memorandum of agreement, and used it for over 20 research briefs, memos, and summaries.
What does this tool do:

> To facilitate trust and transparency, we created a "no-surprises" research release process. We articulated the groups that must review publications prior to release, making sure to include reviewers from both sides of the partnership along the way. In the last two years, the project manager and MMSD co-director have modified this process (see Figure 6.6) to add in explicit steps for 1) giving research participants a chance to provide comments and feedback on draft publications and 2) providing research findings to internal audiences in MMSD – such as principals, central office leaders, school staff and the Board of Education – prior to public release.

How do we use it:

> MEP implements this research release process by designating specific roles to MEP staff, MMSD R&I, and other MMSD and WCER staff:

- The MEP project manager oversees the entire release process, coordinating changes to research products, ensuring we hit our deadlines, and posting the public releases. She also leads on communication with MEP Co-Directors, MEP Steering Committee, MMSD Superintendent, WCER Director, and WCER Communications.
- The MEP Co-Director and MMSD Executive Director of R&I, or MMSD Research Director, coordinate with the MMSD Communications Office prior to release and share embargoed research releases with the MMSD community via standard internal district communications (e.g., weekly administrators bulletin, weekly Board of Education update, biweekly staff newsletter). They also send targeted emails to specific district leaders and coordinate with the MMSD Communications Office about the communications of the research findings.
- Our MMSD content leads (e.g., leaders like the Director of Early Learning) share embargoed and recently released research with

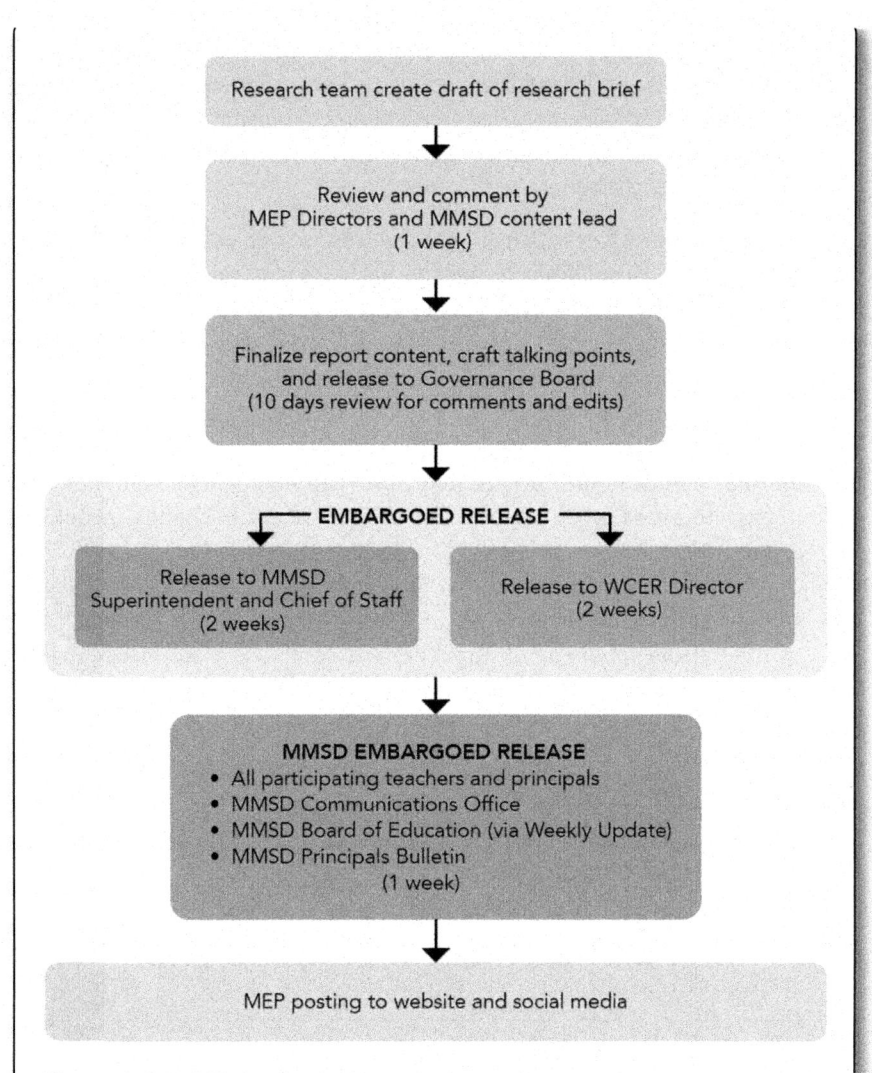

Figure 6.6 MEP's brief release process revised

principals, teachers, and other key stakeholders via their communication channels (e.g., monthly newsletters, monthly professional development sessions).

Throughout the process, these MEP and MMSD members draft and edit release language, share feedback received, and provide updates on when communication has gone out. This consistent communication – mostly via email – helps ensure coordination across releases.

Tips for making the most of this tool:

- Co-create your process before you have research to release. MEP Co-Directors built the initial process in early 2016, prior to having any research findings to release. Building this process together, prior to releasing any publication, helped us identify priorities.
- Revisit the process often. Processes need to change as organizations shift and change to better fit the goals of releasing research.
- Visualize your process. We have found that having a one-page visual that describes the various steps has reduced confusion and made it easy to share what happens in advance as staff change in both organizations.
- Clearly designate roles and communicate your progress. Assigning specific staff members to types of tasks in the release process helps us plan ahead for the work to come, and communicating throughout allows us to coordinate our work along the way.

In the second case, Lisa Sall from the University of Chicago Consortium on School Research shares how she worked with the Latino Policy Forum in Chicago to develop strategies for sharing research from the Consortium. This case illustrates how and why RPP brokers may need to work beyond the main membership of their RPP to support the external communication of their work.

COMMUNICATIONS STRATEGY BRIEF

University of Chicago Consortium on School Research – Latino Policy Forum
Lisa Sall

Researchers, practitioners, and policymakers establish partnerships to ensure educational leaders have practical and useful information to make decisions. Yet, what communications strategies do partnerships use to ensure that educational leaders and stakeholders use research in their decision-making? In short, multiple partners must align on communications goals, audiences, audience motivations, key messages, barriers, etc. One example of a tool used by a partnership to achieve such alignment is a communications strategy brief.

The UChicago Consortium on School Research (the Consortium) and the Latino Policy Forum (the Forum) have partnered together for several years on research analyzing the academic experiences and outcomes of English learners in CPS. Both organizations bring a unique set of skills and perspectives to the research process and the dissemination of findings. The Consortium conducts rigorous research to inform and assess education policy and practice but does not advocate for particular policies or programs. As an advocacy organization, the Forum catalyzes policy change to build a foundation of equity, justice, and economic prosperity for the Latino community, including policies that strengthen bilingual education for English learners. Both partners have expertise in and resources for the communication and dissemination of research findings.

The goal of developing a communication strategy brief was to help the Consortium and the Forum align on a communications plan to reach multiple audiences in both English and Spanish. The first step towards developing a communications strategy brief was a group meeting between researchers and communications staff that began with attendees sharing ideas on high-level questions that raise issues of importance to both organizations. These guiding questions for the strategy brief also helped meeting attendees take a step back from the complex details of the research and become grounded in the problem we were initially trying to solve, our audiences and their motivators, and the single most important message we wanted the audience to take away. As described in the tips that follow, I used creative facilitation and processes to gather as many ideas as possible to include in the communication strategy.

Following the brainstorm meeting, as the communications team lead, I compiled the ideas into the communications strategy brief and shared it with all meeting participants. Participants made edits or signed off on the contents of the strategy brief. The next step was the development of a more detailed communications plan, but this initial brief helped align both organizations on the big picture before planning more detailed communications and outreach efforts.

Tips for making the most of this tool:

- Gather partners involved in research and communications together to brainstorm questions for the strategy brief.
- Provide all participants with sticky notes and markers. Ask them to put one idea per sticky note.
- Ask participants to get up and post their ideas on the wall. Encourage them to read one another's ideas and group similar thoughts and ideas into common themes.
- Work through the questions and discuss as a group rather than ask individuals to complete the brief template and share out. Discussing the questions leads to responses that are conversational and easier to understand compared to written responses that tend to be more formal.
- Press participants to come up with ONE single most important takeaway from the research. This can be challenging, but groups will generally reach consensus.
- Discuss and include how the role of each partner will be positioned in external communications, such as media releases, websites, and presentations.
- See Appendix O for a brief template used as a model for how to organize this work.

ASSESSING AND CONTINUOUSLY IMPROVING THE PARTNERSHIP

Another key role for brokers is continuous improvement and assessment work, which often goes neglected if it isn't intentionally included in someone's portfolio of work. Brokers can design accountability systems, feedback loops, and reflection processes that allow the partnership to identify what it has done well and where it still needs to grow.

Dan Gallagher from Shoreline Public Schools and Bill Penuel from the University of Colorado, who wrote a book titled *Creating Research-Practice Partnerships* in 2017, also created a qualitative rubric to help their partnership assess itself on the strength of its processes and the impact of its work. The ensuing discussions helped members come to consensus on its current status and identify priorities for future collaborative work.

ARE WE A PARTNERSHIP YET? (DIAGNOSTIC RUBRIC)

Critical CS Ed and CS for All: RPP Applicants
Bill Penuel and Dan Gallagher

Effective partnerships do not just happen naturally, but they flourish when partners attend to specific dimensions of effectiveness identified by Erin Henrick, Paul Cobb, Bill Penuel, Kara Jackson, and Tiffany Clark (Henrick et al., 2017). Those dimensions are:

(1) building trust and cultivating partnership relationships
(2) conducting rigorous research to inform action
(3) supporting the partner practice organization in achieving its goals
(4) producing knowledge that can inform educational improvement efforts more broadly
(5) building the capacity of participating researchers, practitioners, practice organizations, and research organizations to engage in partnership work

Using a qualitative rubric based on this framework (Penuel & Gallagher, n.d.; Penuel & Gallagher, 2017), partnership leaders can identify areas for improvement and areas of strength as a partnership. Critical CS Education (2022), a new partnership, has used such a rubric to discuss their partnership's development. The same rubric was used in workshops designed to help prepare applicants to the National Science Foundation's (NSF's) original Computer Science for All: RPP (National Science Foundation, n.d.) competition to describe their partnerships-in-development and create evaluation plans for them.

In Critical CS Ed, the University of Washington and Shoreline and Highline Public Schools recently formed a partnership to prepare justice-focused computer science teachers. After six months, Dan Gallagher from Shoreline Public Schools led a brief partnership check-in activity during a weekly meeting. He shared the rubric with a bit of background before each person responded independently on a survey. Dan then facilitated a discussion on each dimension with particular attention to items that elicited different responses between the partners. Because the partnership is in its early stages, consensus was high – a good sign! – and the group appreciated how the rubric called attention to things that might cause trouble later if neglected now. For example, they are busy developing products for implementation but were reminded of the need to embed plans for research and data use that will drive improvements in their work. Dan will lead a similar partnership check-in six months later, and as the partnership evolves, a shift to more detailed rubrics will become more useful.

Dan's example builds from an earlier use of the rubric in a workshop series for applicants to the NSF's CS for All: RPP competition. Many of the applicants for that competition were new to research-practice partnership work, so the workshops were intended to provide teams of educators and researchers an opportunity to come together to learn about research-practice partnerships (RPPs) and develop common aim statements to guide their proposals. Some teams had already been working together for some time, but not necessarily as an RPP. In a workshop for those teams, Bill Penuel led participants in an activity of looking at the rubric together as a team. Teams quickly discovered that they had different ideas about where they fell on specific dimensions of RPP effectiveness. And in some cases, they agreed on where to place their RPP, but the RPP was judged to be more "early phase" in one dimension and "middle phase" in another dimension. Participants said engaging with the tool helped them to understand better just where they could improve, and a number used the tool to inform the development of their evaluation plans.

Tips for making the most of this tool:

- Use the rubric to prompt discussions about each dimension. Increasing awareness and making sense of these dimensions is just as important as identifying where you think your partnership lands on a continuum.
- Provide a method for each person to respond individually either to a survey or in writing before a group discussion, which will help you identify differences in perspectives and elevate individual voices.
- Look for differences in responses between different roles within a partner institution, not just between partner institutions. Leaders and people closer to different aspects of the work may respond differently.
- Welcome – even celebrate – when responses differ or you find you are not as far along in a dimension compared to others. The purpose is to identify areas for the partners to work on together.

Similarly, Kelly McMahon, Jon Norman, and Dave Sherer, from the Carnegie Foundation for the Advancement of Teaching describe a reflective activity that involves interviewing RPP participants that they worked on to help the Hewlett Foundation's Deeper Learning + Diffusion of Innovation and Scaled Impact RPPs (please see tool in Chapter 4).

NOTES

1. The Youth Data Archive is a research collaborative among youth serving organizations in five California counties, including school districts, county agencies, and non-profit community-based organizations managed by the John W. Gardner Center for Youth and Their Communities at Stanford University. See McLaughlin, M., & London, R. A. (Eds.). (2013). *From data to action: A community approach to improving youth outcomes*. Harvard Education Press.

2. For reference, please review the Code of Ethics for educational researchers adopted by the American Educational Research Association (AERA) in February 2011 (American Educational Research Association, 2011).

REFERENCES

American Education Research Association. (2011). *Code of ethics*. www.aera.net/Portals/38/docs/About_AERA/CodeOfEthics(1).pdf

Critical CS Education. (2022). https://criticalcsed.org

Farrell, C. C., Penuel, W. R., Allen, A., Anderson, E. R., Bohannon, B. X., Coburn, C., & Brown, S. L. (2022). Learning at the boundaries of research and practice: A framework for understanding research – practice partnerships. *Educational Researcher, 51*(3), 197–208.

Henrick, E. C., Cobb, P., Penuel, W. R., Jackson, K., & Clark, T. (2017). *Assessing research-practice partnerships: Five dimensions of effectiveness*. William T. Grant Foundation.

McLaughlin, M., & London, R. A. (Eds.). (2013). *From data to action: A community approach to improving youth outcomes*. Harvard Education Press.

Penuel, W. R., Allen, A. R., Coburn, C. E., & Farrell, C. (2015). Conceptualizing research – practice partnerships as joint work at boundaries. *Journal of Education for Students Placed at Risk, 20*(1), 182–197.

Penuel, W. R., & Gallagher, D. (n.d.). *Diagnostic rubric: Are we a partnership yet?* http://learndbir.org/uploads/Resources/Diagnostic-Tool-Are-We-a-Partnership-Yet.pdf

Penuel, W. R., & Gallagher, D. (2017). *Creating research-practice partnerships*. Harvard Education Press.

Roderick, M., Easton, J., & Sebring, P. (2009). *The consortium on Chicago school research: A new model for the role of research in supporting urban school reform*. Consortium on Chicago School Research.

Science Foundation. (n.d.). *Computer science for all (CSforall: RPP)*. Researcher Practitioner Partnerships. www.nsf.gov/pubs/2018/nsf18537/nsf18537.htm

Chapter 7

Using Cases to Support RPP Broker Work and Development

We have been practicing, researching, and teaching about RPPs and knowledge brokering our entire careers. When the first version of the RPP Brokers Handbook was published on the NNERPP website, we immediately started to think about how to *use* the cases presented within. There are now two editions of the RPP Brokers Handbook, containing 59 cases that pull back the curtain on how brokers support the development of long-term formalized collaborations between researchers and education practitioners to tackle problems of practice. They show, rather than tell, how to do this essential work, so they can help RPP practitioners at all stages of development learn how to do brokering work better and avoid learning things the hard way. At that point, we realized that the cases in this handbook could be used by several audiences in different ways.

This handbook has primarily been developed by NNERPP as a resource for individuals who want to or are engaging in brokering activities within education research-practice partnerships. This may include individuals who serve in formal RPP brokering positions or partners who are engaging in informal knowledge brokering as a part of their larger role (e.g., as a researcher or educator). In addition, the handbook may prove useful to the growing number of university instructors, faculty, and students who are teaching and learning about brokering within education contexts. Furthermore, the handbook may also prove useful to researchers who are studying knowledge brokering as a concept or those researchers who are working with education partners to develop a research-practice partnership and seeking to embed brokering roles into the partnership's architecture to facilitate collaboration and co-engagement. Finally, we see a growing number of non-profit organizations, state or school district departments, and university centers that bring on new staff using the handbook to train these staff on how to engage in RPPs. Within this context, the handbook is designed to serve a number of purposes:

- to introduce a number of techniques for brokering in education research-practice partnerships
- to serve as a guide for the creation of courses, professional development workshops, and other capacity-building activities, in which an experiential model of learning is employed
- to serve as a self-learning guide to avoid roadblocks and frustrations that can occur when "learning on the job"

To provide a deeper understanding of how these cases can be used in different ways, we present three scenarios in which the first iteration of the RPP Brokers Handbook (available at nnerpp.rice.edu) has been used by various actors.

IN A COURSE...

One of the authors of this book, Conaway, has used the Broker's Handbook in her course, Making Data Count, which is geared towards Master of Education students at the Harvard Graduate School of Education. Throughout the course students think about data and research use through the lens of a teaching case about a research project by Castleman and Page on summer melt, conducted in the Fulton County Schools (Jenkins et al., 2012). During one lesson, students consider arguments about why Fulton County might want to invest in an RPP versus an internal research director. Students debate about the appropriate approach, and after which, students hear directly from the case protagonist what actually happened (as it turns out, they did a bit of both). After hearing from the case protagonist, Conaway draws attention to the fact that no matter which strategy Fulton County Schools chooses, someone has to do the work of building the relationships and capacity for the district to benefit from research. This is where the brokering handbook comes in. Students are asked to read the framing part of the handbook (Chapter 3) plus a few selected cases, which they draw on to discuss the following prompt:

- Let's suppose Fulton County Schools hires you as the research director – a role that requires you to act as a broker between researchers/analysts and program staff to infuse more research into the decision-making process. One task will be to continue to build the research partnership with Castleman and Page. What would you do in the first 90 days to get off to a strong start as a broker and set yourself up for long-run success?

Conaway's discussion prompts connections back to the framework, asking students to think about what they'd need to do to strengthen individual partners versus strengthening the partnership. The cases used by Conaway include

"Agenda for a first date," "Mini-coaching over time," "Sustaining through central office churn," and "Structure for engaging partners in research development."

COACHING...

As part of a recent grant, NNERPP has developed a year-long coaching program to deepen the capacity of central office administrators who work as brokers in school districts to translate research evidence into practice. Throughout the year-long program, participants take part in two two-day workshops (fall 2021 and spring 2022) that focus on building participants' skills and knowledge related to brokering in an RPP as defined by the RPP Brokers framework. During the fall workshop, participants were asked to develop individualized goals and plans of action to reach their desired outcomes.

In addition to attending these workshops, participants took part in three one-on-one coaching sessions with an experienced broker throughout the 2021/2022 school year to help participants work towards their goals. In between coaching sessions, coaches asked participants to read the handbook and to think about how they could apply aspects of the framework to improve their own work as an RPP broker. Participants would read the sections of the handbook that align to the goals and action plans they developed. During the coaching sessions, the participants would have conversations with their coach about the framework and how the participant is using the handbook and its materials to work towards their goals.

ONBOARDING RESOURCE...

In preparation for writing this book, we reached out to members of our network to inquire if and how they used earlier iterations of the handbook in their own local contexts. In discussions with one individual, we learned that they recently transitioned into a position that requires engaging in extensive brokering activities and having previously worked in positions that focused more on research and analysis, they used the RPP Brokers Handbook as an onboarding resource to fill knowledge gaps.

> I think the main benefit of having access to the handbook has been that it provides a really useful framework to think intentionally about how I want to approach my role. The handbook has helped me set the right mindset and transition into this new position.

They explained that they treated reading the handbook "like a grad school reading assignment," reading each section of the handbook, and highlighting and summarizing important concepts from the handbook. They then use these notes to self-assess their work.

USING CASES TO SUPPORT RPP BROKER WORK AND DEVELOPMENT

In addition to using the handbook to fill knowledge gaps, they remarked that reading the cases have shown them that they are part of a much larger community of individuals who are engaging in similar work.

> The cases have also been helpful reminders that there's a community of people doing this type of work, who are willing to share their knowledge and resources so that people that are newer to this work like I am, don't have to start from scratch. I work in a small department and sometimes it can become isolating if you're the one person or one of two people in an organization that are focused on this kind of thing. So being able to see examples of other people that have tried and failed, tried and succeeded, and done similar types of work in similar contexts is a nice feeling. It's not just me, in my day-to-day work, trying to make these research partnerships successful and impactful, other people are also working on the same thing.

Finally, they report that they have bookmarked specific tools relating to how to create meeting agendas (Tool: Agenda for a "First Date" Meeting Between a Researcher and Practitioner in Chapter 3), memos (Tool: Quarterly RPP Facilitation Memos in Chapter 6), policy briefs (Tool: An Initial Interview Guide for Writing Policy Briefs in Chapter 5), and DUAs (Tool: DUAs in Chapter 6) for future use and plan to continue using the handbook as guidance, particularly where the handbook provides examples that are similar to circumstances at their institution.

Brokers Uses and Adapting Tools and Cases in Their Practice

The cases in the RPP Brokers Handbook present some initial documentation of tools and models of practice for brokers working in the field to use in their everyday practice. The cases are only the beginning of what is possible for documenting the moves, actions, activities that brokers make to support RPP work. The cases are meant to be a starting point and will hopefully be used across different contexts of RPPs. Consequently, the tools and models of practice will likely need to be adapted to the characteristics unique to the RPP broker. Here we present a case of how an RPP broker used the existing cases in their own work. And we present one case where the tools were adapted to unique characteristics of the RPP context.

RPP Brokers Use of a Case

When the Stanford–Sequoia K–12 Research Collaborative was getting started in 2016, the design of the RPP was built off of the lessons learned from Stanford University Graduate School of Education and California Education Partners leaders work to build the Stanford–SFUSD Partnership. They used Jorge Ruiz de

Velasco's work on DUAs, described in the case documented in the case titled "Data Use Agreements" in Chapter 5. Ruiz de Velasco's case provides some essential tips for any brokers helping their RPP develop a DUA. The case asks questions like which research projects require DUAs and who owns the data. It also suggests providing ongoing training, periodic alignment of DUA language, and use of a DUA template that can be adapted for each project.

In the case of the Stanford–Sequoia Collaborative, the data use agreements were designed based on the DUA template that Ruiz de Velasco offers in his case. The template was originally conceptualized when the John W. Gardner Center was developing its Youth Data Archive. It was subsequently used as a template to develop a DUA template for the Stanford–SFUSD Partnership projects. It was also used to design a data warehousing agreement between Stanford University and SFUSD, so Stanford projects could more easily access SFUSD administrative data (Kim et al., 2020). In the Stanford–Sequoia Collaborative, the DUA template was used to develop individual DUAs with each of the nine school districts in the RPP.

As described in Wentworth et al. (2021), to take the lessons learned from the Stanford–SFUSD Partnership and apply them to the Stanford–Sequoia Collaborative, the RPP leaders had to rely on brokers to maintain relationships across the Stanford researchers and the nine districts. The use of RPP brokers' experience provided the possibility of taking advantage of characteristics of the Stanford–SFUSD Partnership, like the use of Ruiz de Velasco's DUA template from the work of the Youth Data Archive. Additionally, given the district partners' capacities in the Stanford–Sequoia Collaborative, like some district prior RPP work with the John W. Gardner Center prior to forming the Collaborative, some districts were familiar with establishing data use agreement with the Gardner Center through the Youth Data Archive and the language within the DUA template. Generally, the use of Ruiz de Velasco's DUA template allowed the Stanford–Sequoia K–12 Research Collaborative to take advantage of the prior knowledge shared in the case to accelerate formation of data agreements, and ultimately data access, research production, and ultimately use of the research produced by district leaders.

RPP Brokers Adapting a Case

During the development of these cases within the National Network of Education Research Practice Partnerships, one team of RPP brokers adapted one of the original cases written by Wentworth titled, "Agenda for a 'First Date' Meeting Between a Researcher and Practitioner." It was Vaade, Monahan, and Kruger from the MEP who repurposed and consequently adapted the "first date" agenda in the case titled, " 'First Date' Meeting Agenda to Build Community & Find Common Ground." The MEP team wrote the case in hopes of restarting the relationship between RPP brokers managing MEP and the MMSD IRE

Department. According to the case by Vaade, Monahan, and Kruger, "MEP team members felt it difficult to engage IRE team members in their projects, and IRE team members felt as if they didn't always fit in with academics and that their contributions were not needed or appreciated." The MEP team used Wentworth's agenda in the "First Date" case as a template for helping them develop an agenda for finding more common ground between the MEP and the school district IRE team.

What did the MEP team adapt to the "First Date" case? First, they integrated in pre-work, which prepared the MEP and IRE for the meeting. This allowed each team to have some common understanding of the content of the meeting in preparation for finding ways to improve their collaboration. Then, they integrated the review of their existing norms in the beginning of the agenda, as in this case, this meeting was with people who had worked together before, and the Wentworth "First Date" Agenda is with individuals who have not worked together before. Finally, the MEP team used additional facilitation tools like a Venn Diagram to help the two teams find where they could best collaborate.

This adaptation of one of the RPP Brokering cases to fit the needs of another RPP context and current need demonstrates the possibility of these cases of RPP brokering. To borrow from Paul Cobb at Vanderbilt University, RPP brokers could think of these cases as sacrificial offerings. The cases are meant to be used in whichever way possible to support the work of an RPP. If need be, the cases can and should be adapted to the needs of each RPP.

CONCLUSION

The RPP Brokers Handbook can be (and has been!) used in a number of different ways. And by no means are these the only ways in which the handbook can be used — its uses are only limited by your imagination! The handbook and its cases are intended to provide a bridge between broad, high-level overviews of brokering and explicit, detailed guidelines applicable to the needs of specific brokers. Ideally, the handbook should be used to help focus thoughts, increase overall understanding, promote professional development, and act as a catalyst for further action. The handbook is intended for a wide and diverse audience, from those who are only beginning to consider brokering as a career path to practitioners who have already accumulated considerable theoretical and/or practical experience.

REFERENCES

Jenkins, L., Wisdom, M., & Glover, S. (2012). *Increasing college-going rates in Fulton county schools: A summer intervention based on the strategic use of data*. Harvard Education Press.

Kim, M., Shen, J., Wentworth, L., Ming, N., Reininger, M., & Bettinger., E. (2020). The Stanford–SFUSD partnership: Development of data-sharing structures and processes. In S. Cole, I. Dhaliwal, A. Sautmann, & L. Vilhuber (Eds.), *Handbook on using administrative data for and evidence-based policy*. Retrieved October 12, 2022, from https://admindatahandbook.mit.edu/book/v1.0-rc3/sfusd.html

Wentworth, L., Khanna, R., Nayfack, M., & Schwartz, D. (2021). Closing the research-practice gap education. *Stanford Social Innovation Review*, 57–58.

Chapter 8

The Future of Brokering in Research-Practice Partnerships

As we turn towards the last chapter of the book, we take a moment to reflect back on how we got here. One of the first versions of the RPP Brokers Framework contained a seventh dimension that ultimately did not make it into this current version. We called it "blending in," in an effort to capture the idea that part of an RPP broker's work should involve "blending in" to the ecosystems of the partnership member organizations, allowing them to move fluidly between "we the researchers" and "we the practitioners." We abandoned this feature of the framework because we felt it downplayed the explicit work RPP brokers do to create the conditions for meaningful partnership across participating individuals and organizations.

And yet, as we ponder what the future of RPP brokering might look like, we find ourselves returning to this idea of "blending in," albeit with a slightly different take. In our original conception of this aspect of brokering, we imagined only the broker themself shifting their role and identity to blend in with the various organizations taking part in the partnership. This "shape shifting" nature of the broker, we posited, would likely help them reduce the individual and organizational boundaries defining those in the RPP, which would, in turn, help create the conditions for meaningful "joint work" (Farrell et al., 2021).

What we have come to realize, however, is that RPP brokering is not something that just one person – i.e., the designated RPP broker – does in a partnership. In fact, if we were to imagine what an ideal research-practice partnership might look like, especially in terms of brokering, we might expect to see a *constellation* of RPP brokers representing any multitude of engaged organizations, all working collaboratively towards a common education goal. Getting to this scenario would involve the creation of opportunities so that all partnership members could develop their brokering skills. This is where the designated RPP broker would come back in – their role would be to build the skills and knowledge of others in the RPP to broker their own relationships, so that *they too* can "blend in" as they cross institutional boundaries. These efforts, we think, would strengthen

DOI: 10.4324/9781003334385-8 **179**
This chapter has been made available under a CC-BY-NC-ND license.

the foundational network of relational trust across members of the RPP, which ultimately would result in changes to and redesigning of relationships, systems, and institutional structures needed to support partnership research. In short, the more partnership members that know how to "blend in" across boundaries, the stronger the RPP.

Thus, as we imagine the future of RPP brokering, we argue that brokering should grow into an essential activity that all members of an RPP must be able to do or develop over time, to varying degrees depending on their roles in the partnership. The health of the RPP might even be judged by how many RPP members demonstrate brokering moves and how many brokering activities are happening across the RPP, for example. If we connect back to the Henrick et al. (2017) RPP effectiveness framework, a related hypothesis might be that the effectiveness of an RPP will be strongly correlated with the brokering skills and knowledge developed across RPP members. More recent research has additionally suggested that if we are to imagine transformative work in the field of education research, it will require partners to engage in boundary spanning efforts that will allow them to work at and across the boundaries of their roles and institutions (Farrell et al., 2021; see Penuel et al., 2015 for original thesis).

Based on these ideas, we explore three claims related to the argument that all RPP participants should develop brokering proficiency over time as a mechanism for strengthening the RPP itself over time.

BROKERING AIMS TO CHANGE THE STATUS QUO BEHAVIORS AND SYSTEMS OF INDIVIDUALS AND INSTITUTIONS

RPPs require robust brokering because they are ambitious: they aim to transform not just individuals, but organizations and systems as well. Farrell and colleagues (2021) describe RPPs' intended aims as supporting educational improvement and transformation. Other traditions associated with RPPs and collaborative education research talk about RPPs working to break down status quo ways of working together. For example, Penuel and colleagues (2011) described one of the four principles of design-based implementation research (DBIR) as "developing capacity for sustaining change in systems" (p. 332). Similarly, Roderick and colleagues describe how their formation of a research alliance in Chicago required an approach they describe as "conducting research to build capacity" (p. 3). In essence, the University of Chicago researchers changed their behaviors as well as the practices within their research institutions through "a specific set of organizational arrangements that allow [them] to establish coherence across studies, seek broad stakeholder engagement, and make findings accessible" (p. 1). They argue these changes allow them as researchers to work with educators and policymakers to help them manage "decentralized decision-making and school improvement efforts" (p. 1).

As some of these examples suggest, this work is hard – and it falls most heavily on the designated broker. We would bet that most RPP participants engaged in brokering will describe the behaviors as taxing and at times emotionally draining, especially when encountering resistance to change. For example, it sounds simple to co-develop research questions in an RPP by finding common ground between the participants. Yet, co-developing involves working against the incentives of each participant's roles and institutions. Researchers need to answer questions that have the potential to advance theory; education system leaders need to negotiate with a complex array of stakeholders to move systems forward; teachers need to teach to specific standards or curriculum; and students need to pass milestones like completing courses for graduation. By choosing to work together, RPP members need to *broker their way* through co-development by explaining and hearing each other's interests, negotiating common ground, and synthesizing ideas into a manageable set of questions. By answering specific questions that go outside the bounds of their day-to-day work, RPP members will need to try new practices in their classrooms, document new research methodologies during the IRB review at their university, renegotiate the scope of work within a grant award from a funder, and so on.

Consequently, RPP brokering needs to help participants develop the necessary relationships to work together, while also prepare them to support work that requires them to change the systems and structures in their organizations. These individual relationships and changes in behavior are the beginning foundation for larger-scale changes in system-level practices: how a university establishes an agreement with a school district, how a school district shares data with a university, how research produced by universities gets used in policy or practice decisions within a school district, etc. RPP brokering embodies behaviors that work against the traditional means of conducting research or teaching in classrooms. Brokering moves aim to fundamentally change how the individuals and institutions in the research, practice, and community – students, teachers, schools, universities, non-profits, research institutes, professional associations, student unions, policymakers, and others – work together as a means to change undesirable and unjust outcomes in education. As RPPs develop, the types of brokering activities necessary to support the development of the partnership may also change over time.

Because RPP brokering is intended to build capacity to support large-scale systems changes at multiple levels in order to upend the status quo relationships between researchers and community members and the status quo systems producing outcomes where some students and families experience more opportunities and resources than others, we think the more brokers there are working within an RPP, the better.

181

BROKERING ACTIVITIES EXPAND AND SPREAD TO ALL MEMBERS AS AN RPP DEVELOPS

As we've suggested, to achieve the ambitious tenets of an RPP, all RPP participants eventually need to be able to broker (to a certain extent). The need for brokering activities in an RPP changes based on the partnership's developmental trajectory, with the brokering activities being spread across more people as participants learn activities that strengthen their partnering and partnerships.

We have had first-hand experience with this idea. For example, one co-author, Wentworth, started documenting the moves of RPP participants in meetings to demonstrate how brokering moves spread (Kipnis et al., 2020). Wentworth and colleagues collected participant observation data across 83 meetings in two years, from two different partnerships, and noticed an important pattern. In the older of the two RPPs in their sample, the RPP broker spent more time working with the researchers and practitioners to solve problems in the RPP while the research was underway, whereas in the younger RPP, the RPP brokers spent more time working with researchers and practitioners while the research was in development with partners. Also, in the older RPP, the brokers did less facilitation of meetings as the other researchers and practitioners in the RPP took on this role, whereas in the younger RPP, the broker facilitated most meetings.

One way to explain these findings is that the substantive work of an RPP is not stagnant – that is, it grows and develops over time, as we might expect it to. For example, in helping and supporting partnership members who are at the beginning of a line of research, the broker might focus on building the capability of those participants to work together on their own so that they might deepen their newfound relational trust. This helps RPP participants engage in brokering activities themselves and, over time, helps them become less reliant on the initial RPP broker. This, in turn, is likely to strengthen the partnership itself over time, especially as RPP participants continue to nurture their relationships via self-led brokering activities.

We saw this scenario unfold in the younger RPP from the Wentworth example introduced earlier. For example, in developing one of the lines of new research, the RPP members relied heavily on their RPP director to facilitate their meetings at the beginning of the relationship, even after the research activities got started. After a year into the research, the RPP director decided they needed more brokering to help the participants find common ground. The director asked the research team to assign a broker role to one of their team members, in this case a research assistant with good relationship and project management skills. Over two years, the RPP director worked with this newly assigned broker from the research team to help them develop meeting agendas, facilitate meetings, and follow up with practice partners with clear next steps for all participants. This line of research was subsequently integrated into the practice partner's decision-making and resulted in a major practice change based on the findings.

BROKERS LEARN HOW TO DO THIS WORK BOTH EXPLICITLY AND IMPLICITLY

RPP members will implicitly learn brokering skills and knowledge by participating in their RPP work and watching other participants enact brokering moves. Some of our favorite moves as brokers come from watching our mentors and advisors negotiate RPP work in action. We have seen veteran district leaders co-developing questions with seasoned professors. We have seen other district leaders and researchers collaboratively building survey items that help them answer critical questions for both the district and the academy. Aspiring and current brokers do learn by seeing, working with, and experimenting with these brokering moves in situ.

To accelerate the advancement of brokering skills, though, RPP participants also need explicit coaching and teaching of brokering moves. If all RPP members should learn how to broker over the life of the RPP, then partnership participants across roles – teachers, researchers, students, community members, etc. – should have opportunities to explicitly learn brokering moves. For researchers, universities could offer course requirements during their doctoral training or during faculty workshops and retreats. For teachers and school leaders, universities and other organizations training teachers and school leaders could teach brokering in their pre-service training while working towards a certificate. Or, schools and districts could offer professional development opportunities to learn brokering skills. For community members and families, an array of non-profits, local higher education organizations, and other member organizations like parent–teacher associations and school board associations could offer workshops or certificates in brokering. For students, we recommend looking at the approach in collaborative research called Youth Participatory Action Research (YPAR), which supports students to run their own inquiry, associated activism, and community organizing as a place where students can explicitly learn brokering skills. Finally, any organization that is onboarding new staff who will be working in RPPs could provide explicit teaching in brokering to support their RPP work.

NEXT STEPS FOR RPP BROKERING

Brokering is an essential activity that will make or break the effectiveness of an RPP. Brokering activities require participants to reach beyond the traditional, status quo practices in research relationships. As RPPs grow and strengthen, brokering activities should spread across the practices of all participants. Hence, to support the development and spread of RPPs, the field will need more and more RPP participants to have both informal and formal opportunities to learn brokering skill and knowledge.

If the ideas we present above are true, then the next steps for brokering in current and future RPPs are clear. First, research, practice, and community-based organizations will need to recognize brokering efforts as a valuable asset. Currently, brokering activities are buried in job descriptions or are assumed behaviors we expect across various roles. Brokering will need to be more recognized as an important activity in RPPs and across organizations more generally. For example, school districts typically experience intense siloing between departments. If school districts valued, encouraged, and identified the importance of brokering, they could potentially transform their organizations by elevating professionals with brokering skills and knowledge to key roles in the organization and creating organizational structures and routines that help them do their work better. In this vein, some small and large districts have established data analyst positions that work across schools and departments to support data-driven decision-making and integration of research evidence and data analysis into decision-making. We have also seen university-based research centers starting to post "Director of Partnerships" positions, a key role in brokering partnerships with practice or policy partners.

Second, we need to learn more about how RPP brokering helps support partners and partnerships by breaking down status quo relationships, and especially not centering white, middle-class, patriarchal norms. There is a growing literature base about issues in RPPs such as status (e.g., Coburn et al., 2008), racism (Tanksley & Estrada, 2022), and social justice (Vetter et al., 2022). Yet, less is documented about how the concept of brokering intersects with these issues. More information is needed about the types of strategies and practices that RPP brokers can use when engaging in disruptive systems-level work.

Third, we also need more explicit training in brokering across RPP participants—both learning opportunities and formal training. Some professionals come with brokering skills gained through their years teaching in or leading schools and school districts, organizing activism in their communities, or advocating for change in their universities. Other professionals have less expertise in brokering, like researchers who received informal opportunities to work in RPPs while pursuing their PhD. From what we have heard, when RPP leaders go to hire professionals with brokering skills, they will tell you these professionals often need explicit onboarding and training in brokering when they arrive. Consequently, we need more opportunities for explicit training in brokering through workshops, courses, and other opportunities to learn.

We end with our original argument that the future of RPP brokering will always harken back to the three larger themes driving the RPP Brokers Framework. RPP brokers work in specific sociocultural, historical, and political contexts that must be honored and respected. RPP brokers' work aims to strengthen the partners by advancing the relationships, competencies, capabilities, and skills in research production and research use. RPP brokers' work aims to strengthen the RPP itself by helping the structures and governance, communications and routines, and progress monitoring and assessment. The more of these individuals there are working collaboratively in an RPP, the more likely the ambitious aims of RPPs are to be met.

REFERENCES

Coburn, C. E., Bae, S., & Turner, E. O. (2008). Authority, status, and the dynamics of insider-outsider partnerships at the district level. *Peabody Journal of Education*, *83*(3), 364–399.

Farrell, C. C., Penuel, W. R., Coburn, C., Daniel, J., & Steup, L. (2021). *Research-practice partnerships in education: The state of the field*. William T. Grant Foundation.

Henrick, E. C., Cobb, P., Penuel, W. R., Jackson, K., & Clark, T. (2017). *Assessing research-practice partnerships: Five dimensions of effectiveness*. William T. Grant Foundation.

Kipnis, F., Wentworth, L., & Nayfack, M. (2020, April 17–21). *Designing and using measures for improving research-practice partnerships* [Paper presentation]. American Education Research Association Annual Meeting, online.

Penuel, W. R., Allen, A. R., Coburn, C. E., & Farrell, C. (2015). Conceptualizing research – practice partnerships as joint work at boundaries. *Journal of Education for Students Placed at Risk*, *20*(1), 182–197.

Penuel, W. R., Fishman, B. J., Haugan Cheng, B., & Sabelli, N. (2011). Organizing research and development at the intersection of learning, implementation, and design. *Educational Researcher*, *40*(7), 331–337.

Tanksley, T., & Estrada, C. (2022). Toward a critical race RPP: How race, power and positionality inform research practice partnerships. *International Journal of Research & Method in Education*, 1–13.

Vetter, A., Faircloth, B. S., Hewitt, K. K., Gonzalez, L. M., He, Y., & Rock, M. L. (2022). Equity and social justice in research practice partnerships in the United States. *Review of Educational Research*. https://doi.org/10.3102/00346543211070048

Appendix A
Tables Showing the Association Between the Literature and Themes and Activities in the Framework

APPENDIX A

Literature Categorized by Theme and Subtheme

	Brokering to Strengthen the Partnership			Brokering to Strengthen Partnering		
Citation	Developing Partnership Infrastructure	Designing Social Structures and Routines	Assessing and Reflecting on the Partnership	Building Conditions for Research Use and Production	Building Relationships to Weather Challenges	Building Individuals' Knowledge and Skills
Akkerman & Bruining, 2016	X	X	X	X	X	X
Benichou et al., 2019				X		X
Brown, 2017	X	X	X	X	X	X
Buskey et al., 2018	X				X	
Campbell et al., 2017	X	X	X	X	X	X
Coburn et al., 2008	X			X	X	X
Davidson & Penuel, 2020	X	X	X	X	X	X
Denner et al., 2019	X	X	X	X	X	X
Farrell et al., 2019	X	X		X	X	X
Farrell et al., 2018	X	X	X	X	X	X
Farrell et al., 2017	X			X	X	X
Farrell et al., 2019		X		X	X	
Fenwick, 2007	X				X	X
Fenwick, 2004	X	X			X	X

188

Firestone & Fisler, 2002	X	X		X	X
Furtak et al., 2016	X	X	X	X	X
Harrison et al., 2019	X	X	X	X	X
Hartmann & Decristan, 2018	X	X	X	X	X
Hopkins & Penuel, 2019				X	X
Hopkins et al., 2018		X		X	
Johnson et al., 2016			X	X	X
Klar et al., 2018	X	X			X
Kronley & Handley, 2003	X	X	X	X	X
Lasater, 2019	X		X	X	X
Lasater, 2018	X	X	X	X	X
Miller, 2007	X	X		X	X
Miller & Hafner, 2008	X	X		X	X
Muñoz-Muñoz & Ocampo, 2016	X	X	X		X
Nelson et al., 2015	X		X	X	X
Thompson et al., 2019				X	X
Wilcox & Zuckerman, 2019	X	X		X	X
Wilcox et al., 2017		X	X	X	X
Total	24	22	16	26	28	26

Appendix B

References for Records Included in Systematic Review of Brokering Literature

Akkerman, S., & Bruining, T. (2016). Multilevel boundary crossing in a professional development school partnership. *Journal of the Learning Sciences, 25*(2), 240–284. https://doi.org/10.1080/10508406.2016.1147448

Benichou, M., Atias, O., Sagy, O., Kali, Y., & Baram-Tsabari, A. (2019). Citizen science in schools: Supporting implementation of innovative learning environments using design-centric research-practice partnerships. In Lund, K., Niccolai, G. P., Lavoué, E., Hmelo-Silver, C., Gweon, G., & Baker, M. (Eds.), *A Wide Lens: Combining Embodied, Enactive, Extended, and Embedded Learning in Collaborative Settings, 13th International Conference on Computer Supported Collaborative Learning (CSCL) 2019, 2* (pp. 843–844). International Society of the Learning Sciences.

Brown, S. L. (2017). *Negotiating position during the process of design within a researcher-developer-practitioner partnership: An activity systems analysis* [Doctoral dissertation, Florida State University]. FSU Digital Library. Retrieved from http://purl.flvc.org/fsu/fd/FSU_2017SP_Brown_fsu_0071E_13753

Buskey, F. C., Klar, H. W., Huggins, K. S., & Desmangles, J. K. (2018). Spanning boundaries to enhance school leadership. In Reardon, R. M. & Leonard, J. (Eds.), *Innovation and implementation in rural places: School-university-community collaboration in education* (pp. 57–80). Information Age Publishing.

Campbell, C., Pollock, K., Briscoe, P., Carr-Harris, S., & Tuters, S. (2017). Developing a knowledge network for applied education research to mobilise evidence in and for educational practice. *Educational Research, 59*(2), 209–227. https://doi.org/10.1080/00131881.2017.1310364

Coburn, C. E., Bae, S., & Turner, E. O. (2008). Authority, status, and the dynamics of insider-outsider partnerships at the district level. *Peabody Journal of Education, 83*(3), 364–399. Retrieved from www.jstor.org/stable/25594798

Davidson, K. L., & Penuel, W. R. (2020). Chapter 11: The role of brokers in sustaining partnership work in education. In Malin, J., and Brown, C. (Eds.), *The role of knowledge brokers in education: Connecting the dots between research and practice* (pp. 154–167). Routledge.

Denner, J., Bean, S., Campe, S., Martinez, J., & Torres, D. (2019). Negotiating trust, power, and culture in a research–practice partnership. *AERA Open*. https://doi.org/10.1177/2332858419858635

Farrell, C. C., Coburn, C. E., & Chong, S. (2019). Under what conditions do school districts learn from external partners? The role of absorptive capacity. *American Educational Research Journal, 56*(3), 955–994. https://doi.org/10.3102/0002831218808219

Farrell, C. C., Davidson, K. L., Repko-Erwin, M. E., Penuel, W. R., Quantz, M., Wong, H., Riedy, R., & Brink, Z. (2018). *A descriptive study of the IES researcher–practitioner partnerships in education research program: Final report* (Technical Report No. 3). National Center for Research in Policy and Practice. Available at: https://files.eric.ed.gov/fulltext/ED599980.pdf

Farrell, C. C., Davidson, K. L., Repko-Erwin, M. E., Penuel, W. R., Herlihy, C., Potvin A.S., & Hill, H.C. (2018). *A descriptive study of the IES researcher–practitioner partnerships in education research program: Final report* (Technical Report No. 2). National Center for Research in Policy and Practice. Available at: http://ncrpp.org/assets/documents/RPP-Technical-Report_Feb-2017.pdf

Farrell, C. C., Harrison, C., & Coburn, C. E. (2019). "What the hell is this, and who the hell are you?": Role and identity negotiation in research-practice partnerships. *AERA Open*. https://doi.org/10.1177/2332858419849595

Fenwick, T. (2007). Organisational learning in the "knots": Discursive capacities emerging in a school-university collaboration. *Journal of Educational Administration, 45*(2), 138–153. https://doi-org.udel.idm.oclc.org/10.1108/09578230710732934

Fenwick, T. (2004). Discursive work for educational administrators: Tensions in negotiating partnerships. *Discourses: Studies in the Cultural Politics of Education, 25*(2), 171–187. https://doi.org/10.1080/01596300410001692139

Firestone, W. A., & Fisler, J. L. (2002). Politics, community, and leadership in a school-university partnership. *Educational Administration Quarterly, 38*(4), 449–493. https://doi.org/10.1177/001316102237669

Furtak, E. M., Henson, K., & Buell, J. Y. (2016, April). Negotiating goals around formative assessment in a research-practice partnership. In annual meeting of the National Association of Research in Science Teaching, Baltimore, MD. Retrieved from https://www.researchgate.net/profile/Erin_Furtak/publication/301301901_Negotiating_Goals_around_Formative_Assessment_in_a_Research-Practice_Partnership/links/57113c2408aeebe07c02417c.pdf

Harrison, C., Wāchen, J., Brown, S. & Cohen-Vogel, L. (2019). A view from within: Lessons learned from partnering for continuous improvement. *Teachers College Record, 121*(9). Retrieved from https://eric.ed.gov/?id=EJ1225420

Hartmann, U., & Decristan, J. (2018). Brokering activities and learning mechanisms at the boundary of educational research and school practice. *Teaching and Teacher Education, 74*, 114–124. https://doi.org/10.1016/j.tate.2018.04.016

Hopkins, M., Weddle, H., Gluckman, M., & Gautsch, L. (2019). Boundary crossing in a professional association: The dynamics of research use among state leaders and researchers in a research-practice partnership. *AERA Open.* https://doi.org/10.1177/2332858419891964

Hopkins, M., Wiley, K. E., Penuel, W. R., & Farrell, C. C. (2018). Brokering research in science education policy implementation: The case of a professional association. *Evidence & Policy: A Journal of Research, Debate and Practice, 14*(3), 459–476. https://doi.org/10.1332/174426418X15299595170910

Johnson, R., Severance, S., Penuel, W. R., & Leary, H. (2016). Teachers, tasks, and tensions: Lessons from a research–practice partnership. *Journal of Mathematics Teacher Education, 19*(2/3), 169–185. https://doi.org/10.1007/s10857-015-9338-3

Klar, H.W., Huggins, K.S., Buskey, F.C., Desmangles, J.K., Phelps-Ward, R.J. (2018). Developing social capital for collaboration in a research-practice partnership. *Journal of Professional Capital and Community, 3*(4), 287–305. https://doi.org/10.1108/JPCC-01-2018-0005

Kronley, R. A., & Handley, C. (2003). Reforming relationships: School districts, external organizations, and systemic change. Annenberg Institute for School Reform. Retrieved from https://eric.ed.gov/?id=ED479779

Lasater, K. (2019). Developing authentic family-school partnerships in a rural high school: Results of a longitudinal action research study. *School Community Journal, 29*(2), 157–182. Retrieved from https://eric.ed.gov/?id=EJ1236596

Lasater, K. (2018). Using the researcher–practitioner partnership to build family–school partnerships in a rural high school. In Reardon, R.M. & Leonard, J. (Eds.), *Innovation and implementation in rural places: School-university-community collaboration in education* (pp.233–256). Information Age Publishing.

Miller, P. M. (2007). "Getting on the balcony to see the patterns on the dance floor below": Considering organizational culture in a university–school–community collaboration. *Journal of School Leadership, 17*(2), 222–245. https://doi.org/10.1177/105268460701700204

Miller, P. M., & Hafner, M. M. (2008). Moving toward dialogical collaboration: A critical examination of a university-school-community partnership. *Educational Administration Quarterly, 44*(1), 66–110. https://doi.org/10.1177/0013161X07309469

Muñoz-Muñoz, E., & Ocampo, A. (2016). A three-way partnership to bridge and connect institutional perspectives on English Language Learner instruction. In Slater, J.J., Ravid, R., & Reardon, R.M. (Eds.), *Building and maintaining collaborative communities: Schools, university, and community organizations* (pp. 229–240). Information Age Publishing

Nelson, I. A., London, R. A., & Strobel, K. R. (2015). Reinventing the role of the university researcher. *Educational Researcher, 44*(1), 17–26. https://doi.org/10.3102/0013189X15570387

Thompson, J., Richards, J., Shim, S.-Y., Lohwasser, K., Von Esch, K. S., Chew, C., Sjoberg, B., & Morris, A. (2019). Launching networked PLCs: Footholds into creating and improving knowledge of ambitious and equitable teaching practices in an RPP. *AERA Open.* https://doi.org/10.1177/2332858419875718

Wilcox, K. C., & Zuckerman, S. J. (2019). Building will and capacity for improvement in a rural research-practice partnership. *The Rural Educator, 40*(1), 73–90. Retrieved from https://journals.library.msstate.edu/ruraled/article/view/534

Wilcox, K. C., Lawson, H. A., & Angelis, J. I. (2017). COMPASS-AIM: A university/p-12 partnership innovation for continuous improvement. *Peabody Journal of Education, 92*(5), 649–674. https://doi.org/10.1080/0161956X.2017.1368654

Appendix C

Literature Included in Review About Racism, Power Differences and RPPs

Sullivan, et al. (2001). Researchers and researched-community perspectives: toward bridging the gap. *Health Education & Behavior, 28*(2), 130–149.

Chavez, V. (2005). Silence speaks: the language of internalized oppression and privilege in community-based research. *Metropolitan Universities Journal, 16*(1).

Wallerstein, N. B., & Duran, B. (2006). Using community-based participatory research to address health disparities. *Health Promotion Practice, 7*(3), 312–323.

Coburn, C. E., Bae, S., & Turner, E. O. (2008). Authority, status, and the dynamics of insider-outsider partnerships at the district level. *Peabody Journal of Education, 83*(3), 364–399.

Campano, G. Chiso, M. P., Welch, B. (2015). Ethical and professional norms in community-based research. *Harvard Education Review, 85*(1), 29–49.

Vakil, S., de Royston, M. M., Nasir, N. S., & Kirshner, B. (2016). Rethinking race and power in design-based research: reflections from the field. *Cognition and Instruction, 34*(3), 194–209.

Gutiérrez, K. D., & Jurow, A. S. (2016). Social design experiments: toward equity by design, *Journal of the Learning Sciences, 25*(4), 565–598.

Penuel, W. R. (2017) Research-Practice Partnerships as a strategy for promoting equitable science teaching and learning through leveraging everyday science. *Science Education, 101*, 520–525.

Denner, J., Bean, S., Campe, S., Martinez, J., & Torres, D. (2019). Negotiating trust, power, and culture in a research practice partnership. *AERA Open, 5*(2), 1–11.

Greenberg, D. Barton, A. C., Turner, C., Hardy, K., Roper, A., Williams, C., Herrenkohl, L. R., David, E. A., & Tasker, T. (2020). Community infrastructuring as necessary ingenuity in the COVID-19 pandemic. *Educational Researcher, 49*(7), 518–523.

Henderson, J. W., & Laman, T. T. (2020). "This ain't gonna work for me": the role of the afrocentric praxis of eldering in creating more equitable research partnerships. *Urban Education, 55*(6), 892–910.

Ho, D., Dawene, D., Roberts, K., & Hing, J. J. (2020). A systematic review of boundary-crossing partnerships in designing equity-oriented special education services for culturally and linguistically diverse students with disabilities. *Remedial and Special Education*, *42*(6), 412–425.

McMahon, K., Henrick, E., & Sullivan, F. (2022). *Partnering to Scale Instructional Improvement: A Framework for Organizing Research-Practice Partnerships*. Stanford, CA: The Carnegie Foundation for the Advancement of Teaching.

Ortiz, K., Nash, J., Shea, L., Oetzel, J., Garoutte, J., Sanchez-Youngman, S., & Wallerstein, N. (2020). Partnerships, processes, and outcomes: a health equity–focused scoping meta-review of community engaged scholarship. *Annual Review of Public Health*, *41*, 177–199.

Appendix D

San Francisco Unified School Districts' Tools for Reviewing Research Applications

Our ABC's of Research

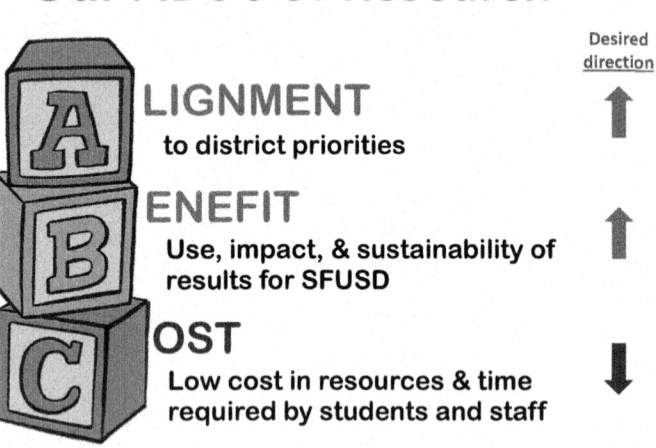

Desired direction

ALIGNMENT
to district priorities ↑

BENEFIT
Use, impact, & sustainability of results for SFUSD ↑

COST
Low cost in resources & time required by students and staff ↓

SFUSD

Last revised 15 Sep 2017

RPA

APPENDIX D

Alignment of Research

Practitioners rate, reviewers confirm:

☐ How strong is the alignment of the proposed project to your department's priorities?

Consider:
- ☐ connection to district/department theory of improvement
- ☐ prioritization of improvement goals, evaluation needs, research questions
- ☐ relevance to existing initiatives
- ☐ compatibility with resources/capacity/needs
- ☐ timeliness for upcoming important decisions

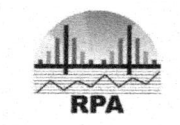

Last revised 15 Sep 2017

197

APPENDIX D

Benefit of Research

Practitioners rate, reviewers confirm:

☐ **Usefulness:**
  ☐ What actions might you take if the study....
    ☐ yielded favorable results?
    ☐ yielded neutral / unfavorable results?

☐ **Impact:**
  ☐ How would those new actions lead to improvements in students' outcomes?
  ☐ What impact, how much, for whom?

Reviewers also rate:

☐ How worthwhile is the research question?

☐ How much would the knowledge advance the district's learning agenda?

☐ How strong is the methodological rigor?

Last revised 28 Aug 2018

APPENDIX D

Cost of Research

Practitioners rate, reviewers confirm:

☐ **Partnership:**
  ☐ Identify concrete discussion topics or deliverables for ≥3 possible meetings with the researchers.
  ☐ Identify key district leaders / stakeholders for these meetings.

☐ **Operationalizing study:**
  ☐ Identify staff to help operationalize data-gathering.

Reviewers also rate:

☐ **Time:**
  ☐ Duration × sample

☐ **Resources:**
  ☐ Data extraction
  ☐ Additional support to execute project

☐ **Burden to people:**
  ☐ Instructional time
  ☐ Surveys, interviews, observations
  ☐ Ethics/equity of research burden

Last revised 28 Aug 2018

199

Appendix E

San Francisco Unified School Districts' Internal Review Template

Study Title: Click or tap here to enter text.
PI & Res Org: Click or tap here to enter text.

Reviewed by: Click or tap here to enter text.
Review Date: Click or tap here to enter text.

	SUMMARIZE	ASSESS
WHAT	*Problem to be solved* Click or tap here to enter text. *RQ to be explored* Click or tap here to enter text.	*Alignment & significance of problem* Click or tap here to enter text. *Benefits: usefulness & potential impact of knowledge gained* Click or tap here to enter text.
HOW	*Research design to answer the RQ* Click or tap here to enter text. *Personnel, partnership, resources* Click or tap here to enter text.	*Benefits: validity of design* Click or tap here to enter text. *Benefits: likelihood of productive findings* Click or tap here to enter text. *Costs* Click or tap here to enter text.

Questions or issues to discuss
Click or tap here to enter text.

Next steps
Click or tap here to enter text.

Copyright material from Laura Wentworth, Paula Arce-Trigatti, Carrie Conaway, and Samantha Shewchuk (2023), *Brokering in Education Research-Practice Partnerships*, Routledge

Appendix F

San Francisco Unified School Districts' Roles and Responsibilities for Research Partnership Matrix

APPENDIX F

Stage in Research Life Cycle		SFUSD Admin. Sponsor(s)	RPA's Research Support Team	External Research Team
Priority-setting	Build district/department learning agenda	Articulate priorities, programs, and practices/policies to study. Coordinate with key stakeholders.	Facilitate meetings to set research priorities. Share existing research; match with potential partners.	N/A
Developing	Co-develop potential research ideas	Advise on actionable lines of inquiry, desired populations, feasible contexts, and useful measures.	Support refining research questions and designs given likely actions and practical constraints.	Propose potential research questions and designs to address information needs.
	Establish roles and timeline	Identify decision-making windows. Clarify roles (leaders/stakeholders).	Facilitate and advise as needed.	Confirm timeline for sharing information.
Reviewing	Complete research application	Advise on alignment, benefits, and costs (ABCs); sign if approving.	Review research application materials and data request.	Submit application and data request. Revise as needed.
Supporting	Collect & analyze primary data	Assist with outreach, recruitment, scheduling, sharing artifacts, etc.	N/A	Conduct interviews, surveys, observations, etc. Analyze.
	Exchange & analyze secondary data	N/A	Securely provide data. Address questions about data.	Securely receive data. Analyze data.
	Monitor progress and adapt research	Discuss updates and implications; adapt implementation as needed.	Facilitate discussions and/or advise as needed.	Share preliminary findings; adapt research as needed.

APPENDIX F

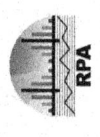

Integrating	Present and discuss findings	Identify audience; co-plan meeting. Discuss context, potential actions.	Advise on meeting design; review slides. Co-facilitate discussion.	Co-plan meeting. Present findings; discuss implications.
	Disseminate results	Review drafts before submission. Share reports with key stakeholders.	Coordinate feedback on drafts. Circulate final reports.	Draft initial reports; revise as needed. Share publications.
	Implement evidence-based policies/practices	Integrate learning and action in continuous improvement cycles.	Share related evidence; embed findings in artifacts; advise on testing and evaluating adaptations.	N/A

Last modified 11 March 2021

203

Appendix G

Partnership Agreement Between San Francisco Unified School District (SFUSD) and The University of California, Berkeley (UC Berkeley)

This document sets forth the agreed-upon partnership values and processes between SFUSD and UC Berkeley to establish an ongoing research practice partnership (RPP) for the purpose of reducing inequities among SFUSD students, improving the applicability of cross-disciplinary research in an education setting, and promoting the inclusion of student-generated evidence in decision-making and practices.

RATIONALE

Traditional approaches to research tend to be primarily investigator-driven and historically do not prioritize alignment between research and the priorities of community partners. Learning from the activities and applicable research from RPPs across the country, SFUSD and UC Berkeley seek to enter a partnership that is characterized by a long-term, mutualistic collaboration that is organized to investigate problems of practice and solutions for improving outcomes in the lives of community members. We aim to establish a formal RPP structure to help bridge the research/practice gap and enhance the relevance of our research to the challenges faced by our local communities.

PURPOSE

This partnership agreement makes clear the following shared values and practices between the UC Berkeley and SFUSD partners. Our understanding is that faculty and staff of the two partners are agreeing to work together in the spirit of these values and practices and to raise concerns in a constructive and timely way when those arise.

OVERARCHING FOCUS ON EQUITY

Our RPP starts from the equity-focused questions and problems of practice prioritized by SFUSD to generate research aimed at improving equitable outcomes for San Francisco youth. We are committed to promoting equity and social justice, interdisciplinary approaches to addressing social problems, co production of knowledge including participatory research, studying interventions not just outcomes, growing research use in addition to facilitating new research, and a full-cycle collaborative process from co-creating research agendas to evaluating research-based interventions.

SHARED VALUES

We have agreed on five guiding values:
1) **Trust:** Trust involves understanding, respecting, and valuing each partner's role in the partnership. Building trust between all partners is crucial for a successful partnership.
2) **Flexibility:** Flexibility involves humility, tolerance, and a willingness to compromise when necessary for the betterment of the partnership.
3) **Diversity:** Diversity is more than ethnic and racial diversity; it also includes diversity of experience and ideas.
4) **Shared Assets:** Students are our greatest asset. Uplifting the voice of students in research fulfills our mission and leads to rigorous research findings.
5) **Research utility:** Generating useful research that responds to problems of practice yields better research, practice, and policy.

COMPONENTS AND PROCESSES OF SFUSD-UCB-BERKELEY PARTNERSHIP

This section is intended to clarify the research process under this RPP with special attention to how it can add value beyond the status quo investigator-driven research model.

1) Sustained leadership structure and process with regular standing meetings provide a forum where SFUSD can voice research needs, ongoing projects

can report on progress, and new researchers can bring project proposals for pre-submission review.
2) Shared initiation and targeting of research questions and opportunities will keep researchers in conversation about how our research addresses relevant questions and challenges for SFUSD, rather than only investigator-initiated questions and projects. Research priorities will be driven by the needs and interests of SFUSD practitioners, administrators, students, families, and community members. SFUSD will identify and nurture preliminary research interests from these stakeholders, in order to facilitate more targeted and productive discussions with researchers to further refine the research agenda.
3) A multidisciplinary network of researchers will facilitate stronger coordination and strengthening of the research itself, as well as the identification of shared research and funding opportunities.
4) Ongoing engagement with students and families in participatory approaches will strengthen the likelihood that the work of SFUSD and UC Berkeley researchers is informed by diverse stakeholders, especially those not already represented via existing mechanisms.
5) Timely ongoing communication of knowledge generate·d with practitioners, administrators, other researchers, and policymakers will deepen research impact and uptake: we envision more regular discussion and report-back, beyond the current expectations of a report at the end.
6) Facilitation of data-sharing and access will mean there is a formalized process for sharing information.
7) Yearly or twice yearly "meet and greet" networking meetings to enable generation of ideas and inclusion of new faculty, trainees, and staff.
8) Quarterly working group meetings around more specific questions or domains for incubation and workshopping of findings and methods and collaborative challenges.

RESEARCH AGENDA

We encourage a range of research projects across disciplines and questions to be fostered by this partnership, all aligned with the values expressed here and strengthening opportunities for all, and with an emphasis on innovative and participatory approaches to student and practitioner engagement in school improvement and equity efforts. Some specific domains of interest that have emerged thus far include:

- Sharing and generating research evidence to support SFUSD's initiatives to promote success for all, especially in narrowing opportunity and

achievement gaps for our historically underserved populations, particularly African American, Latinx, English learner, special education, and socio-economically disadvantaged students
- Targeting of chronic absenteeism as a key driver of opportunity and achievement gaps in SFUSD
- Defining and measuring success for students in multiple domains that go beyond the traditional academic and cognitive domains (i.e. content, skills, dispositions), utilizing innovative participatory approaches to build on students' experience and expertise
- Continuous improvement efforts[1] at school sites and at central office
- Testing and scaling of youth voice and participatory research models
- Understanding the impact of the rich array of services and student and family supports offered through SFUSD's Student, Family, and Community Support Division (e.g., School Health Programs such as the Wellness Initiative, Foster Youth Services)

PROPOSED ORGANIZATIONAL STRUCTURE:

At SFUSD, the partnership will sit with RPA leadership and key staff including Norma Ming (Supervisor of Research & Evaluation) and Devin Corrigan (Educational Policy Analyst). RPA is uniquely suited to lead this work for SFUSD, as the department has a long history of engaging with external researchers (including through other RPPs) and has already established processes for vetting research projects with other SFUSD departments and school sites, and integrating research into SFUSD's continuous improvement processes.

At UC Berkeley, we have established a steering committee of 1–2 point people from key units including Public Health (SPH), Graduate School of Education (GSE), School of Social Welfare (SSW), and the Psychology department, who will serve for 2 year terms for continuity. Note: In 2019–20, we will determine processes for future transitions of steering committee members).

Staffing: There is mutual interest in a Berkeley-SFUSD liaison with research and practice expertise to help support the development and nurturing of collaborative research relationships, manage communications and networks, share best practices to ensure high-quality research applications, and facilitate mutual learning and research-practice integration. Such a staff member would reside formally at SFUSD but spend time in both places. Graduate and undergraduate trainees will work within the RPP broadly and also with particular projects under the RPP umbrella.

SFUSD:

- 2019–20: Clarification of steering committee and meeting structure; development of other structures that formally include other units in addition to RPA
- Berkeley-SFUSD liaison
- Engaged CBO's embedded within SFUSD
- Student participants

UC Berkeley:

- As of July 2019: Leadership/steering committee with current faculty from the School of Public Health, School of Social Welfare, Graduate School of Education, and Psychology Department
- Broader network of investigators working within RPP through Innovations for Youth (14V) and others will be invited to join.
- Cohorts of graduate and undergraduate research trainees with shared seminar and training workshop opportunities (content on equity framing, ethics, collaborative and participatory research approaches, diverse research methods)
- Specifics of funding model and how support by units and central campus will be determined requires strategic planning and input from steering committee, external advisory board, and success of funding proposals and cross-unit philanthropic efforts.

MEETING STRUCTURE

Following the initial 2018–19 intensive planning phase of monthly meetings, we plan for 2019–20 and beyond a quarterly standing leadership meeting structure including the steering committee members with the following goals:

1. Build and maintain a research agenda
2. Share updates on the progress of current research initiatives
3. Target new research questions and opportunities
4. Engage new faculty and maintain a multidisciplinary focus

Meetings will alternate locations between UC Berkeley and San Francisco. At each meeting, researchers will bring short (~20 minute) presentations about current research being conducted in the district and give updates on current projects; SFUSD will come prepared to share project wishlists and updates on current district needs to generate research and evaluation ideas.

We recognize that both parties (SFUSD and UC Berkeley) have existing partnerships. Our goal is to support the development of multiple Research-Practice Partnerships to learn from partnered scholarship across diverse settings and sectors, share lessons learned and best practices across RPP's, and promote the relevance and impact of Berkeley's portfolio of research on reducing inequalities. The Berkeley-SF USO partnership is intentionally focused on promoting equity within SFUSD, connecting research on reducing educational inequalities with other systems and sectors in San Francisco and the region, and on studying the implementation of research into practice.

REPORTING

To be determined during planning period: Consider how we will evaluate effectiveness and adherence to the agreement and when evaluation will happen.

FUNDING

This partnership agreement is not a commitment of funds. Funds will be only be committed via formal scope of work agreements approved by the authorized officials of SFUSD and UC-Berkeley. This partnership agreement indicates our shared interest in seeking funding in joint proposals.

DATA SHARING

It is SFUSD's policy that data-sharing agreements are negotiated after funding and project proposals are approved, due to the intensive nature of negotiating those agreements. We note that there are already approved data-sharing agreements and approved research proposals that involve data-sharing among the Berkeley faculty with leadership roles in this RPP, including Dr. Susan Stone.

DURATION

This partnership agreement is at-will and may be modified by mutual consent of authorized officials from SFUSD or UC Berkeley. This partnership agreement is active upon signature and will remain in effect until modified or terminated by any one of the partners by mutual consent.

NOTE

1   The cycle of continuous improvement is used for improving outcomes and creating a reflective mindset within the education system. It is an iterative, problem-solving method for making rapid, incremental improvements while gaining valuable

APPENDIX G

learning and knowledge from the practice. Starting in school year 2018–19, all school sites are charged with identifying and executing a continuous improvement project as part of their school improvement plans (with support from central office).

Contact Information
Partner name: UC-Berkeley
Partner representative: Emily J. Ozer, Ph.D.
Position: Professor
Address: School of Public Health
E-mail: eozer@berkeley.edu

Emily Ozer   8/27/2019
Emily Ozer, Professor
School of Public Health, UC Berkeley

Partner name: San Francisco Unified School District
Partner representative: Norma Ming, Ph.D.
Position: Supervisor of Research and Evaluation
Address: 555 Franklin Street, San Francisco CA 94102-4456
E-mail: MingN@sfusd.edu

Norma Ming   8/27/2019
Norma Ming, Supervisor
Research, Planning, and Assessment; San Francisco Unified School District

Appendix H
Process for Generating a Portrait

Process for Generating a Portrait

Identify Guiding Questions ⇨ Negotiate Access if Needed ⇨ Develop Interview Questions ⇨ Identify Potential Interviewees ⇩ Conduct Interviews & Gather Artifacts ⇦ Analyze Interviews & Write Memos ⇦ Draft Portrait ⇦ Share Portrait Draft with RPP Leaders ⇄ Revise Portrait Draft as Needed ⇨ Share Final Draft of Portrait & Use as a Tool for Conversation & Learning

Appendix I

Shortened EFI Sprint Protocol for RPP Members: Hewlett Deeper Learning Network

Below you will find an example set of questions that can be used to understand an RPP according to the Evidence for Improvement Framework. This example consists of four core questions **(in bold)** followed by a set of probes that can be used, time permitting, to dive deeper. These questions are intended for members of the RPP, but they can be adapted to serve those working with the RPP (such as teachers or administrators).

THEORY OF PARTNERSHIP

> **Note:** *the following questions are meant to elicit the RPP members' understanding of how their partnership is organized and how they collaborate, make decisions, and learn together from the work.*

> **(1) How does this partnership work together? On a day-to-day basis, how does work get done in the partnership?**
> (a) How are *different roles* in the partnership structured?
> (b) How do you make *decisions* in the partnership? If the partnership faces a challenging decision point, how do you decide what to do?
>   (i) Can you provide an example?
> (c) How do the members of the partnership *learn from the work* in order to improve it?
>   (i) Please describe any learning routines that may be in place (e.g., specific meetings to stop and reflect, data analysis sessions, etc.).
>   (ii) Please describe how you are learning from the more formal research you are conducting in the partnership.

THEORY OF IMPROVEMENT

Note: *the following questions are meant to elicit the RPP members' understanding of their project's theory of improvement and how they will realize the improvements or innovations that they seek to make. We are interested in understanding the outcomes that are being targeted, the activities that are being enacted in order to accomplish those outcomes, and the causal logic that connects activities to outcomes. We are especially interested in following this casual chain all the way to the classroom.*

(2) **Can you tell me what your partnership is trying to accomplish?**
   (a) Help me understand more specifically what activities you are engaging in to accomplish these goals?
   (b) How do these activities relate to the outcomes you want to achieve? (For example, "We want to improve_____[outcomes]; one way we do that is to focus on_____by doing _____.")

(3) **What evidence, if any, are you collecting about your approach?**
   (a) **Note:** Be sure to inquire about both the processes that the partnership is engaging in to achieve its outcome, and the partnership's more formal outcomes.
   (b) [For each type of evidence identified] How often are you gathering this information?
   (c) To what extent are you looking at variation in performance across contexts and/or subgroups within your program? For example, if you are working with multiple schools, how are you learning from the fact that one school may be more successful?

THEORY OF SCALING

Note: *The following questions are meant to elicit explicit or implicit theories about the RPP's work to scale. In particular, we want to understand the extent to which they are thinking about six domains that we believe may be particularly important to scaling (see Q4 probes a–f).*

(4) **What is your theory about how you might scale? If not mentioned . . .**
   (a) How will *materials* you develop (e.g., curricula, protocols, handbooks) play a role in scaling?
   (b) How does *capacity building* for leaders and practitioners (through training, workshops, learning networks, etc.) play a role in your approach to scaling?
   (c) How are you thinking about generating ongoing *revenue* to support scale up?

(d) How are you thinking about the *political context* surrounding the work and how that may relate to your efforts at scaling, if at all?
(e) How is your work *aligned* with other efforts in the district and the state? If there are challenges with alignment, how are you thinking about overcoming them?
(f) How do you see *communication* and messaging as connected to your approach to scaling, if at all?
(g) How will you expand beyond the early adopters of your innovation to those who may be more initially reluctant to engage?

Appendix J

Generic School District DUA

AGREEMENT FOR CONFIDENTIAL DATA EXCHANGE BETWEEN [SCHOOL DISTRICT] AND THE JOHN W. GARDNER CENTER FOR YOUTH AND THEIR COMMUNITIES AT STANFORD UNIVERSITY

This Data Exchange and Confidentiality Agreement ("Agreement") between School district (hereinafter referred to as SD), The Board of Trustees of the Leland Stanford Junior University by and through its John W. Gardner Center for Youth and Their Communities (hereinafter referred to as JGC) describes the means to be used by JGC to ensure the confidentiality and security of information and data exchanged between SD and JGC for the purposes stated below.

I. GENERAL TERMS

A. PURPOSE

The JGC will develop a data archive of matched longitudinal administrative data for conducting policy analyses and program improvement studies for school leaders and practitioners. The archive will link student participation data from School District with student data from participating after-school providers and early learning centers that provide youth and family services at schools within School District. Policy questions to be addressed using the archive will be developed in collaboration with the participating public agencies and representatives of local community-based organizations.

[*A sentence describing/listing the research* questions (or general public policy purposes) or *making reference to the applicable grant agreement or approved research proposal, DATED XX.XX.XXX may be added here.*]

To ensure that this data archive is a valuable resource for all agencies contributing data, the project may also work with SD to identify one or more additional research questions that will be included in the project scope on behalf of SD.

B. NATURE OF DATA

To further the achievement of the above stated purpose, SD will at its discretion provide JGC with data extracts from the SD data systems to include data elements identified in **Attachment A**, as well as any additional items required to answer research questions defined by SD alone or in collaboration with other participants in the project data archive.

SD warrants that it has the authority to provide such data to the JGC under the terms of this Agreement, and that SD will not be in breach of any law or representations to any person by providing such information to the JGC

These data extracts will include historical information wherever possible. Additional data elements may be provided at the discretion of SD.

Because the research project will match individual student level data, these data are expected to contain confidential information, the disclosure of which is restricted by a provision of law. Some examples of "confidential information" include, but are not limited to, "personal information" about individuals as defined in California Civil Code Section 1798.3 of the Information Practices Act and "personal information" about students as defined by the Code of Federal Regulations CFR Title 34 Volume 1 Part 99.3.

C. TRANSFER OF DATA

SD and JGC shall use a secure, mutually agreed upon means and schedule for transferring confidential information. SD will create data extracts and validate the data. Extracts will be updated using a mutually agreed upon schedule. At no time will data be sent electronically to or from the parties except via a secure file transfer protocol.

D. PERIOD OF AGREEMENT

This Agreement shall be effective per specifications in **Attachment B**, unless terminated earlier by either party pursuant to Section F.

E. JGC RESPONSIBILITIES

JGC agrees to the following confidentiality statements:

1. JGC acknowledges that these data are confidential data and proprietary to SD, and agree to protect such information from unauthorized disclosures and comply with all applicable confidentiality laws which may include but is not limited to, the Health Insurance Portability and Accountability Act (HIPAA), the California Education Code and the Family Education Rights and Privacy Act (FERPA) as set forth in this agreement. JGC is responsible for complying with all District, Local, State and Federal confidentiality applicable laws and regulations.

2. JGC will use appropriate safeguards to prevent the use or disclosure of the information other than as provided by this data use Agreement.
3. JGC shall (a) instruct all staff with access to confidential information about the requirements for handling confidential information (b) provide all staff with access to confidential information statements of organizational policies and procedures for the protection of human subjects and data confidentiality and (c) notify staff of the sanctions against unauthorized disclosure or use of confidential and private information. JGC will ensure that all staff and subcontractors to whom they provide the limited data sets obtained under this Agreement, agree to the same restrictions and conditions that apply to JGC in this Agreement with respect to such information. Other than as provided herein, no confidential data will be released by JGC.
4. JGC shall not assign this Agreement or any portion thereof to a third party without the prior written consent of SD, and any attempted assignment without such prior written consent in violation of this Section shall automatically terminate this Agreement.
5. JGC will use any information which could potentially allow the identification of any individual only for the purpose of creating the data sets using aggregate data and analyzing the data. JGC will not use or further disclose the information accessed or received other than as permitted by this Data Use Agreement or as otherwise required by law.
6. JGC will report only aggregate data and will not report any individual data, nor will data be reported in a manner that permits indirect identification of any individual. This paragraph will survive the termination of this Agreement.
7. JGC will not contact the individuals included in the data sets.
8. JGC agrees to obtain written approval from SD prior to engaging any subcontractors to perform any services requiring access to any individually identifiable information.
9. JGC shall not re-disclose any individual-level data with or without identifying information to any other requesting individuals, agencies, or organizations without prior written authorization by SD.
10. JGC shall use the data only for the purpose stated above. These data shall not be used for personal gain or profit.
11. JGC shall keep all information furnished by SD in a space physically and electronically secure from unauthorized access. Information and data shall be stored and processed in a way that unauthorized persons cannot retrieve nor alter the information by means of a computer, remote terminal, or

other means. Following stringent security protocols approved by Stanford IT, no data will be archived on unencrypted laptop computers or other portable computing devices or media, e.g., flash drives, etc.
12. JGC shall permit examination and on-site inspections by SD upon reasonable advance notice for the purpose of ascertaining whether the terms of this Agreement are being met.

F. TERMINATION

1. This Agreement may be terminated as follows, after notification via the United States Postal Service (certified mail or registered mail) or recognized overnight delivery service (e.g., UPS, or FedEx):
   a. By JGC or SD immediately in the event of a material breach of this Agreement by the other party.
   b. By JGC or SD upon 30 day notice to the other party.
2. Upon ninety (90) days written notice from SD, JGC shall delete all confidential and/or sensitive information promptly so that it is no longer accessible for analysis and exists only on a temporary back-up server that is encrypted. JGC shall also securely destroy all physical media (e.g., data on CDs or USB drives) containing confidential and/or sensitive information utilizing a mutually approved method of confidential destruction, which may include shredding, burning, or certified/witnessed destruction for physical materials and verified erasure of magnetic media using approved methods of electronic file destruction. In the absence of such notice, JGC may continue to use such data for research, education or related purposes.

G. GENERAL UNDERSTANDING

1. This Agreement contains the entire understanding of the parties and may only be amended in writing signed by the parties.
2. This Agreement shall be governed by and construed under the laws of the State of California.
3. Any waiver by any party of the violation of any provision of this Agreement shall not bar any action for subsequent violations of the Agreement.

Signed:	
FOR SCHOOL DISTRICT	**FOR THE JOHN W. GARDNER CENTER FOR YOUTH AND THEIR COMMUNITIES**
Signatory, Job Title	Amy Gerstein, Executive Director
Date	Date

II. ORGANIZATION-SPECIFIC AGREEMENTS: ATTACHMENTS

ATTACHMENT A: SPECIFIC DATA ELEMENTS

- Student identifiers and demographic information
  - Student name
  - Student date of birth
  - GENERIC SD identifier
  - Address
  - Identifier
  - Address
  - Ethnicity
  - Gender
  - Primary language
  - English language fluency/learner status
  - Special education
  - Parent name (if available)
  - Parent education level
  - Free and reduced-price lunch
- Student enrollment
  - Current and past schools attended
  - Enrollment date
  - Withdrawal date
  - Reason for withdrawal
- School attendance
  - Student absences, excused, and unexcused
- Academic achievement
  - Units attempted and completed
  - Grades by subject area
  - Cumulative GPA, GPA by semester (if available)
  - UC/CSU eligibility
  - State assessment data (CST, CELDT, CAHSEE)
  - Local Benchmark Assessment data
  - Graduation

Copyright material from Laura Wentworth, Paula Arce-Trigatti, Carrie Conaway, and Samantha Shewchuk (2023), *Brokering in Education Research-Practice Partnerships*, Routledge

- Student services participation
  - After School Program participation – include hours or days attended
- Disciplinary data
  - Suspensions disaggregated by offense
  - Number of days suspended
  - 504 involvement

ATTACHMENT B: PERIOD OF AGREEMENT

This agreement shall be effective beginning XX Month 2013 through XX Month 2015, unless terminated earlier by either party pursuant to Section F. The effective dates of this agreement may be modified by written amendment subject to acceptance of both parties.

ATTACHMENT C: VARIOUS OTHER ORGANIZATION-SPECIFIC AGREEMENTS RE E. JGC RESPONSIBILITIES

JGC will not conduct any analyses using SD data without prior approval by an authorized SD representative. JGC will not publish findings obtained using SD data without prior review by an authorized SD representative. SD shall designate the following person(s) as authorized representatives for this project/RPP:

Name Title
Name Title
Name Title

Ver: 10/2020

Appendix K
Data SafeGuards

john w. gardner center for youth and their communities

[Template: One-page handout for Partner Induction]

DATA SAFEGUARDS

The Gardner Center has several ways of protecting the individual-level data we obtain for use in our research partnerships. We discuss these data safeguards in four categories below.

PROCEDURAL DATA SAFEGUARDS

- Unless agreed otherwise, Partners retain ownership of data they contribute. Gardner Center staff will not share partners' data with third parties without written consent.
- We will use the data only as appropriate for the agreed-upon analysis.
- We will report all research findings in aggregate only. As such, it would be highly improbable that anyone might indirectly identify any individual whose information we use for a research project.

PHYSICAL DATA SAFEGUARDS

- We use a Secure File Transfer Protocol to transfer data. If we transfer data via portable media – like a CD or thumb drive – we destroy the media once we upload the files to a secure server that is not connected to the internet.

- We store data in a secure data center with strictly controlled access. Only those Gardner Center researchers with proper training and permission can access the data.

ELECTRONIC DATA SAFEGUARDS

- Stanford University Information Technology Services (ITS) provides the firewall-protected server on which we store confidential data. Stanford ITS adheres to strict policies to keep restricted data confidential and secure.
- Gardner Center researchers can only access the data through encrypted connections that require two-step authentication – both a Stanford ID and another password obtained through a secondary device.
- There is no way to access the data on the internet.

LEGAL DATA SAFEGUARDS

- All Gardner Center research projects must meet the requirements set by Stanford University's Institutional Review Board (IRB) for research involving human subjects.
- Projects linking data across agencies comply with the California Education Code, as well as FERPA and HIPAA regulations, where applicable.

For more information, consult the Server Documentation & Information Security Policies report prepared by Stanford University Information Technology Services. A copy is available upon request.

12/2020

Appendix L

DUA Correspondence Template

john w. gardner center for youth and their communities

DUA WALK-THROUGH MEETINGS

- I am writing to schedule a brief telephone conversation between you and my colleague, [insert Associate here] (cc'ed here), so that s/he can go over the agreement with you in detail, answer any questions you may have about our partnership, fill you in on our process for signing the DUA, and get a sense of the data that your organization currently collects.
- Attached please find a sample copy of our DUA, which will give you a sense of what the agreement will cover. The attached is just an example; it is not ready for you to sign.
- After this conversation, we'll prepare a new DUA for your review that we will customize for your organization.

FOLLOW-UP EMAIL: AFTER THE DUA WALK-THROUGH

Dear [name of contact(s)],

Thank you for meeting with [insert name] last week regarding your organization's Data Use Agreement (DUA) with the John W. Gardner Center as part of your participation in [insert project name]. Attached please find your organization's customized DUA, which is ready for your review and signature. Once

Copyright material from Laura Wentworth, Paula Arce-Trigatti, Carrie Conaway, and Samantha Shewchuk (2023), *Brokering in Education Research-Practice Partnerships*, Routledge

you've reviewed the DUA, do not hesitate to reach out to me with any questions I can help answer as you review the document and prepare to sign it.

We are hoping to get signed DUAs back by [insert specific date here, ideally within 1–2 weeks] so that we may begin [describe analysis]. Please print and sign **two copies** of your DUA and return them to us via snail mail (c/o [insert your name]) at the following address: [insert our address].

Once we receive them, our Executive Director, Amy Gerstein, will sign both copies. We'll keep one copy for our files and return the other copy to you for your files.

Many thanks,
[your name here]

FOLLOW-UP EMAIL: AFTER ED SIGNS DUA

Dear [name of contact],

Thank you so much for signing the Data Use Agreement. [Insert details about timeline for data transfer] I will be in touch with you about this within the next few weeks. This promises to be important and compelling work and we are excited to partner with all of you.

Our Executive Director Amy Gerstein has signed your DUA and we have mailed your copy back to you. A copy for your files should be arriving shortly.

Please do not hesitate to ask me any questions regarding this work. Many thanks!

[your name here]

DATA EXTRACTS

Dear [signatory and, if relevant, person who attended the original DUA meeting],

Recently you and I met/you met with my colleague(s) [insert name(s) here] regarding your Data Use Agreement, and we are now ready to gather all of the student-level data for the youth your organization serves. I spoke with [name of Gardner Center colleague(s)] about the data you collect, and [pronoun] informed me that [describe what we know of their data/the format/etc.].

We would like to get all of the data by [one week from the date of email]. For security purposes, we stress that you should not send us data over email; instead, we will get the data from in you in person. I will follow up with a phone call to talk through the data extraction process with you.

Once I have your data, we will upload everything onto our secure server located here on campus. Only trained, appointed staff are able to access the server.

Thanks again for all of your help! Please feel free to call or email me with any questions. We're really looking forward to collaborating with you.

Copyright material from Laura Wentworth, Paula Arce-Trigatti, Carrie Conaway, and Samantha Shewchuk (2023), *Brokering in Education Research-Practice Partnerships*, Routledge

DATA TRANSFER

- We typically receive data on an encrypted flash drive, with either the drive or files password- protected, or through a secure transfer method like an FTP (SFTP) site.
- We prefer the data to be in an Excel file or delimited Text file (tab or comma).
- Make sure to state that neither the data nor the passwords is sent over email.
- Passwords should be given verbally in person or over the phone.
- Reiterate that we need the data for individual students going back X number of years.
- The data need to be electronic. If you do not have electronic data, we can make you a template for entering your data into a database.
- The data should include individual students' identifying information and participation records.
- If the project requires that we match your data to those of other organizations (e.g., an afterschool partner) we will need, for each student, their name, birthdate, and any other identifying information that you collect, such as ethnicity, gender, address, school, etc. These help us to match your youth to data from other organizations.
- We will also need participation in relevant programs in whatever way you collect it for each youth. That can be daily attendance or hourly – whatever level of detail you have.
- If they say that they have something else like student surveys or anything else and do we want it, the answer is yes as long as it is individually identifiable.
- We will take data for as far back as they have records (but we don't need anything before 2005).

RENEWALS

In addition to project-specific contextual information, please adapt the following text:

- The time has come to renew the [org name] DUA, which is set to expire on [date].
- We are initiating this process early, as we don't want our agreement to lapse.
- I am attaching your current DUA as well as a draft of your new DUA.
- Please note that some language has changed in the past year or two, and I have highlighted those changes in the new DUA attached. [Briefly summarize changes]

- Please review the attached materials and let us know what you think.
- We would be happy to talk with you in person or by telephone to discuss any questions that may arise.
- If you are happy with the new DUA attached, please print out two copies and have [insert signatory's name] sign them. Mail the copies – c/o [insert your name] – to the address in my signature below. I'll have our Executive Director sign both copies and return an original to you for your file.

11/02/22ver

Appendix M

Northwestern-Evanston Education Research Alliance Partnership Agreement

Northwestern
OFFICE OF COMMUNITY
EDUCATION PARTNERSHIPS
School of Education and Social Policy

School District Research Partnerships
Northwestern-Evanston Education Research Alliance (NEERA) Chicago Public Schools Northwestern Partnership

INTRODUCTION

School District Research Agreement

Northwestern University is dedicated to innovative research and community engagement. These missions align to help surrounding school districts by providing research on issues significant to them as well as communities around the world. We are uniquely positioned to advance research in diverse arenas such as policy, learning, and health, for example, to advance well-being and improve our communities.

Our success in achieving these missions will not be measured solely by the number of academic papers published, but by the extent to which we inform and ultimately improve teaching, learning, and the well-being of our communities and develop mutually beneficial partnerships. Research questions explored with our local school districts will thus be informed both by faculty members' research trajectories and by the needs of our educational resource providing partners.

The School of Education and Social Policy's Office of Community Education Partnerships (OCEP) facilitates research partnerships between researchers and school districts. It is the districts' point of contact for data sharing and a resource for both the school districts and researchers. At the core of OCEP's mission is engaging in actionable scholarship and partnerships that improve learning and well-being in our communities, including their school districts. Therefore, OCEP facilitates discussions between the districts and researchers that advance scholarship in areas such as learning, policy, and health; address questions that are of direct and immediate importance to the school districts; and develop partnerships for research between faculty, staff, students, and community partners and practitioners.

Researcher Commitments

Researchers who agree to work on projects through OCEP will have the opportunity to directly inform local districts. Their projects will benefit from access to a high-quality, longitudinal data, partnership with key staff within the districts and larger communities, and dissemination of findings to area education leaders and practitioners.

In exchange, researchers who agree to work on data from these districts commit to:

- Abiding by Policies
  - Respecting privacy and confidentiality of individual and institutional research subjects. Individual districts' data sharing agreements further lay out details.
  - Supervising and aiding student, other research assistants and associates, and subcontractors in meeting the expectations outlined in these research agreements.
  - Sourcing district data and seeking approval for research projects with the district always in conjunction with OCEP.
- Ensuring Reliability of Research
  - Providing adequate supervision to students and inexperienced researchers either via faculty or district research staff advisors.
- Coordinating with Other Researchers as Appropriate
  - Streamlining data collection between projects, e.g. collaboratively designing and administering surveys.
  - Resolving timing or experimental conflicts internally as much as possible.

- Sharing district and data context knowledge.
- Collaborating with Practitioners from Design through Publication. Each collaborative process will be project specific, but see companion documents for suggestions and exemplar deliverables.
  - Creating a process and schedule or timeline that allows sufficient time for feedback and collaboration regarding:
    - research design checks
    - implementation
    - status updates
    - interim and final result reporting
  - Designing research with district feedback and context in mind, e.g. choosing a feasible randomization level, finding ways to recruit students for a focus group, or selecting cohorts with fairly complete data.
  - Implementing treatments or using data in compliance with district policies.
  - Communicating with the district according to its preferences.
  - Reporting results to districts in a user-friendly way, with at least 2 months for them to review before making results public.
- Keeping OCEP in the Loop
  - Notifying OCEP of questions or issues with each research collaboration process.
  - Participating in meetings set up by OCEP with other researchers or practitioners working in the district(s) as appropriate.
  - Keeping OCEP, IRB, and districts apprised of changes to research plans.
  - Bringing any new context knowledge obtained. This will be particularly useful for any new researchers brought into work with the district(s).
  - Allowing OCEP at least 5 business days to review and provide feedback on drafts of results for districts, and at least 10 for drafts of public-facing documents. OCEP will NOT censor results. This review is to ensure that results shared within districts are user-friendly, that those shared outside districts contain appropriate contextual information, and that districts can anticipate public responses.

The purpose of this document is to make expectations of research conducted with K–12 school districts under the auspices of OCEP explicit. Each researcher who works with school districts must sign this document before working with any district. This does not displace any prior research approvals or agreements held with the district(s). Signing it acknowledges the importance of:

- maintaining good working relationships with K–12 school districts,
- using their feedback to produce the best research possible, and
- giving useful, relevant feedback to them to improve district policies and practices.

APPENDIX M

Additional questions may be directed to the Research Data Analyst Leads who are the primary OCEP contacts for data partnerships at ed_partnerships@northwestern.edu or:

Northwestern-Evanston Education Research Alliance (NEERA) Chicago Public Schools Northwestern Partnership	
Lila K. S. Goldstein 847-491-8709 lila.goldstein@northwestern.edu	Love Sanchon Morgan 847-491-7870 love.morgan@northwestern.edu
Printed Name: Employee/Student ID:	Signature: Date:

Detailed Application Process and Information on Data Access

The purpose of this document is to be a quick reference about how researchers gain access to district data and how that data is kept from the partnerships with school districts. The School of Education and Social Policy's Office of Community Education Partnerships (OCEP) facilitates research partnerships between researchers and school districts and is the districts' point of contact for data sharing, and a resource for both the school districts and researchers. The districts' data sharing agreements differ slightly from one another, and this quick reference takes the more conservative line with those differences. The agreements themselves should be read in full before embarking on research with the districts and referred to if anything is ever in question. Data always belongs to the district, so if there are still questions or requests beyond these agreements, the researcher must get written consent from the district(s).

Data Application

OCEP entertains requests for data access from qualified applicants within the Northwestern University research community. Researchers who propose work with the school districts or their data will be asked to commit to working with OCEP throughout the research process from design through release as described below. All documents that need to be reviewed and completed are in blue and available in this Box folder: School District Research Partnerships

1. Review the following documents and sign as appropriate:
   a. Data Sharing Agreement and Affidavit of Nondisclosure for the relevant district.
   b. School District Research Agreement (including Researcher Commitments) and Detailed Application Process and Information on Data Access
   c. Suggestions for Collaboration with Practitioners

APPENDIX M

      d. Sample Memo and Sample PowerPoint
2. Meet with OCEP for guidance on the district's research interests, potential research questions, and contacts within the district.
3. Use the Initial Research Proposal form to give sufficient detail on the project for OCEP and district(s) to evaluate it.
4. Submit the proposal to OCEP for guidance and district review. OCEP will provide guidance and facilitation but does not approve or reject proposals. Be prepared to answer questions, make changes, or coordinate with other researchers as needed.
5. Obtain background clearance, safety training, etc. as applicable.
6. Apply for IRB approval.

Once the project has been run by OCEP and IRB:

7. Draw up a Statement of Work (SOW) using the templates in the district Data Agreement. Districts approve, reject, or ask for modifications in SOWs.
8. Compile the SOW and all other documents and submit to OCEP at ed_partnerships@northwestern.edu

Individual and Institutional Privacy

- Treat data as though it is confidential unless it is collected from a publicly available source or is otherwise available publicly.
- Publish results of research using confidential data in ways that protect the privacy of the individuals and institutions reflected in the data. Do not publish any individually identifiable information or results for any group of fewer than 10 students.
- Allow districts 60 days before intended release of information to review and strike any identifying information for individuals and institutions (such as district or school names).

Data Locations and Transfers

- Keep data only in district-specific folders within Northwestern's secure access server, \\resfilesaudit.northwestern.edu, OCEP-created project-specific folders within Northwestern Box, or hard copy in physically secure locations. Do not save it on a thumb drive or laptop.
- Delete or shred copies and versions of data as soon as the approved project ends.
- Transfer data only encrypted and through SESP Nextcloud, a secure FTP. Do not send data via email or internet sites like Google Drive. Give passwords separately.

Signing below indicates having read the relevant data sharing agreement.

APPENDIX M

| Printed Name: | Employee/Student ID: |
| Signature: | Date: |

Suggestions for Collaboration and Partnership between Researchers and Practitioners

The bullets below provide examples or options, but are not exhaustive.

Timeline

Hold meetings and deliver items at mutually agreed upon intervals. Ultimately, timelines should set expectations for all involved. Some suggested high contact timelines:
- 2 months: meetings bookending, biweekly phone calls, 1 final policy memo
- School year: email as needed, triweekly phone calls, a presentation per semester
- 4 years: phone calls as needed, a meeting per semester, yearly research briefs, multiple final presentations

Design Feedback

Solicit district feedback on a design plan and allow sufficient time for the district to respond.
- Propose and hash out details in person, distributing design in writing after
- List options and pros/cons in a memo, then a phone call for questions and selection
- Give a complete design proposal with plenty of time for questions and new drafts

Implementation

Get approval on general plans for implementation before beginning any research activity. Get approval on more detailed plans for any piece of implementation before beginning each piece. For example, planning to survey teachers would need approval before any work such as classroom observations or treatment implementation were to begin. However, details of how and when to distribute the survey may wait to be approved later but before the survey begins.

Status Updates

Update the district, regardless of work completed, as frequently as the timeline indicates.

Interim and Final Results

Report results to any district whose data is being used at least a month before public release. Report results concisely and in formats that are convenient for them. Districts may use results to make decisions, so share certainty levels, and prepare to share details or advice as solicited.

- 2 page policy or research brief recommending a policy change or measure to track
- 30 minute presentation to leadership launching discussion of potential policy levers
- 45 minute presentation to educators getting buy in for new initiatives
- 3-5 key takeaways and a contact person for ongoing discussion

School of Education and Social Policy | Office of Community Education Partnerships

OCEP's mission is to promote, build capacity for, and engage in actionable scholarship and partnerships that improve learning and well-being in our home communities of Evanston and Chicago, and beyond.

Summary of OCEP: Situated within the School of Education and Social Policy (SESP) at Northwestern University, OCEP's mission stands on three pillars: scholarship, infrastructure and capacity building, and community partnerships.

- *Scholarship.* OCEP promotes and leverages SESP's scholarly expertise and resources to advance research, develop programs, and engage in teaching and service-related activities that help to understand and improve learning, public policy, and well-being in our home communities of Evanston and Chicago, and beyond.
- *Infrastructure and Capacity Building.* OCEP provides infrastructure and builds capacity for researchers, practitioners, students, and diverse community stakeholders to work together. Providing institutional support for cooperation, coordination, and collaboration among these stakeholders allows us to build, share, and maximize human and financial resources; be more efficient and effective in our work; more easily identify new opportunities for engagement; and therefore, amplifies impact and makes our efforts more sustainable and scalable.
- *Community Partnerships.* Improving learning and human development requires new ways of working together in and across communities. Thus, OCEP is committed to developing community partnerships that are based on collaboration and mutual respect; common vision and goals; community needs and priorities; and the valuing and sharing of resources and

expertise and seeks to document and share models and promising practices for university-community partnerships.

In sum, OCEP works to bridge the research, practice, and service missions of SESP and Northwestern University to create initiatives and partnerships that positively impact our home communities of Evanston and Chicago, but that can be shared and scaled far beyond.

For more information about OCEP please contact:

Nichole Pinkard, Ph.D., Faculty Director nichole.pinkard@northwestern.com

Amy Pratt, Ph.D., Assistant Dean for Community Education Partnerships amy.pratt@northwestern.edu

Appendix N

Template for a Quarterly RPP Facilitation Memo

NC STATE UNIVERSITY

THE WILLIAM & IDA
FRIDAY INSTITUTE
FOR EDUCATIONAL INNOVATION

The Friday Institute for
Educational Innovation
NC State College of Education
fi.ncsu.edu
Campus Box 7249
1890 Main Campus Drive
Raleigh, NC 27606
P: 919.513.8500

To: Names of PI, Principal, Magnet Coordinator
From: Callie Edwards, Associate Director of Research and Evaluation
CC: Sr. Director of Research and Evaluation
Date: XXXXX
Re: RCMMS/FI Research Practice Partnership Facilitation Memo #X

The purpose of this quarterly memo is to briefly summarize the Research-Practice Partnership (RPP) facilitation provided by Callie Edwards (NCSU FIRE Team) to the Reedy Creek Magnet Middle School Center for Digital Sciences (RCMMS)/Friday Institute for Educational Innovation (FI) RPP from XXXX 202X–XXXX 202X.

This memo is organized into four sections: the first provides an update on the action items that were identified in the XXXX 202X memo, the second describes RPP facilitation activities that occurred during this quarter, the third outlines action items for the upcoming quarter, and the fourth provides an update on longer-term considerations for 202X–2X academic year that were initially proposed during the 20XX–2X academic year. You may click the above hyperlinks to go directly to the listed section.

UPDATE

In [previous memo name and link], XXX action items were identified. XX action items have been completed, XX action item is planned and will be completed on

APPENDIX N

Table 1 [Semester Year] action items

#	Action Item	Current Status
1	XXXX	Planned XXXXX
2	XXXX	Completed – XXX
3	XXXX	Completed – XXXX
4	XXXX	Completed – XXXX
5	XXXX	In Progress – XXXX

XXXX, 202X, and the final action item is in progress. Table 1 (below) outlines the action items and their current status.

RPP FACILITATION ACTIVITIES

[Month Year]

In [month], Callie engaged in XXX partnership meetings, XXXX of which she facilitated. Most partnership meetings in January centered around XXXX. Please see Table 2 for more information about the [Month Year] partnership meetings.

Throughout the quarter, Callie and [practitioner contact] frequently communicated via email regarding recent activities and next steps. [Additional details about communication]

Two NNERPP related activities occurred in [month]:
(1) XXXX
(2) XXXX

Table 2 [Month Year] partnership meetings

#	Date and Time	Topic	Attendees
1	XXXX	PD Planning Call*	XXXX
2	XXXX	Bi-weekly RPP Check-In Meeting*	XXXX
3	XXXX	PD Planning Call*	XXXX
4	XXXX	EcoCS Internal Meeting	XXXX
5	XXXX	Bi-weekly RPP Check-In Meeting*	XXXX
6	XXXX	Digital Sciences Team Meeting	XXXX
7	XXXX	Reedy Creek/FI PD Planning*	XXXX
8	XXXX	AERA Paper Planning*	XXXX
9	XXXXXXXX	Bi-weekly RPP Check-In Meeting*	XXXX

Asterisk (*) indicates Callie facilitated the meeting. [Month Year]

APPENDIX N

In [month], most RPP facilitation activities focused on XXXXX.

To begin, Callie and [practitioner contact] co-developed and administered a survey to gauge teacher feedback on the session. The survey responses indicate that the session was very well received by Reedy Creek teachers. The full anonymous raw survey data is available [link here].

[Overview of survey results]

Throughout the month of February, Callie and [practitioner contact] communicated frequently via email, phone, and Zoom conversations to discuss the strengths and areas of improvement highlighted in the survey feedback.

[Additional details about communication]

As another follow up to the professional development session, Callie created a recap document [insert link] for the research team to categorize strengths, challenges, lessons learned, and next steps.

[Additional details about document]

Two NNERPP related activities occurred in [month]:
(1) XXXX
(2) XXXX

Table 3 highlights the eight partnership meetings that Callie participated in [month year], four of which she facilitated. Please note, this table does not include impromptu phone calls or text messages in between meetings. The team was in constant communication in [month]. Moreover, the Digital Sciences Team did not meet in [month], but decided to correspond via email regarding teacher leader updates.

It is also important to note that in [month], Callie volunteered to coordinate scheduling for the internal and full EcoCS meetings. Within this administrative capacity, she creates and shares monthly Doodle polls for both teams, selects the most ideal time frame, and sends a calendar invitation with Zoom meeting links and agendas to participants.

Table 3 [Month Year] partnership meetings

#	Date and Time	Topic	Attendees
1	XXXX	RCMMS/FI Professional Development Session	XXXX
2	XXXX	EcoCS Full Team Meeting	XXXX
3	XXXX	Bi-weekly RPP Check-In Meeting*	XXXX
4	XXXX	NNERPP Steering Committee Meeting	XXXX
5	XXXX	Bi-weekly RPP Check-In Meeting*	XXXX
6	XXXX	Food Web Lesson Run-Through	XXXX
7	XXXX	Bi-weekly RPP Check-In Meeting*	XXXX
8	XXXX	Reedy Creek PD Planning*	XXXX

APPENDIX N

Asterisk (*) indicates Callie facilitated the meeting. [Month Year]

Many of the RPP facilitation activities in [month] were focused on XXXX. Other major RPP facilitation activities in [month] included XXXX.

Two NNERPP related activities occurred in March:
(1) XXXX
(2) XXXX

Table 4 outlines the eight partnership meetings that Callie participated in [month], four of which she facilitated. Three pre-scheduled check-in meetings were canceled as there were no major updates to report outside of the frequent email communication.

Also in [month], Callie continued to coordinate scheduling for the upcoming internal and full EcoCS meetings.

Table 4 March 2021 partnership meetings

#	Date and Time	Topic	Attendees
1	XXXX	Bi-weekly RPP Check-In Meeting*	XXXX
2	XXXX	AERA Planning Meeting*	XXXX
3	XXXX	Bi-weekly RPP Check-In Meeting*	XXXX
4	XXXX	DST Meeting	XXXX
5	XXXX	NNERPP Steering Committee Meeting	XXXX
6	XXXX	EcoCS Internal Meeting	XXXX
7	XXXX	EcoCS Full Team Meeting	XXXX
8	XXXX	AERA Paper Planning/Practice*	XXXX

ACTION ITEMS

The following action items are slated for the next quarter:
1. XXXX
2. XXXX
3. XXXX
4. XXXX

In addition, two action items are slated for the following quarter:
1. XXXX
2. XXXX

FUTURE CONSIDERATIONS

The following are quarterly updates to Callie's three main goals that were initially proposed during the 20XX–XX academic year:
1. XXXX
2. XXXX
3. XXXX

The mission of the William & Ida Friday Institute for Educational Innovation at NC State's College of Education is to advance education through innovation in teaching, learning, and leadership. Bringing together educational professionals, researchers, policymakers, and other community members, the Friday Institute is a center for fostering collaborations to improve education. We conduct research, develop educational resources, provide professional development programs for educators, advocate to improve teaching and learning, and help inform policymaking.

Visit fi.ncsu.edu to learn more.

Appendix O

Communications Strategy Brief

Communications Strategy Brief

UCHICAGO Consortium
on School Research

Project	PI	Comms Team Lead
New Insights on Academic Progress of English Learners		

Alignment with Consortium Goal: Focus on experience of groups of students

Why are we doing this? What problem are we trying to solve?	
What must be accomplished?	
Who is the primary target audience?	
Who is the secondary target audience?	
Why is our research important to the target audience? Why should they care?	
What do we want our audience to think, say, feel, or do? What does success look like?	
How will we measure success?	
What are possible barriers to success?	
What are key messages?	
What is the single most important thing our audience needs to know?	
What resources will we need to be successful?	
Timeline/Key Dates	
Budget	

Note: the document has a watermark that reads, "internal use only," to remind users that this is an internal strategy development tool and not a public document for communicating research.

6/18/2019

Appendix P

TERA Research Brief Process:
Initial Interview Guide

About this Guide:

This tool is designed to guide the author of a non-technical brief in interviewing a researcher about a specific research study or set of studies. The guide provides a line of questioning intended to prompt researchers to clarify, in non-technical speak, the key points of their work and their relevance to important problems of practice.

The Importance of Initial Interviews:

TERA's primary goal is to inform education policy and practice with rigorous research. Policymakers and practitioners don't have time to sort through new information and figure out on their own what's most important and how it relates to their work. Part of TERA's job is to do this for them, and an initial interview between the brief's author and the researcher is a critical part of how we accomplish this. Through focused dialogue, the researcher and the brief's author formulate a set of well-supported and explained key takeaways appropriate for a non-technical audience. This benefits the researcher and the author as they build a shared understanding of how to talk about research with the people TERA aims to inform.

Keep in mind a TERA brief is more than a jargon-free summary of a research paper – developing one is not a matter of cutting, pasting, and editing what's in a technical piece. Research findings, as written in most research reports, are far less useful to policymakers and practitioners than are ***insights that help them better understand a problem and how they might address it***. Such insights are rarely stated explicitly or prominently in technical papers. As such, writing a TERA brief entails more than translation. Working with the researcher, the author articulates and elevates key messages for non-technical audiences that may have only been hinted at in the academic article.

Technical and non-technical audiences differ in what they look for most in research	
Researchers tend to care most about...	Policymakers/practitioners care most about...
How does this study add to previous research?	How does this study inform what I do?

Presented at the NNERPP Annual Forum
July 9, 2019

APPENDIX P

Interview Process:

Assignment:	Reading:	Interview Preparation:	Interview:	Summarizing Key Points and Explanations:
Assigner explains why a brief is needed, how it relates to other TERA work, agrees with author on timeline for development	Author of brief reviews the researcher's study and identifies what seem to be key points + what seems important but unclear	Author adapts/selects from questions in this guide to create a set of prompts for the interview	Author interviews researcher (asking clarifying questions and paraphrasing, etc). Author takes notes and records audio	Author drafts outline/ PowerPoint (with notes)

Guidance for reading research papers:

In reviewing the technical paper before the interview, it is expected that the brief author will not understand or absorb everything in it. Here's some additional guidance on reading:

- Pay the closest attention to the Results/Discussions/Conclusions sections.
- As you read, highlight sentences where the author seems to be saying something especially new or important. Annotate such sentences, or some of them, with notes on your own understanding of the idea expressed.
- Flag anything that seems contradictory (i.e. one finding that seems to contradict another) so you can ask the researcher to reconcile them.
- Look for charts (or figures) that seem to show clear patterns; find the text in the paper that explains the charts and try to piece together what the charts are showing you. Consider annotating charts with your own attempt at a headline that calls out the pattern they show. (Note that technical papers often include many tables of data, which are less illuminating.)

Presented at the NNERPP Annual Forum
July 9, 2019

APPENDIX P

TN EDUCATION RESEARCH ALLIANCE

Knowledge Design Partners LLC

TOPIC QUESTION

(To be answered by brief author before preparing interview questions)

What is this study about?

This study is about: _____

_____

_____

> Examples of what you're after:
> ...turnover among teachers of color in Tennessee schools.
> ...improvement in teachers' effectiveness as they gain more experience.

GUIDING QUESTIONS FOR INTERVIEW

RELEVANCE /CONTEXT

1. **Relevance: Why is this topic important to study?**

   Possible variations/deeper dives:
   - What is the Tennessee context that makes this study relevant?
   - What do we know or not yet know from previous research that tells us this is important to study?
   - How is this study situated within previous TERA research?

   > Examples of what you're after:
   > - Previous research suggests that students benefit from a diverse teacher workforce, *so it's important to* know what's driving/hindering teacher diversity. We know that principals impact teaching and learning in schools, *so it's important to* know if effective principals are in the schools that need them the most.
   > - Previous TERA research demonstrated how principals are key to driving school success. Building on that knowledge, we now know that schools with the most challenging leadership environments in Tennessee also tend to have less effective principals.

2. **Caveats: What can't this study tell us that would be important to know?**

   Possible variations/deeper dives:
   - What cautions should we keep in mind when interpreting the results?

   > Examples of what you're after:
   > - We don't know if principal supervisors really do recognize effective school leadership or if they just give good ratings when they see that a principal's school is performing well.

Presented at the NNERPP Annual Forum
July 9, 2019

APPENDIX P

DATA/METHODS

4. **Methods: In non-technical language, could you please walk through what methods you used in this analysis?**

   Possible variations/deeper dives:

   - What measures did you use, and what question did your analysis ask of the data?
   - What data were included in the study? Who was included and what information about them was included?
   - If applicable, what comparisons were made and how? What claim does this study allow us to make?

   > Examples of what you're after:
   > - We measured growth in teacher effectiveness by looking at changes in the evaluation scores of individual teachers over time. With that data we asked: to what extent do teachers continue to become more effective over the course of their careers?

In this section, walk through each headline one-by-one. In other words, proceed through question 8 for first headline, then return to question 5 for the second one, until you've covered them all.

FINDINGS

5. **Key Takeaways: Let's talk through what you see as the big headlines/takeaways from this study. Taking all the findings into account, what would you say are the key/major takeaways from this research?**

   > Examples of what you're after:
   > - Teachers of color leave their schools at higher rates because they tend to teach in more challenging situations.
   > - Contrary to popular belief, teachers generally continue to improve over the course their career.
   > - TN's principal evaluation system identifies school leaders who retain effective teachers.
   > - TN's most effective principals are working where they are least needed.
   > - In TN, low-performing teachers are being reassigned to early grades, where state testing doesn't take place.

Presented at the NNERPP Annual Forum
July 9, 2019

6. **Findings:** Circling back to the first big takeaway (restate), what findings from your research support that headline/takeaway? (e.g. specific numbers/results from analysis)

> Examples of what you're after:
> • Schools with fewer teachers of color experience higher turnover rates among such teachers.

Possible variations/deeper dives:

- What results from your analysis lead you to make that statement?

7. **Significance:** How would you explain how big or small those findings are to non-research person?

> Examples of what you're after:
> • The growth in effectiveness among participating teachers was equal to gaining one point on TN's four-point measure for teacher evaluation.

Possible variations/deeper dives:

- Can you give a sense of how big the differences were in terms that a non-technical person might understand?

8. **Visualization:** What kind of charts or graphs would best clarify those findings for a non-research person?

> Examples of what you're after:
> • We could show the rate at which effective teachers leave their schools when their principal is rated a 1,2,3,4, or 5 in the state's principal evaluation system.

Possible variations/deeper dives:

- How could you present the data so that the key relationships or patterns are crystal clear?
- Do you already have charts showing that, or could you create one?
- Or, what charts in the research report best capture the finding. Tell me what the chart is showing.

9. **Interpretation:** What are some possible explanations for what you see in the results?

> Examples of what you're after:
> • It might be that the districts where teachers are becoming more effective at faster rates have created conditions that are especially conducive to professional learning.

Possible variations/deeper dives:

- What do you think might be going on here to produce these results?

Presented at the NNERPP Annual Forum
July 9, 2019

10. **Misinterpretation: How might these results be misinterpreted by a general audience?**

Possible variations/deeper dives:

- What would you not want a general audience to take away from these results?

> Examples of what you're after:
> - Possibly that early grades are just a dumping ground for ineffective teachers. We don't actually know this; we just know that less-effective teachers tend to be reassigned to lower grades

Go on to Question 11 after you've been through Qs 5-10 for each key takeaway.

11. **Implications: Who do you think most needs to understand the results of this study, and what would you suggest they do or think about as a result of it?**

> Examples of what you're after:
> - Principal preparation programs could explore ways to help principals understand how to better support a diverse teaching workforce.

Possible variations/deeper dives:

- Whose work would benefit most from this study? State officials, district leaders, principals, teacher leaders?
- What might each of these groups do differently based on this work?

CURRENT CONTEXT/FUTURE RESEARCH

12. **Contribution: How does this study add to or challenge our previous understandings about this topic?**

> Examples of what you're after:
> - The conventional wisdom is teachers don't improve after 3-5 years in the profession. This shows that isn't true.

Possible variations/deeper dives:

- Do its findings challenge or confirm the conventional wisdom? If so, how?
- Does it point to a major problem? If so, what?
- Does it tell us that something is working as intended? If so, what?

Presented at the NNERPP Annual Forum
July 9, 2019

13. **Future research: Based on this study, what additional research questions do you think should be asked on this topic? Why?**

   Possible variations/deeper dives:
   - What do we still not understand about this topic that should be explored in further research?

   > Examples of what you're after:
   > - We should find out if there are conditions in those districts that predict the likelihood of teachers becoming more effective over time. If we understood those conditions, we might find ways to bring them about in more places.

Presented at the NNERPP Annual Forum
July 9, 2019

Index

Note: Page numbers in *italic* indicate a figure, and page numbers in **bold** indicate a table on the corresponding page. Page numbers followed by n indicate text found in a note.

ABC's of research 196
action 104, *105*
administrative structures 21, 55, 140–152
Advanced Partnership Research 70
agency, collective 86
agreement for confidential data exchange 215–220
agreement, generating 45
alignment of research 197
American Institute for Research 142
anti-racism 83–87
Arce-Trigatti, P. 13, 20
Archer, J. 130
assessment of partnership 66, 168–171
authority 70–71

Barron, B. 1, 2
Barton, A. 70
Baumgartner, E. 128, 160
benefits of research 198
Bevan, B. 70
Bijur, k. 39, 40
Blass, L. 1–3
Blekic, M. 155, 156
blending in 179–180
book club 83–87, *85*
Booker, L. 135

Boston P-3 Partnership 153–155
boundary infrastructure 139
boundary spanning 44–45
Bradley, K. 49
Branson-Thayer, M. 149
briefs: policy 130–132; practitioner 132–134, *134*
Brokering Activities Framework 15
broker moves 15, *15*, **16**
brokers/brokering: activities of 5–6, *6*, 9; activity types xii; to address differences 119–123; cases, use of 172–177; competency, building 48–54; critical lens 72–73; defined 15, **16**; embedding 117–119; expansion of 182–183; framework in RPP *see* RPP brokers framework; future of 179–185; importance of 10; informal 122–123; literature on RPPs 184; mini-coaching 52–54; multi-layered 109–111, 119–121; next steps 183–185; personal scope of practice 14; processes of 5; relationships, nurturing 44–46, 109–118; research production and use 42–44, 49–54; role of xii–xiv, 4–5, 40–41, 181; skills 48–49, 100–103, 183; to strengthen

248

partners 41–54, *41*, 99–136, *100*; to strengthen partnerships 54–71, 139–171; to support research use 123–136; value of 184; *see also* research-practice partnership (RPP)

California Education Partners 1, 24, 39, 58, 66
Cambero, S. 83, 84, 155
Campbell, C. 3
Carnegie Foundation for the Advancement of Teaching 93, 94–97, 104
Carter, P. 90
cases: brokering to address differences 122–123; brokering to strengthen partnerships 139–171; communications strategy briefs 166–168; conferences and events design 155–157; consensus building 119–121; contrasting 135–136; data dictionary wiki *143*; data use agreements 141–142; diagnostic rubric 169–170; embedding 117–119; "first date" meeting 112–114; free workshops 100–103; IDEA data discussion protocol 103–107; meeting routines 152–155; multi-layered brokering 109–111; newsletters 161–163, *162*; partnership agreements 144–147; policy briefs 130–132; practitioner briefs 132–134; quarterly RPP facilitation memos 158–160; research agendas 147–152, *151, 152*; research release process 163–166, *165*; research road shows 128–130; strategic planning 107–109; superintendent dinners 114–116; whether to conduct research 124–128
Center for the Analysis of Longitudinal Data in Education Research 108
Center to Support Excellence in Teaching 109–111
Chavez, V. 25

Chicago Public Schools 142–144
Clark, T. 169
coaching 174
Cobb, P. 169, 177
code switching 45
collaborations, long-term 78–79
collective agency 86
common vision 56
communication: developing 61–62; elements of 45; literature reviews 25; managing internal and external 157–168; memos 158–160; newsletters 161–163, *162*; plans *64*; of research findings 128–136; research release process 163–166, *165*; strategy briefs 166–168
community building 86
competency, building 48–54, 88, 99–109, *100*
Conaway, C. 13, 15, 17, 18, 20, 107, 172
conferences and events design 155–157
conference seating chart 46–47, *47*
connections 79–80, 110
consensus building 119–121
consultation 128
context 48, 76–97
contrasting case studies 135–136
core DNA 77, 97
correspondence template, DUA 223–226
Corrigan, D. 49, 89, 90, 145
Corson, A. 142
cost of research 199
course work 173–174
Creating Research-Practice Partnerships (Gallagher and Penuel) 168
culture 58

Dafonte, C. 160
data analysis 67–68, *67*
data dictionary wiki 142–144, *143*
Data Exchange and Confidentiality Agreement 215–220
data infrastructure 140–145

INDEX

data safeguards 221–222
data transfer 216, 225
data use agreements (DUAs): correspondences for 223–226; example of 140–143; explained 141; as partnership documents 56; for Stanford–SFUSD Partnership 176
Davidson, K. L. 5
Deliverology planning framework 108
description 104, *105*
diagnostic rubric 169–170
Diamond, J. B. 68, *71*
district partners 79
diversity 82–83, 92–93
Dodd, M. 1, 2
Duran, B. 25

educational improvement 97
Edwards, C. 158
EFI sprint protocol 212–214
embedding 117–119
equitable transformation 97
equity 8–9, 69, *71*; see also inequality, systemic
Evidence for Improvement Framework 94, 212–214
evidence-informed practice 3
expansion of brokering 182–183
expectations 53
expertise, diversity of 82–83, 92–93
explanation 104, *105*

Farley-Ripple, E. 4
Farrell, C. C. 4, 139, 180
FI Branded Google documents 160
"first date" meeting 43–44, 112–114, 176–177
Friday Institute 235–239
Fulton County Schools 172

Gallagher, D. 169–170
Georgia Policy Labs (GPL) 100–103
goals 53, 84–87

Goldstein, L. K. S. 124, 145
Google documents 160
governance and administrative structures 21, 55, 140–152
Greenberg, M. 25

Hayes, K. 121, 122
Henderson, J. W. 24
Henrick, E. C. 66, 69, 169, 180
Hewlett Foundation 94–97
Highline Public Schools 169
Ho, D. 24
Holter, J. 130
Houston Education Research Consortium (HERC) 119, 128–130, 160–163
Houston Independent School District (HISD) 160–163
Hughes Gibson, E. 1–3

IDEA data discussion protocol 103–107, *105*, *106*
identity 58, 89–92
inequality, systemic xi; see also equity
infrastructure 9–10
intention 104, *105*
intentional organization 82–83
internal brokers 72
interviews 130–132
introductions 80–82, *81*

Jackson, K. 169
John Gardner Center 140, 176, 215–220, 221–222, 223–226
Joseph, G. 149
journaling 85–86

Kennedy, A. 50
Khanna, R. 89, 90
Kim, M. 116, 117–119
Kipnis, F. 67
Klaus, B. 1
Klein, K. 79, 114
knowledge mobilization 5, 42

knowledge of self 48
Kruger, A. 111, 112–114, 132, 163, 176–177
Kwun, N. 83, 155

Laman, T. T 24
Las Lomitas Elementary School District 109–111
Latino Policy Forum 166, 166–168
Le, Q. 50
Lesnick, J. 147
Levinson, A. 1, 2
Limlingan, M. C. 149
literature: partners' competency, building **30–31**; partnership governance and administrative structures **22–23**; partnership, improving **26**; processes and communication routines **25**; references for brokering 190–193; references for racism and power differences 194–195; relationships, nurturing **28–29**; research production and use **27–28**; RPP issues 184; by theme and substance **188–189**
local context 48
long-term collaborations 78–79
Los Angeles Educational Research Institute (LAERI) 122–123

Madison Education Partnership (MEP) 111, 112–114, *112*, 132–134, 163
Madison Metropolitan School District (MMSD) 112
Maghes, M. 50
Massachusetts Department of Elementary and Secondary Education 107–109
McGee, S. 69
McMahon, K. 93, 94, 171
meet and greet email *81*
meetings 62–63, 121, 153–155
memorandum of understanding (MOU) 56, 146
memos 158–160

Ming, N. 50, 63, 89, 90, 103, 145
mini-coaching 52–54
Monahan, B. 111, 112–114, 132, 163, 176–177
Moore, C. A. 39, 40
Moriarty, T. 109
multi-layered brokering 109–111, 119–121

National Network of Education Research-Practice Partnerships (NNERPP) 8, 13, *15*, **16**, 17, 18, 34n1
Nayfack, M. 63, 114, 115–116
NC State College of Education 235–239
NEERA *see* Northwestern-Evanston Education Research Alliance (NEERA)
negotiation 44, 53, 55
Nelson, J. 3
newsletters 161–163, *162*
next steps 183–185
NNERPP *see* National Network of Education Research-Practice Partnerships (NNERPP)
Norman, J. 93, 94, 171
norms and values 155
Northwestern-Evanston Education Research Alliance (NEERA) 79–82, 114, 124–128, 145, 227–234
Northwestern University 142

Oakland Unified School District–UC Berkeley RPP 116, 117–119
OCEAN 83–87
onboarding 174–175
Orange County Educational Advancement Network (OCEAN) 83–87
Oregon Department of Education 155, 156
Oregon State University 155, 156
organization: clarity in 72–73; intentional 82–83
Ozer, E. 89, 90, 92, 145

Padilla, A. 70
partnering, defined 8

251

INDEX

partners: cases for strengthening 99–136; competency, building 48–54, 99–109, *100*; "first date" meeting 112–114; identifying 56; relationships *see* relationships; research production and use 42–44; strengthening **19**, 41–54, *41*

partnership agreement 89–92, *91*, 144–147

partnerships: assessment and improvement 66, 168–171; cases for strengthening 139–171; common vision 56; communication 61–62, 64, 153–168, 158–168; data analysis 67–68, *67*; equity 69; goals and expectations 53; governance and administrative structures 55, 140–152; identity and culture 58; improving **26**; key aspects of 77; meetings 62–63; multiple 73; negotiation 53; power differences 68–69, 70–71; processes, designing 152–168; racism 69; readiness to engage 56–57; reflective activity 94–97; research agendas 147–152; RPP role in 8, 9–10; social opportunities 62–63; stages of *54*; strengthening **19–20**, 54–71

Penuel, W. 69

Penuel, W. R. 5, 169, 170, 180

personal scope of practice 14

Philadelphia Education Research Consortium (PERC) 147

Phillips-Sved, S. 38, 40

Pierson, A. 149

PLE pilot 1–3

policy briefs 130–132

Polito, B. 109

Poonen Levien, Z. 1–3, *2*, *3*

portraits, of RPPs 94–97, *211*

Potter, D. 119

power dynamics 24, **32–34**, 68–69, 70–71, 88, 89, 93

practice-based reflection 15–16

practitioner briefs 132–134, *134*

PRISMA flow diagram *18*

processes **25**, 50, 61–62, 88, 152–168

professional development 100–103

program evaluation 127

racism 24, 26, **32–34**, 38–40, 69, 70–71, *71*, 83–87

readiness to engage 56–57

Reedy Creek Magnet Middle School Center for the Digital Sciences/Friday Institute for Educational Innovation (RCMMS/FI) 158–160

reflection: activity 94–97; practice-based 15–16; strategic planning and 107–109

relationships: to address differences 118–123; developing and nurturing 44–46; "first date" meeting 43–44, 112–114; literature reviews **28–29**; meetings to promote 121; multi-layered 109–111, 119–121; superintendent dinners 115–116; to support research use 123–136

renewals 225–226

research: ABC's of 196; alignment of 197; benefits of 198; cost of 199; literature reviews **27–28**; production and use 42–44, 49–54; resources for 127; support of 123–136; whether to conduct 124–128, *125–127*

research agendas 147–152, *151*, *152*

research and practice cycles 86–87

research brokers 72

research-practice partnership (RPP): defined 4, 77; dimensions of effectiveness 66; education initiatives 13; infrastructure 9–10; key aspects of 77; principles of 4; road shows 128–130; roles and responsibilities **201–203**, 216–218, 220; sociocultural context 8; strategies for 4; typology of 98n1; *see also* brokers/brokering; partnerships

252

research production and use: agendas and guidelines for 49–52; conditions for 42–44; life cycle *50*; literature **27–28**; skills for 48–49
research release process 163–166, *165*
reviews, structured 20–34
road shows 128–130
Roderick, M. 180
Rogers, T. 100
RPP *see* research-practice partnership (RPP)
RPP brokers framework 14, 20–34; activities 6–7, 7, 21, **22–23**, **25**, **26**, **27–29**; development of 13–14; final draft **31–32**; literature review *see* literature; perspectives from other brokers 17–20; power dynamics 24, **32–34**, 88, 89, 93; practice-based reflection 15–16; PRISMA flow diagram *18*; racism 24, 26, **32–34**; RPP definition and 78–97; second version **19–20**; themes 17
Ruiz de Velasco, J. 140, 176

Sall, L. 166
San Francisco Peer Resources 90
San Francisco Unified School District (SFUSD) 89, 103–107, 204–210; internal review template 200; *see also* Stanford–SFUSD Partnership
Schwartz, N. 135
scope of practice, personal 14
Seesaw 3
Sequoia Collaborative 115–116
Sexton, S. 69
Sherer, D. 93, 94, 171
Shewchuk, S. 20
Shoreline Public Schools 169
skills 48–49, 100–103, 183
social justice 83–84
social opportunities 62–63
social structures and routines 21
Speth, T. 149

staff turnover 79–82
Stanford Graduate School of Education (GSE) 69
Stanford–Sequoia Collaborative for Leadership 109–111
Stanford–Sequoia K–12 Research Collaborative 114, 115–116, 175–176
Stanford–SFUSD Partnership 176; annual meeting 59–61, *60*, *61*; conference seating chart 46–47, *47*; governance and administration 58–59; mini-coaching 52–54; origin of 1–3; partner matching 45; and race issues 38–40; research production 42–44, 49–52; timeline of projects 63–65, *65*
Stanford University 140
status 70–71
status quo behaviors and systems 180–181
STEM teachers 83, 84, 87
Stone, S. 92
strategic planning 107–109
strategic research production 124–128
Sullivan, M. 24
superintendent dinners 115–116
support staff 80
sustainability 86
systems and routines 103–109

targeted meetings 53–54
Taylor, A. 153–155
Tennessee Department of Education 135–136
Tennessee Education Research Alliance (TERA) 130–132
termination of agreement 218
theory of improvement 213
theory of partnership 212
theory of scaling 213–214
Thompson, K. 155, 156
timelines 63, 64–65, *65*
tools: for brief writing 130–131; brokers/brokering 17–18; to meet goals 85; meeting agenda 154

training 184
transformation 180–181
Turner, A. 147

UC Irvine CalTeach 83–87, *85*
University of California, Berkeley 89, 204–210
University of Chicago 142
University of Chicago Consortium on School Research 166, 166–168
University of Washington 169

Vaade, B. 111, 112–114, 132, 163, 176–177
Vakil, S. 24
value proposition 79–80
values 155

Vasan, J. 128
Vetter, A. 69
vignettes 18
Villa, B. 92

Wallerstein, N. B. 25
Wentworth, L. 1–2, 3, 13, 15, 17, 18, 20, 24, 39, 40, 43, 45, 52, 59, 63, 67, 70, 113, 177, 182
Wisconsin Center for Education Research (WCER) 112
workshops 100–103, 174

Youth Data Archive 140

Zinger, D. 83, 84, 155